$2 ⁷⁹⁶

Worship and Sin

PETER LANG
New York • Washington, D.C./Baltimore • Bern
Frankfurt am Main • Berlin • Brussels • Vienna • Oxford

Karel Kurst-Swanger

Worship and Sin

AN EXPLORATION
OF RELIGION-RELATED CRIME
IN THE UNITED STATES

PETER LANG
New York • Washington, D.C./Baltimore • Bern
Frankfurt am Main • Berlin • Brussels • Vienna • Oxford

Library of Congress Cataloging-in-Publication Data

Kurst-Swanger, Karel.
Worship and sin: an exploration of religion-related crime in the United States /
Karel Kurst-Swanger.
p. cm.
Includes bibliographical references and index.
1. Violence—Religious aspects. 2. Violence—United States. I. Title.
BL65.V55K87   364.2'56—dc22   2008000225
ISBN 978-0-8204-6387-2

Bibliographic information published by **Die Deutsche Bibliothek**.
Die Deutsche Bibliothek lists this publication in the "Deutsche
Nationalbibliografie"; detailed bibliographic data is available
on the Internet at http://dnb.ddb.de/.

Cover design by Clear Point Designs

The paper in this book meets the guidelines for permanence and durability
of the Committee on Production Guidelines for Book Longevity
of the Council of Library Resources.

Printed in the United States of America

Contents

Preface

This volume brings together scholarly research into various types of religion-related crime. A three-pronged typology is presented as a conceptual framework to distinguish the dynamics of various forms of religion-related crime in the United States. My intention is that this typology will serve as a useful beginning point from which to conceptualize crime in which religion is a core feature. I have taken great care to present a comprehensive overview of religion-related crime to demonstrate its complexity and multidimensionality. I draw on empirical findings from many academic perspectives and consider the practical issues facing practitioners.

I present case examples to reveal the multifaceted nature of religion-related crime. In many instances I have provided direct quotations from judges, lawmakers, and others associated with the specific cases or issues that I am describing. To make specific points, I also take the liberty of quoting the exact passages that appear on the Web pages of various religious organizations. This provides readers the opportunity to interpret for themselves the inherent meanings of the passages quoted. Although I have attempted to focus on cases that were long ago disposed of, it was difficult to resist discussing new cases as they have emerged in the news media or in court documents. Thus, some of the cases presented here are ongoing and may be resolved long after this book is published. This approach may be construed as anecdotal, but I balance this with empirical research and statistical data whenever possible. My hope is that my approach will prompt others to see value in classifying religion-related crime as a distinct category and will view this text as a starting point for future research and inquiry.

This book is likely to confront you on different levels. Although this is a book about crime, rather than a book about religion, it is likely that your religious beliefs, or lack of them, will play a role in how you digest the material presented.

I encourage you to take stock of your religious traditions and to reflect upon them as you work your way through the text. Whether you categorize yourself as a religious person or not, the cases and issues explored in this text are likely to resonate with you in some substantial way, since diverse religious ideas are presented throughout. For me, this book was truly a learning expedition. I do not consider myself a religious person and, given the topics explored here, I find it especially ironic that my journey with this text has ended with a new level of respect for and understanding of a diverse set of religious traditions and a desire to learn more about them in the future.

The text is divided into five major parts. Part I provides an overview of the issues presented in the text. Chapter 1 defines religion-related crime and explores a typology describing three different categories of religion-related crime. This framework provides an opportunity to examine the distinctive issues related to each of the three categories. *Theologically based crimes* are those that result from a particular religious custom, practice, or belief, whereas *reactive/defensive crimes* come about more as a result of social or political tensions between the religious individual or group and the broader secular community. The third type of religion-related crime identified is *the abuse of religious authority*. This category explores crimes committed by clergy who have taken advantage of their social, political, and religious status. The remaining parts of the text are organized around this conceptual framework.

Chapter 2 explores concepts related to religion and to the academic study of religion, such as the definition of religion, religiosity, conversion, and the organization of religious groups. Chapter 3 presents a historical perspective on the First Amendment of the U.S. Constitution and explores a variety of U.S. Supreme Court decisions in cases of religion-related crime.

Part II of the text focuses on examples of theologically based religion-related crimes. Chapter 4 explores crimes committed against children, and Chapter 5 investigates crimes against women. Chapter 6 highlights the use of illicit drugs in religious practice or to reach desired states of spiritual awareness.

Part III investigates crimes that are reactive or defensive in nature—crimes that religious individuals or groups commit in response to some external pressure or threat. These crimes are usually influenced by theology or specific religious beliefs. The external pressure may be real or imagined; it may be manufactured by the group leader to meet his or her own hidden agenda. In such cases, criminal activity is prompted by a need or desire to protect a belief system or a group of believers. Chapter 7 explores the nature and function of destructive religious groups. Chapter 8 provides an overview of specific crimes associated with violence against reproductive health providers. Chapter 9 highlights the problem of hate crime in which religion is a factor.

Part IV of the text explores my third type of religion-related crime, the abuse of religious authority. Here we focus on crimes committed by clergy. Chapter 10 provides and overview of the issue, and Chapter 11 provides examples of economic and personal crimes.

The book concludes with Part V, Chapter 12: "Final Thoughts and Future Directions." In this chapter, I highlight some of the major themes raised in the text and give some preliminary recommendations for future research and for those who work with these issues daily. As I will state many times throughout the text, this book is intended to spark continued dialogue about, and scholarly inquiry into, the issues raised and to argue that religion-related crime should be considered a distinct subset of crime worthy of continued investigation. I believe that learning more about religion-related crime can only help us better understand the human condition.

Part I
Overview

Religion-Related Crime: An Introduction

On September 3, 2003, former Presbyterian minister Paul Hill was executed in a Florida state prison for the murders of Dr. John Bayard Britton, a physician who performed abortions, and retired Air Force Lt. Col. James Herman Barrett, who served as Dr. Britton's bodyguard. Hill also wounded June Barrett during the attack on July 29, 1994. Paul Hill, a member of the Army of God, was one of many anti-choice extremists who believe that violent acts against abortion clinics are justified and necessary to protect the life of unborn babies. Up to the point of his execution, Hill continued to urge anti-abortion supporters to stop abortion, no matter what the cost. Although most would consider Paul Hill a vicious killer, his supporters consider him a hero of the faith.

Sadly, this heinous crime is not an isolated incident. Health care providers and their staff have had to take additional security measures in recent years to protect themselves from such violence. According to the National Abortion Federation, a total of 5,622 acts of violence against abortion providers were reported between 1977 and 2007, with 1,285 acts of violence reported during 2005–2007 alone (NAF, 2007). It would be impossible to determine whether all such attacks were motivated by specific religious beliefs; however, it is safe to assume that at least a percentage of them were, since religious principles are often at the core of the debate about reproductive rights. Since mainstream pro-life supporters condone such violence, how and under what circumstances does religion become a core feature of the type of violence I have just described? How does religion have the power to move people to commit such heinous acts?

Approximately one week after the execution of Paul Hill, the Catholic archdiocese of Boston agreed to pay a settlement of $85 million to 552 victims of sexual abuse by priests—one of the largest lump-sum settlements paid by any diocese in the United States. Sexual abuse by priests was first identified as an issue in the early 1980s, and the U.S. Roman Catholic Church continues to struggle with this problem nationally. The Boston archdiocese is only one of many dioceses across the country that have had to face lawsuits and deal with the arrest and conviction of clergy in their employ. Although specific religious beliefs are not at issue in these cases, the carte blanche social power granted to religious authorities in the United States creates a climate in which such crimes can be committed.

As you will discover in this text, as in these two cases, religion plays a prominent role in a vast array of criminal behaviors. There is no denying that religion is fundamental to the fabric of American life. Religion has been a multidimensional, complex force in American history, and despite our ardent commitment to secular approaches to law, government, and economic prosperity, it remains central. Intuitively we all have some idea of what religion is and what it means to individuals and to societies, yet it is difficult to define religion exactly. Perhaps Karl Marx had an understanding of the power of religion: "Religion is the sigh of the oppressed creature, the heart of the heartless world, just as it is the spirit of a spiritless situation. It is the opiate of the people" (quoted by Bowker, 2000, p. xviii).

Karl Marx is just one of many scholars and theologians to have attempted to define religion and how and why it is such an important organizing principle in people's lives. Perhaps religion has the opiate properties Marx describes. Charles Kimball (2002) states that "religion is arguably the most powerful and pervasive force on earth" (p. 1). It is certainly true that religion provides millions with fervent spiritual guidance, strong social bonds, and principles to guide decision making and behavior. Faith, regardless of specific religious affiliation, endures as an instrument of healing and hope during difficult times. Faith communities have played a role in healing neighborhoods broken by drugs, crime, poverty, and natural disasters, and religious leaders in particular have been central to this effort. For many, religious beliefs bring understanding and meaning to life.

For the most part, religion is regarded as an integral and positive component of American culture. After all, early U.S. history was centered on the religious vision held dear by colonists who fled religious persecution and on the strength and richness of religious beliefs held by African Americans and Native Americans. Throughout American history, religion has been a focal point for political discourse and the impetus for public policy reform. As Butler, Wacker, and Balmer (2003) note, religion has changed, and in turn has been changed by, events in U.S. history. In fact, it is probably fair to say that despite the evolutionary changes of American culture over time, Americans have sustained a high degree of faith, even though that faith is represented in a diverse set of religions beliefs, traditions, customs, and practices. Surveys indicate that Americans have a high rate of religious participation and donate a considerable amount of human and financial resources to religious organizations (Sherkat & Ellison, 1999).

Therefore, it should not be surprising to us to find that religiosity continues to be a dominant theme in modern-day American politics and public policy debates. Many may argue that religion has always been fundamental to such dialogues; however, there does appear to have been a renewed interest in exploring the role of religion in America in recent years. A changing political environment in which faith-based discourse is tolerated, and perhaps in some circumstances even embraced, is bringing such a dialogue to the forefront, in part through the political momentum built by religious conservatives and the expressed religiosity of President George W. Bush Jr. Debates on the relationship between morality, politics, and law continue to rage in reference to a number of issues, including pornography, drugs, crime, divorce, sexual orientation, and reproductive rights. The growth in scientific inquiry into the sociology of religion reflects a revival of interest in religion on the part of social scientists as well (Sherkat & Ellison, 1999).

Technological advances in communications and mass media have provided us an opportunity to observe, in a way that just was not possible even twenty years ago, the interaction between religion and society in a variety of settings. The Internet, the 24/7 availability of news programming, and instantaneous access to news stories worldwide have provided a new venue in which we can observe religiosity in action. The execution of Paul Hill is just one of many events with religious overtones to dominate the news agenda in recent years. For example, the horror of September 11, 2001, the sexual abuse scandal of the Catholic Church, and the tragedies of the Branch Davidians and Heaven's Gate have been captured on film and will, therefore, forever be ingrained in our collective memory.

Moreover, the World Wide Web has become a venue for both new religious movements and more established religious organizations to preach their views and to recruit new members across the nation and the world. The information age has certainly prompted numerous changes in how we interact as a society and has provided a new forum for religious discourse.

This renewed interest in exploring the role of religion is reflected in a number of ways; however, political arguments have centered on the purported role of religion in healing all social ills—in particular, crime, drug abuse, and teenage pregnancy (Kaminer, 1997). For example, William J. Bennett (former U.S. Drug Czar) and John P. Walters (the current director of the Office of National Drug Control Policy), together with professor John Dilulio, insist that America's problems with drugs and crime are a direct result of a moral decay they refer to as "moral poverty." They offer religion as a solution to such social problems (Bennett, Dilulio, & Walters, 1996). A recent survey of 2,600 Americans showed some support for this notion, with 70 percent of respondents claiming they wanted religion to play a greater role in American society. However, the majority believed this role should be at the personal level, not at the governmental level (Gallop-Goodman, 2001).

While the focus of the political dialogue is the appropriate role for religion in the establishment of political agendas and public policy, Americans are also on the cusp of a different type of national dialogue, one that has been ignited by recent tragic events, scandals, acts of terrorism, and legal challenges. This dialogue has not yet fully emerged, but it is simmering just below the surface. It is a dialogue that we are fearful of starting. Certainly, the events of September 11, 2001, have served as a wake-up call to the potential deadly consequences of religious fervor. Yet, despite the active discourse on terrorism, the issue has still largely been safely defined within the dichotomous terms of "us versus them." In other words, this is a dialogue in which "their" (the terrorists') religious views are somehow considered separate and distinct from "our" own, although it is very clear that Americans do not have one common religious palate. Acts of terrorism, such as those experienced on September 11 or those committed by Paul Hill, involve a number of different factors that must be understood from psychological, social, and political perspectives. Religion may well be the central organizing factor that pulls together the other psychosocial or political concerns to mobilize belief into action.

Although a national dialogue has begun to materialize, as citizens we have been reluctant to acknowledge the crime and violence that members of "our" own religious communities have perpetrated. We appear to be comfortable discussing the connection between violence and religion in the context of violence perpetrated by foreigners on foreign soil, yet we are unable to articulate fully what such a discussion might mean domestically. For example, the arrest of Eric Rudolph in June 2003 for the bombings of two abortion clinics, a gay nightclub, and the 1996 Atlanta Olympics generated a flurry of media commentaries on whether it is appropriate to refer to Rudolph as a "Christian terrorist," not unlike referring to Osama Bin Laden as a "Muslim or Islamic terrorist."

Definitional dilemmas such as how to characterize the actions of someone like Eric Rudolph raise a number of interesting questions that we have not yet been able fully to digest. Perhaps such questions are part and parcel of the dynamics of social change and are indicative of the dawn of a new religious era in America, or perhaps they were buried long ago and are now just beginning to resurface. History is replete with examples of the horrors of religious tyranny and war, so it is not clear why we would be in denial that such religious conflicts could flourish in the United States. Whether we are ready to hear it or not, the reality is that religion is central to some crime and violence problems in the United States.

Worship and Sin: An Exploration of Religion-Related Crime in the United States asks not what the moral community can do for a social problem such as crime, but under what circumstances such a moral community becomes the source of the problem. The darker side of religion is exposed to advance a framework within which to describe and comprehend what Kurst-Swanger and Ryniker (2003) termed "religion-related crime." Some will find the contents of this book fascinating; others will find them unsettling. This book combines both theoretical and practical concerns and may raise more questions than it answers. It will explore a variety of theoretical concepts, provide an overview of the different types of religion-related crimes, examine the dilemmas faced by religious and secular authorities, review current public policy and legal challenges and ramifications, and make recommendations for practitioners and researchers. The subject matter is approached from a multidisciplinary perspective, but the specific purpose of this book is to provide a beginning point from which to conceptualize crime of which religion is a core feature. My hope is that others will see value in characterizing religion-related crime as a distinct subset of criminology. Future research and discourse are important to advance our understanding of the issues this category of crime raises—issues that this book only begins to explore.

Religion and Criminology: A Brief Overview

The relationship between religion and crime has been studied in the past by sociologists, criminologists, and historians; however, this research has been limited to three essential domains: the influence of religion on the evolution of law and public policy, the role of religion in correctional environments and the development of correctional alternatives, and the influence of religion as a mechanism of social control and legal conformity.

Scholars have explored the historical influences of religion in the development of American jurisprudence (Holbrook, 1987) and penology (Mackey, 1987; Skotnicki, 2000). Religion has helped shape the American system of justice as well as other justice systems around the world. In fact, religious dialogue continues to influence the evolution of restorative justice models (Grimsrud & Zehr, 2002; Hadley, 2001; Marshall, 2001). In addition, religious views have been found to be connected to public opinion about appropriate responses to crime, including rehabilitative and punitive policy choices (Applegate, Cullen, & Fisher, 2000). In particular, religious arguments have been made to support or to refute the death penalty (Hanks, 1997; Harvey, 1986; Marshall, 2001).

Others have inquired into religion as a mechanism of social control, its influence in rehabilitating offenders, its potential as a remedy for crime, and its efficacy in correctional management. Scholars have investigated the role of religion in offender rehabilitation (Jensen & Gibbons, 2002; Johnson, 1987, 2004; O'Connor & Perreyclear, 2002), prison adjustment and disciplinary problems (Clear & Sumter, 2002; Johnson, Larson, & Pitts, 1999), and the correctional environment (Dammer, 2002; Johnson, 1987). Others have examined the role of faith-based organizations in offender recovery (Camp et al., 2006; Earley, 2005; Johnson, 2004).

The courts have grappled with religious freedom issues as they pertain to prison inmates and have afforded prisoners rights to pursue religious practices (*Cruz v. Beto*, 1972) provided those practices do not violate the safety concerns of the prison administration or involve the use of contraband drugs. For example, in *Dettmer v. Landon* (1985), a federal district court ruled that an inmate could legitimately practice Wicca and should therefore be provided with items that relate to Wicca worship. However, the U.S. Court of Appeals for the Fourth Circuit later ruled that prison security becomes paramount if a prisoner's possession of religious items conflicts with prison security (*Dettmer v. Landon*, 1986).

Scholars also have taken great interest in exploring whether religious beliefs can actually deter individuals from engaging in deviant behavior, thereby potentially preventing crime. A number of studies have been conducted, with varied results (Bainbridge, 1989, 1992; Hirschi & Stark, 1969; Stark, 1987). A recent study by Colin Baier and Bradley Wright (2001) examined sixty previous studies on this topic. Their findings indicate that the effect of religion on criminal behavior is moderate, and they note that it is likely studies have found varying effects of religion on criminal behavior because of differences in their conceptual and methodological approaches. Recently, Chu (2007) investigated the potential role of religiosity in the initiation of and the desistance from drug use.

It is clear from this brief overview that criminology has begun to develop a body of literature to examine the place of religion within the broad theme of crime and justice. Zehr (2005) and Hostetter (2005) both argue that religious beliefs and practices play a substantial role in shaping our cultural views about crime and punishment and thus that religious study is important to the study of criminology. Yet, despite this growing body of literature, there appears to be a missing link. Little attention has been paid to the role of religion and religiosity in the commission of crimes. There has been little to no acknowledgement that religious people or groups (with the exception of those groups labeled "cults") can be the cause of criminal problems within their communities. This text is intended to shed some light on this topic by providing a comprehensive, if not exhaustive, overview and a framework within which to explore religion-related crime. Let us now outline the terminology that will be utilized throughout the text.

Religion-Related Crime Defined

As I suggested earlier, the time has come for America to confront the reality that sometimes, and in certain circumstances, religion, religiosity, or the sacred position of religious authority in American society becomes the central element of criminal behavior. I used the term "religion-related crime" originally to describe crimes that had been committed within a variety of religious contexts (Kurst-Swanger & Ryniker, 2003), since I could find no other term to describe such a broad array of crimes in any scholarly or popular writings. Some scholars have written extensively about specific aspects of religion-related crime, such as clergy malfeasance (Jenkins, 1996; Shupe, Stacey, & Darnell, 2000), cults (Galanter, 1999; Jenkins, 2000), and terrorism (Hoffman, 2006; Reich, 1998; White, 2005). Others have focused on specific religious groups, noting their interactions with crime and the criminal justice system. For example, Michael Barkun (1997) traces the origins of the Christian Identity Movement, and Jon Krakauer (2004) traces the evolution of the Church of the Latter-Day Saints and the growth of the Fundamental Latter-Day Saints.

However, little attention has been paid to examining these aspects comprehensively. Criminologists have identified and categorized other types of criminal behavior such as organized crime, occupational crime, white-collar crime, hate crime, family violence, environmental crime, political crime, and victimless crime. These categories help to distinguish each crime category and provide a framework within which to study these distinctive elements in greater depth. This text argues that religion-related crime should be similarly distinguished. It is one cluster of criminal behavior that has yet to be fully described and defined. As we come to learn in this volume, religion-related crime is extensive, and elements of it exist in a variety of contexts, not just those few areas that have gotten the attention of scholars and the media. Owing to its complexity, conceptualizing religion-related crime requires a flexible definition and framework. I define religion-related crime as "[a]ny illegal or socially injurious act which is committed within the auspices of religious practice or as a result of a particular religious belief" (Kurst-Swanger & Ryniker, 2003, p. 63).

This definition acknowledges the broad array of situations in which religion plays a central role in the commission of illegal and/or socially harmful acts, as when

- theology is used to instigate or justify criminal behavior to meet personal, social, or political agendas.
- religious practices are not in line with secular law.
- religious organizations use their sacred social position to cover up criminal behavior.
- religious organizations provide individuals with opportunities to commit crime.
- crimes are committed to support the religious group or its agenda financially.
- individuals or groups are targets for victimization because of their religious affiliation.

Religion-Related Crime: A Typology

I have suggested elsewhere (Kurst-Swanger & Ryniker, 2003) a three-pronged typology as a potential conceptual framework. A couple of caveats are in order. First, it is important to note that this framework is intended to explore religion-related crime within the social, cultural, and legal environment of the United States. The crimes examined here are all domestic and involve perpetrators who are U.S. citizens.

Second, one can easily argue that some of the examples I provide within the text could fall into more than one of the three categories I define:

- theologically based religion-related crime
- reactive/defensive religion- related crime
- abuse of religious authority

These three categories are intended to distinguish the features of crime to help us better understand the specific role that theology, religious practice, belief systems, and religious organizations play in the motives and behaviors of the religious people who violate secular law. Yet these three categories are not necessarily mutually exclusive. Like other kinds of crime, religion-related crime can have many dimensions, of which religion may be only one; therefore, it is not always clear how best to conceptualize certain criminal acts. Thus, the typology presented here has been created more to provide an organized framework for discussion than as a concrete theoretical proposition. Although these three categories are driven in part by the relationship between religion and motive, they are intended to be viewed as descriptive rather than explanatory.

Theologically Based Religion-Related Crime

The first category comprises crime committed as a result of particular religious practice or as an extension of a specific religious belief. Violation of the law results from the dissonance between religious beliefs or theology and secular law. In some instances, crimes are committed as a direct result of a particular religious belief or practice. In other cases, religiosity may play a role in perpetuating criminal victimization. Three chapters of this text are devoted to exploring crime in which theology plays a major role. The examples provided here are crimes against children, crimes against women, and the use of illicit drugs.

Reactive/Defensive Religion-Related Crime

This second category comprises cases in which a religious leader or group (defined as two or more people) commits a crime in reaction to, or in defense of, some type of external force or conflict. Such external forces can be social, political, or legal and are probably reflective of the inherent conflicts between Church, state, and the broader secular society. In some instances, crime is committed to facilitate or initiate change in the social order, ultimately to defend specific religious principles. In other words, religious adherents may become criminal actors to influence secular society. Thus, crimes of this nature are generally reactionary or revolutionary. In this vein, this category of religion-related crime may be similar to what criminologists have described as political crime. Since social change often requires financial resources, religious followers may commit additional crimes to support their intended religious missions.

In other instances, crimes in this category are more defensive in nature, meaning that a crime is committed to protect religious followers or belief systems from the threat of external influences. In some cases, religious followers engage in criminal actions that are harmful to themselves and their families to defend or protect themselves from the pressures exerted by secular forces.

Reactive/defensive religion-related crimes tend to be more violent in nature, since the aim is to maintain, defend, or alter the existing political, legal, or social structure. The loss of life and destruction of property have taken their toll on many communities, and law enforcement officials are challenged to seek preventive measures to contain explosive violence related to religious zeal. It is important to note that what distinguishes the crimes described here from those described as theologically based is their eruption as a reactionary or defensive mechanism to some external threat, whether that threat is considered in theological, legal, social, or political terms. This difference may be a subtle one, but it is an important distinguishing feature to help us understand the social and psychological factors involved in this crime category. Three chapters are devoted to an exploration of this domain. These chapters explore the notion of destructive religious groups, crimes perpetrated against reproductive health providers, and hate crimes.

Abuse of Religious Authority

The third type of religion-related crime comprises situations in which clergy, lay leaders, or high-level Church officials abuse their religious authority for personal or institutional gain. This category also includes religious institutions that either actively participate in crime or, through neglect, place the institution and their parishioners at risk of criminal victimization. Unlike with the other types of religion-related crime described in this text, religion or theology has little to do with the commission of the crimes of interest here. Rather, religion provides the social context in which such crimes can flourish because of the "holy" or "divine" role that faith leaders have in American society. When clergy take advantage of this special role by committing crime or when religious leaders cover up such crime to protect the institution, they abuse the authority they have been granted by their religious institutions and their followers. In this sense, the abuse of religious authority as a type of religion-related crime is most closely associated with what criminologists have defined as occupational or corporate crime. This text explores this category in two chapters. The first explores the conceptualization of the abuse of religious authority, and the second provides examples of economic, personal, and organizational crime.

2

What is Religion?

Many things in life are difficult to describe. Art, wisdom, and beauty are three that come to mind. We know what these terms imply, yet we might be hard pressed to formalize a precise definition of each, given their subjective nature. It may well be that religion also falls in this category. Consider for a moment how you might pen a definition of religion, one that transcends your own personal belief system and can accommodate a wide range of traditions. If you are having difficulty defining religion, then you are in good company, since there is no universal agreement as to what religion is.

In fact, defining religion may prove to be more difficult than conceptualizing religion-related crime. Scholars, faith leaders, and the courts have all grappled to find a cogent definition of religion that can adequately represent all kinds and types of traditions, beliefs, and worldviews. This is complicated by the fact that in some cultures religious traditions are considered in organizational or institutional terms (denominations, sects, churches, etc.), whereas in other cultures religion is not considered a separate or distinct phenomenon but rather is fully embodied in both the public and private lives of citizens.

Thus, defining religion has become a rather controversial matter. Regardless of the specific definition one chooses to adopt, most scholars would acknowledge that religion is part of human life in all cultures. It is experienced in cognitive, emotional, and behavioral terms (Argyle, 2002) and has both social and cultural dimensions. Religions are not stagnant; they evolve and change to meet individual, social, and cultural challenges (Partridge, 2004) and are inextricably woven into world events.

For the sake of simplicity, I will adopt Rossano's (2006) definition of religion as "beliefs or actions predicated on the existence of supernatural entities or forces with powers of agency that can intervene in or otherwise affect human affairs" (p. 346) since this definition is consistent with those of several other scholars. Although this definition may not be satisfying to everyone, it suits our purposes here since this book is intended to explore crime in which religion is a factor. The individuals and religious groups mentioned in this text reflect a wide range of religious traditions, all of which fit this general definition.

Religiosity

As difficult as is it to provide a tangible, concrete definition for a concept as abstract as religion, it is equally difficult to capture an adequate measurement of religiosity. Religiosity is the extent to which a person is religious or is involved in or committed to religion. Himmelfarb (1975) defines religious involvement as "the degree to which a person's religion occupies his or her interests, beliefs, or activities" (p. 607). For several decades researchers have attempted to qualify and quantify religiosity and have looked to explain determinants of religious behavior. For instance, Glock (1962) expanded the conceptualization of religiosity by proposing that it involved five different dimensions: experiential (feeling/emotion), ritualistic (relating to religious behavior, such as going to church), ideological (the degree to which a person acknowledges specific beliefs or tenets), intellectual (knowledge), and consequential (the effects of religious involvement on secular things). Later, Stark and Glock (1968) revised the schema to include only four dimensions: belief, practice, knowledge, and experience. Other researchers have since tested this typology or proposed different ways to conceptualize religiosity (Clayton, 1968, 1971; Cornwall et al., 1986; Faulkner & de Jong, 1966; Himmelfarb, 1975; King & Hunt, 1969, 1972). Many scholars would agree that religiosity is a complex concept with both personal and social dimensions that relate to cognitive, affective, and behavioral domains.

It is especially important to consider the social dimensions of religiosity, for religious worldviews and behavior are not developed within a vacuum; they are socially constructed. As sociologists posit, the structure of social arrangements, environments, and the interactions between individuals and groups all have an impact on individual behavior. In fact, much criminological theory is based on this assumption. In terms of religion-related crime, the social dimension of religiosity is likely to be particularly relevant, since it is within a religious environment or community that such crime occurs. Group involvement and personal community relationships, as well as religious socialization, seem to play a role in religious behavior (Cornwall, 1989). Thus, to understand religion-related crime more fully, we must appreciate the social space in which some religious individuals, groups, and communities function.

Religious Conversion

Another important feature of religion and religiosity is the concept of religious conversion. Loosely defined, conversion is the embracing of a new religious belief system, or the renewal or reaffirmation of a familiar religious identity, or the transition from one religious conceptualization to another. Snow and Machalek (1984) note that conversion is a "displacement of one universe of discourse by another" (p. 170).

Conversion, like religion itself, is difficult to conceptualize. It appears to involve some aspect of a core change, although scholars are reluctant to specify the degree or type of change (Snow & Machalek, 1984) that must occur before the term "conversion" or "convert" is applied. Roof (1989) notes that about one-third of U.S. adults have changed religions at some point in their life, and research suggests that switching religions is a complex phenomenon (Loveland, 2003).

The word "conversion" is derived from the Latin word *converiere*, which means to "resolve" or to "turn around" or "head in a different direction" (Flinn, 1987). Research suggests that conversion is driven by a number of different factors, including economic, social, orgasmic, psychic, and ethical deprivation (Glock, 1964) or the belief that enduring personal problems are best resolved within a religious perspective (Lofland & Stark, 1965). Conversion means different things in different religious traditions, and our understanding of the psychological and neurophysiological facets of conversion is incomplete (Bowker, 2000).

Religious conversion is likely to occur in stages, since the adoption of a new religious identity is not something that occurs without thought and deliberation. Although conversion can be initiated by specific events, Rambo (1993) describes conversion as a dynamic process of change that occurs over time and is influenced by a complex mix of cultural, social, personal, and religious factors. It involves a variety of "forces, ideas, institutions, rituals, myths, and symbols" (Rambo, 1993, p. 11) and is best understood from a multidisciplinary perspective. Thus, it is impossible to identify one set cause of conversion or one specific process that is shared by all converts, especially since individual faith traditions define conversion in a way that is consistent with their particular theological beliefs.

Rambo (1993) describes conversion as a series of seven stages that involve many relationships, circumstances, and situations. It is especially useful to conceptualize conversion utilizing his stage model because the model helps to explain the richness and complexity of conversion—both of which are important to our understanding of how and why religion-related crime occurs. Stage 1 is *context*, which explores the backdrop for conversion, in which influences from education, training, ideologies, institutions, the media, and people shape the thoughts, feelings, desires, or aspirations of the potential convert. It should be considered the "total environment in which conversion transpires" (p. 20).

Stage 2 of Rambo's model is *crisis*; that is, religious conversion is usually preceded by some type of crisis, whether personal, emotional, religious, or cultural. Of particular importance are crises that are life changing in some cumulative or substantial way. Crises may arise internally within the individual or may be caused by external forces.

Crises serve as a catalyst for change. Stage 3 of the model proposes that the process of resolving such crises is a *quest*. Questing is the process by which individuals actively try to resolve their crises, seek answers to their questions about life, and look to secure meaning and purpose in their lives. Questing for a better, more meaningful life is a complex undertaking, but one that is shared by many of those who undergo religious conversion.

Stage 4 of the model involves an *encounter* between the potential convert and members of the religious community, who are referred to as "advocates." Rambo notes the importance of the dynamic interaction during the encounter phase, when those seeking alternatives and resolution are introduced or reintroduced to advocates with a different orientation. It is during this stage that potential converts may be impressed by the charismatic authority of a particular religious leader or individual. Not all encounters result in conversion, but encounters can help to educate or orientate the potential convert to the options available to him or her.

Interaction between the advocate and potential convert is the fifth stage. It is during this stage that an ongoing relationship develops between the potential convert and the advocate. The convert becomes more involved in learning about the religious group, their religious beliefs, rituals, language, practices, and customs. The scope of this stage varies among religious traditions; the potential convert may be invited to participate in religious activities and rituals, may develop personal attachments to the group, and may learn a new language and embody new roles in life. This process tends to be intense—a process by which the potential convert is immersed in the new religion. In essence, this interaction involves the socialization of the new convert in the ways of the religious community.

This intense interaction between advocates and potential converts is an important entrée to the sixth stage of conversion, *commitment.* Commitment is the decision to embrace the new religion and all its rituals and traditions. Commitment is demonstrated through practicing the religion's key rituals, such as following a specific diet, changing one's clothing, altering one's personal schedule for prayer and rituals, and so on. The adoption of the norms, mores, and symbols of the new religion serves to cement the convert's commitment to the new religion and to signal the shedding of the "old" life of the convert. In some religious traditions, commitment is marked by a specific transformation ceremony or ritual in which the convert is officially welcomed into the religious community.

The final stage of Rambo's model relates to the *consequences* of conversion. These consequences are often evident in the earlier stages, but since conversion is a process, they may not be discovered until one has fully committed or surrendered oneself to the new religion. The consequences of conversion can be positive or negative as converts continually evaluate their experiences. Conversion requires ongoing support and affirmation if it is to be permanent.

In addition to viewing conversion as a process, it is helpful to consider conversion as an experience that has a variety of patterns or types. Lofland and Skonovd (1981) describe conversion in terms of "conversion motifs." Motif experiences are those elements that are most vivid or brilliant to the convert. Lofland and Skonovd identify six different conversion motifs, which represent the most defining or illuminating experiences of the conversion process: intellectual, mystical, experimental, affectional, revivalist, and coercive.

In *intellectual conversion*, the potential convert immerses him- or herself in researching the new religion and actively pursues information through books, magazines, television, videos, and so on. In this type of conversion, there is little social pressure to convert, since converts can often take advantage of the plethora of information that is readily available on different religious traditions. Lofland and Skonovd note the emergence of "electronic churches" that reach out to potential converts via television, thereby providing an opportunity for individuals to connect to various religious options in the privacy of their own home.

In *mystical conversion*, the experience is marked by a sudden and overwhelming experience that is life changing and difficult to describe in objective terms. Such experiences may involve visions, voices, or hallucinations. The time in which conversion is achieved is generally quite short; however, it is usually preceded by a period of stress that could extend much further back.

In *experimental conversion*, the potential convert takes the opportunity to "try out" the new religion to see whether it will suit his or her needs. Potential converts experiment with the religion by participating in it but withholding full or genuine conversion after a sense of involvement has yielded positive benefits.

In *affectional conversion*, the convert is positively affected by the interpersonal social bonds created by interacting with other members of the faith. Converts feel affirmed, accepted, and loved by the leader or other members of the group. The central experience is said to be affection, and belief arises out of regular participation in the religious group.

Revivalist conversion, which has declined in recent times, involves a conversion experience in which the group applies pressure to the potential convert through highly emotionally charged group activities. The revivalist type of conversion involves groups of people involved in "ecstatic arousals" that can have an impact on new converts. Group behavior might include events and activities that serve to stimulate intense fear, guilt, and joy within the convert, such as singing, chanting, and hand holding.

Finally, *coercive conversion* is a very rare form in which the convert is exposed to "brainwashing," or thought-reform, programs or to coercive persuasion through a deliberate and intense process of pressure from other group members. Converts are coerced into participation, conformity to the group norms, and confession.

Rambo's (1993) stages and Lofland and Skonovd's (1981) conversion motifs confirm that conversion is a complex process that is experienced in cognitive, emotional, and social domains. Conversion—especially when it involves a new religious movement whose beliefs and practices are not well understood—can be very controversial, especially if it is coercive. In fact, hundreds of court cases have involved claims that conversion into such groups was coerced or that new members were "brainwashed" (Richardson & Ginsburg, 1998). For instance, in *U.S. v. Fishman* (1990), Steven Fishman was indicted on eleven counts of mail fraud for obtaining settlement monies and securities in connection with shareholder class action lawsuits during 1983–1988. He filed an insanity defense, claiming that the Church of Scientology (of which he was a member) had practiced influencing techniques, or brainwashing, that disturbed his state of mind at the time of the offenses. In furtherance of his defense, he planned to call two witnesses to the stand to testify to the nature of coercive persuasion in religious movements. The court rejected this specific testimony as inadmissible on the basis that such coercive practices had not been sufficiently established within the scientific community.

Although many individuals devote their time to "deprogramming" individuals after involvement in a religious movement, many scholars argue that there is little scientific evidence to support the claim that individuals are routinely brainwashed into converting (Dawson, 1998; Richardson & Ginsberg, 1998).

Richardson (1994) argued that individuals who join such groups are in search of personal change, and, consequently, conversion is not coercive. Galanter (1999) found that the religious followers in his study all reported that their emotional state improved after joining a new religious group, whether or not they were seriously distressed before joining. "Such emotional gains reinforce members' involvement in the group by effectively 'rewarding' them for their fealty to it" (Galanter, 1999, p. 33). Levine (1984) notes that young people are particularly good candidates for conversion because they are generally not fully committed to careers or families of their own. Like the elderly, they are free to move into or to try out an alternative religious environment. In fact, research suggests that participation in new religious movements is rather fluid, with most participants leaving of their own volition after a short time (Anthony & Robbins, 2003; Bird & Reiner, 1982; Dawson, 1998; Richardson & Ginsberg, 1998).

Yet, as Kent and Hall (2000) point out, although brainwashing has been dismissed as a generic principle of conversion to new religious movements, little attention has been paid to the possible application of the brainwashing concept to a religious group's efforts to "retain" or "reconvert" members. Through their research with members of the Children of God/the Family, Kent and Hall found evidence of deliberate brainwashing by church leaders of their adolescent members through Teen Training Camps. Since the teenagers were members of the religious group by default, they did not have the opportunity to experience real conversion as their parents had. Thus, the purpose of these intense "training" programs was to make adolescent members of the group compliant and dependent upon the leaders and their doctrines. The research found evidence of physical, psychological, and socioemotional abuse and confinement during the training programs in the 1980s. Thus, the type of treatment these young people suffered at the hands of their church elders was held to be consistent with how scholars define the critical elements of a thought-reform program.

Church-Sect Typology

Our understanding of religions and how they relate to the larger society has been enhanced by the categorization of religions along a continuum generally referred to as "the church-sect typology." First introduced by Max Weber, and later expanded by Ernest Troeltsch, the church-sect typology attempts to classify religious groups according to their relationship with their external environment. This typology was first used to compare and contrast different kinds of religious groups—namely, the polar opposites of churches and sects (Swatos, 1998). The church-sect typology has been used by sociologists as a framework to describe the different organizational elements of religious groups. It also serves as a theoretical proposition for how religions evolve.

A religious group's relationship with the broader community is an important facet of various religion-related crimes. As we will discover, in some instances the theology of religious groups is at odds with secular society, and violation of the law is the result of the dissonance between theology and secular law. In other instances, religious groups conflict with their external environments intentionally to change or adapt to various external forces. In yet other situations, clergy can take advantage of the harmonious relationship their religious group enjoys with the external community. This text provides some evidence that crime exists in religious groups of all types. Thus, our understanding of the motives and causes of specific types of crime is enhanced by understanding the role of a particular religious group in the community. Although it is beyond the scope of this book to detail the historical evolution of the religious groups of interest here, it is important to note that religious groups do evolve and change over time. They take on different organizational forms and elements. They are influenced by the political, social, and cultural events of their time, and, in turn, they often directly influence those events.

There follows a basic review of the general terminology used to describe different types of religious organizations. Keep in mind that the media have often popularized these terms and applied the same labels to different types of religious groups and that some religious groups debate the terminology used to describe them.

Churches

A church is a religious organization that "accepts the social order and integrates existing cultural definitions into its religious ideology" (Dynes, 1955, p. 555). In addition, churches are closely affiliated with the state, their members are organized hierarchically, they employ appropriately credentialed clergy, and generally they gain new members through reproduction and the socialization of young children into the religion (Johnstone, 1983). Thus, a church both accepts and reinforces the broader secular society and is an institutionalized part of the community.

Sects

In contrast to churches, sects are religious organizations that protest the traditional, more established religious groups and often reject the broader secular society

(Johnstone, 1983). They are often considered to be small religious organizations that deviate from an established church or denomination. They are generally dissenting religious groups whose formation is a direct result of some disagreement or division from the religion of origin. Sects tend to hold most of the same beliefs as the religion of origin; however, a number of differences distinguish them from that religion. Sects generally do not desire to change secular society; rather, they are satisfied to be left to their own practices (Sommerville, 2000). Partridge (2004) notes that sects often claim to be the "true" defenders of the faith in the "face of a church or religion that has become 'lukewarm' and barely distinguishable from the surrounding society and culture" (pp. 17–18).

Denomination

A denomination is a religious group within a major religion. The denomination shares the same faith and organization as the major religion. Denominations were originally conceptualized as part of the evolution of a sect or considered a more advanced stage of a sect. As sects evolve, they become more entrenched in their communities and thus grow to be seen as acceptable by others in the community. This growth results in a more stable religious institution, one that is able to embrace the notion of individualism while more closely aligning itself with the social order in which it exists. Martin (1962) notes that denominations tend to flourish in countries, such as the United States, where social change advances at a steady pace.

Cults/New Religious Movements/Alternative Spiritualities

Cults, often referred to today as "new religious movements" or "alternative spiritualities," are religious groups with a novel set of beliefs, practices, and customs. They tend to have a high degree of conflict or tension with the mainstream culture and thus are more alienated from secular society. Scholars have noted a proliferation of new religions in recent years, likely due, at least in part, to the evolution of a global market and the ease with which one can travel to, or access information about, other cultures and societies (Partridge, 2004). In fact, today the United States is considered the most religiously diverse nations in the world (Eck, 2001). It is also interesting to note that all the major religions of the world, including Christianity, Islam, and Buddhism, began as alternative movements considered deviant by the larger society of the time (Zellner & Petrowsky, 1998).

Does Religion Cause Crime?

As I have noted, criminologists have focused their attention on religion and religiosity as a potential deterrent to crime. Yet this text is poised to argue that religion and religiosity may also play a substantial role in the commission of various crimes, including arson, physical and sexual assault, fraud, embezzlement, and drug trafficking and possession. Although this book provides ample evidence to support this position, is religion really the problem? Certainly Charles Kimball (2002) was not exaggerating when he stated that "more wars have been waged, more people killed, and these days more evil perpetrated in the name of religion than by any other institutional force in human history" (p. 1). Wellman and Tokuno (2004) note that tension or conflict exists in all religious groups and is critical to their identity and group mobilization; violence is not an uncommon result of that conflict. They argue that religion "is a nexus of independent power, which by its very nature threatens political centers, no matter their shape or size" (p. 293). It is within the scope of this independent power that religious members and leaders possess a social clout that can marshal groups of people toward whatever goals they seek to attain, even if the goals invoke violence or involve violating the law. Since religion is such an omnipresent force, and religious conflict has been so pervasive throughout history, it is likely that religious violence will persist in modern cultures.

Today, religion is studied within different academic disciplines, including history, political science, sociology, psychology, anthropology, archaeology, medicine, ecology, economics, law, philosophy, music, art, and literature. The academic, secular study of religion, often referred to as "Religious Studies," generally involves a multidisciplinary approach to the study of religion and comparative religion. In contrast, the term "Theology," whose definition is also rather controversial, refers more specifically to the study of the beliefs, texts, and doctrines on of a particular religious tradition. The term has its origins in Greek (*theo* ["god"] + *logos* [discourse]) and was used to describe poets, such as Hesiod and Homer, who wrote about the gods (Bowker, 2000). Rooted in Christian traditions, theology has broadened to the study of the nature of many different religious traditions.

To understand the complex dynamics of religion-related crime, such a multidisciplinary approach is truly necessary. We cannot simply argue that religion itself is the cause of crime, since most people of strong faith live as law-abiding citizens, and many individuals who commit crime are not religious. Nevertheless, there does appear to be a relationship in some cases. What is the essence of that relationship? Well, unfortunately, there are no simple answers to that question. In fact, religion's relationship to crime involves factors best examined across *micro, meso,* and *macro* levels of analysis.

Micro levels of analysis seek to explain social problems, such as crime, on an individual level. That is, we seek to understand the phenomenon by examining the features and characteristics of individual behavior. Explaining religion-related crime at a micro level involves an understanding of the role of religion in the lives of the individuals involved and the impact of religion, religiosity, religious experiences, conversion, or religious beliefs on human functioning and behavior. It is at this level of analysis that psychological, psychobiological, and psychopathological theories of crime may have the greatest relevance.

Meso levels of analysis seek to explain social problems from the group perspective, by examining how individuals and groups affect each other and how environmental influences affect the group. This level of analysis involves the study of the social-psychological features of crime that result from the relationships between individuals and the intimate groups of which they are members. This level of analysis considers individual and group interactions to be important determinants of behavior. Thus, the interaction between religious groups and their members, and how such groups interact with the external environment, are particularly pertinent to the discussion of some types of religion-related crime.

Finally, macro levels of analysis seek to explain social problems in terms of the larger arrangements of society, institutions, and organizations. This level of analysis considers the interactions between individuals, groups, and the various structures of society. Of importance are the interplay between social institutions, cultural values, and the norms of groups and their members.

These three levels of analysis provide a framework within which to recognize the multidimensional aspects of religion-related crime. Since religion has both personal and social dimensions, it is reasonable to assert that religion-related crime should be understood in similar terms, since no one level of analysis can adequately explain all types of religion-related crime. As this book intends to illustrate, religion-related crime involves a wide range of criminal activity, a variety of motives and dynamic personal and social factors that interact and converge in specific ways. Thus, understanding the types of criminal behavior explored in this text will require an acknowledgement that religion can lead to crime in a number of different ways. This is because of the place religion occupies in the lives of the individuals involved, religious doctrines that are sometimes inconsistent with secular law, the sheer diversity of religious organizations and institutions and their unique practices and customs, and the arrangements in American society that both support and limit religious expression.

3

Religion, Crime, and the First Amendment

A core principle of the American tradition is the vigilant protection of religious freedom. American history cannot be recounted without careful consideration of the role that religion has played in shaping the growth and development of our nation. Today, religion continues to be inextricably linked to typically secular affairs such as politics, law, and economics. In fact, religion and the pursuit of religious practice have been the cornerstone of numerous court battles throughout U.S. history, regarding a wide range of seemingly secular legal issues, including zoning and land use, taxes, door-to-door solicitation, education, voting and naturalization rights, property disputes, and family law. No contemporary political debate would be complete without religious consideration or reference.

In fact, many of us may take for granted that our religious beliefs, or lack or them, are fully guaranteed to us as Americans. Historian Edwin Gaustad (2003) reminds us that this was not always the case. Before the establishment of the United States in 1776, the U.S. Constitution in 1788, and the Bill of Rights in 1791, religious oppression was common. Sanctions such as incarceration, physical punishment, death, and exile were applied to individuals whose religious affiliations or practices were deemed unsuitable, and little legal protection was available against such persecution. Religious liberty was ultimately considered a concern of the states. Scholars cite the ratification of the First Amendment in 1791, which states "Congress shall make no law respecting an establishment of religion, or prohibiting the free exercise thereof," as the official proclamation of a formal federal commitment to religious independence. Although religious persecution and bigotry persist within the United States in a variety of circumstances, the notion of federally protected religious freedom has remained a fundamental tenet of the American way of life since the ratification of the Bill of Rights.

Yet, since 1791, the courts have grappled with the interpretation of this guarantee in its application to everyday situations. As First Amendment issues have been brought to the courts for determination, the opening phrase of the First Amendment has been dealt with as two distinct clauses: the establishment clause and the free exercise clause. Since most cases addressing religion have generally been related to one aspect or the other, examining cases via these two clauses has served a useful purpose.

The establishment clause, "shall make no law respecting an establishment of religion," continues to attract controversy over the original intention of the framers in crafting such deliberate language. Many have come to associate the First Amendment with the phrase "separation of church and state." Scholars argue that the establishment clause was intended to limit the ability of the new federal government to establish a federal religion and to prevent Congress from interfering in state affairs regarding religious issues (Fisher, 2002; Gordon, 2002) and from passing legislation on religious matters (Butler, Wacker, & Balmer, 2003). Generally speaking, the establishment clause prevents the federal government from establishing a particular religion, advancing one religion over another (Gaustad, 2003), or creating statutes that might appear to move the federal government toward the establishment of a particular religion (Witte, 2000).

The free exercise clause, "or prohibiting the free exercise thereof," protects religious beliefs and practices from the interference of the federal government. As with the establishment clause, interpreting the specific language of the free exercise clause remains a task of the courts. Such interpretation is critical to our understanding of the complex legal issues at stake when the activities or behaviors of individuals, in pursuit of their religion, conflict with federal, state, or local criminal or civil codes or ordinances.

This chapter is a brief historical overview of free exercise litigation, exploring in particular how the U.S. Supreme Court has analyzed and defined the meaning of the free exercise clause over time. The chapter is divided into four general sections, marked by pertinent cases that illustrate the major legal principles considered by the U.S. Supreme Court. Particular attention is paid to the views of the Justices as evidenced by their formal written opinions. Their words paint a vivid picture of how such legal issues were viewed by the Justices at the time.

Free Exercise Clause: The Early Years

Both clauses of the First Amendment speak only to the role of the federal government in enacting laws related to religious matters. The First Amendment reflected the diversity of religious development that flourished in colonial America, a pluralism that did not exist in other societies (Butler, Wacker, & Balmer, 2003). With it came a governmental pledge of six basic principles or essential rights: liberty of conscience, free exercise, religious equality, religious pluralism, disestablishment of religion, and the notion of the separation of church and state (Witte, 2000). States were left with the task of determining and resolving questions regarding these principles of religious liberty through their individual constitutions. About 135 different state constitutions were developed during the years 1787 to 1947, with some states adopting several different constitutions during this period (Witte, 2000).

The state constitutions did not balance all six principles of religious liberty, nor did all the states define the principles in the same manner. Most state and local governments granted basic rights of conscience, exercise, and equality to accepted religious groups, while struggling to apply such principles to marginal religious groups. All constitutions had provisions for the state courts to hear constitutional questions, and thus thousands of cases came before state courts on issues related to religious liberty (Witte, 2000). Since states were free to determine and define religious liberty, the U.S. Supreme Court had little influence in the early interpretation of the establishment and free exercise clauses of the First Amendment. In fact, from 1815 to 1940, the Court issued decisions in only thirty-two cases related to religious matters. Most of these cases dealt with church property, education, polygamy, and naturalization (Esbeck, 1994). This was so until two landmark U.S. Supreme Court cases in the 1940s—*Cantwell v. Connecticut* (1940) and *Everson v. Board of Education* (1947)—in which the religion clauses of the First Amendment were extended to the states. Both of these cases are discussed later in this section.

The first hundred years after the ratification of the First Amendment were marked by rapid expansion in both the diversity of religious groups and the sheer number of followers. This was, in large part, due to the vast wave of immigration that took place during this period. Millions flocked to the United States, bringing with them their religious beliefs and practices. Although a plethora of different religious organizations sprouted across the nation, by the late eighteenth century the notion of a civil or public religion was firmly embedded in the practices of state and local governments. In general terms, civil religion is a set of beliefs and attitudes of a given society that explain the purpose or meaning of that society in spiritual terms. Michael Angrosino (2002) states, "American civil religion is an institutionalized set of beliefs about the nation, including a faith in a transcendent deity who will protect and guide the United States as long as its people and government abide by his laws" (p. 240). He further describes three different viewpoints on civil religion: civil religion as culture, as religious nationalism, and as transcendent religion. In this light, civil religion viewed as religious nationalism demonstrated the role religion had in legitimizing and guiding the activities of the new republic. For example, during this period, state and local governments approved of religious symbols, ceremonies, and prayer in a variety of contexts. Civil religion developed within a Christian or Protestant tradition and was reflected in policy, practices, and political discourse.

Religious groups whose beliefs were compatible with the civil religion of the new nation were at ease with the adoption of such unifying messages. Since the states were free to set boundaries on religious freedom, they did so in a variety of ways, often minimizing the rights of various groups or sects, especially those who were perceived to be fringe religious groups. As a result, minority religious groups found themselves fleeing to the open frontier and moving about the states in search of a place to call home (Witte, 2002). With the notion of civil religion firmly established and religious liberty being defined and applied in distinctly different ways across the country, marginalized religious groups eventually sought relief from the federal judiciary.

It was not until the late 1800s that the U.S. Supreme Court confronted the interpretation of the free exercise clause, in two cases related specifically to plural marriage, which was a core religious practice of the Mormons. The first case, *Reynolds v. United States* (1879), involved a dispute over the constitutionality, in terms of the free exercise clause, of the Morrill Anti-Bigamy Act, legislation passed by Congress in 1862 specifically to outlaw plural marriage as practiced by the Mormons. George Reynolds, a Mormon with two wives, was selected by the Mormon community to serve as a test case. The criminal trial of George Reynolds resulted in a conviction, which was reversed upon appeal by the territorial Supreme Court on the grounds that the grand jury had been improperly installed. Federal prosecutors retried Reynolds and were successful in sustaining a conviction. Representing the Mormons, Reynolds appealed to the U.S. Supreme Court, intending to test the First Amendment's protection of a religious practice that the rest of the nation so vehemently opposed (Gordon, 2002). The Court upheld Reynolds' conviction and thus the federal anti-bigamy law, arguing that the First Amendment protects the right to believe in any religious principles one chooses but that it does not necessarily free one to act upon such beliefs.

In 1890, the Court decided *Davis v. Beason*, in which they upheld a statute of the Idaho Territory that prohibited bigamists or polygamists from voting. The territory statute, among other things, required male voters to take an oath that they did not engage in the practice of polygamy and were not involved in the teaching, advising, or encouragement of the practice. The District Court of the territory convicted Mr. Davis for conspiracy to swear falsely on such an oath. The U.S. Supreme Court upheld the jurisdiction of the territorial court and affirmed its decision. In a unanimous decision, Justice Stephen Field wrote, "However free the exercise of religion may be, it must be subordinate to the criminal laws of the country, passed with reference to actions regarded by general consent as properly the subjects of punitive legislation."

The *Reynolds* and *Davis* decisions reflect the strong antipolygamist sentiment shared by much of the nation at the time. (We discuss additional issues and cases related to the practice of polygamy in Chapter 5.) *Reynolds* and *Davis* also cemented an interpretation of the free exercise clause in which the right to believe in religious principles does not presuppose the right to act on those principles. The decisions in *Reynolds* and *Davis* formed a distinction between belief and action that became the Court's doctrine in the years to come.

The Court further examined the doctrine in *Cantwell v. Connecticut* (1940). In this landmark case, Newton Cantwell and his two sons were arrested and convicted of charges in violation of a Connecticut statute that prohibited solicitation of goods and services without a permit. The Cantwells, members of a religious group called the Jehovah's Witnesses, engaged in the distribution of pamphlets and books on religious topics and also played messages from a phonograph for those who passed by in a busy neighborhood where the residents were mainly Roman Catholics. The Cantwells asked permission before playing the verbal messages; however, the records contained material that was clearly anti-Catholic, and some residents found it offensive. The Cantwells were arrested for disturbing the peace as well as violating the solicitation statute. Citing both *Reynolds* and *Davis*, the Court reaffirmed the distinction between belief and action and supported the state's interest in protecting its citizenry against fraudulent conduct. Yet Justice Roberts wrote, "In every case the power to regulate must be so exercised as not, in attaining a permissible end, unduly to infringe the protected freedom." The Court reaffirmed the distinction between belief and action yet acknowledged that although belief is fully protected by the Constitution, action may also be afforded such a guarantee. In addition, the Court found that the statute itself deprived the Cantwells of their liberty without due process of law as guaranteed in the Fourteenth Amendment, thereby declaring the local statute unconstitutional. Justice Roberts stated, "The Fourteenth Amendment has rendered the legislatures of the states as incompetent as Congress to enact such laws." This made the free exercise clause applicable to the states.

In *Everson v. Board of Education* (1947), the Court considered a New Jersey statute that authorized local school districts to make rules and engage in contracts for the transportation of children to school and the implementation of one school district's reimbursement pursuant to the state statute. In this case, the school district reimbursed parents of children attending Catholic school for the costs associated with transportation to and from school. A taxpayer filed suit, arguing that the statute, and the Board of Education's subsequent policy, violated the establishment clause of both the state and the federal constitutions. The Court affirmed the decision of the New Jersey Court of Errors and Appeals, which found the New Jersey statute to be constitutional. The majority opinion, delivered by Justice Black, likened school transportation in function and service to other general government services such as police and fire protection, sewage disposal, and highway maintenance. Justice Black delivered the majority opinion: "The [First] Amendment requires the state to be neutral in its relations with groups of religious believers and non-believers, it does not require the state to be their adversary. State power is no more to be used so as to handicap religions, than it is to favor them." The Court ruled that in this instance, transportation to school does not constitute the establishment of religion and applied the establishment clause as a right that extended to the states through the due process clause of Fourteenth Amendment.

Both of these cases, *Cantwell v. Connecticut* (1940) and *Everson v. Board of Education* (1947), represent the incorporation of the First Amendment religion clauses into the due process clause of the Fourteenth Amendment. The Incorporation Doctrine refers to the gradual incorporation by the Court of most of the Bill of Rights into the due process clause of the Fourteenth Amendment by applying such rights to the states. The incorporation achieved in *Cantwell* and *Everson* represents a rebirth in the essential meaning of religious liberty, creating a standard by which all levels of government must now abide. These landmark decisions marked the beginning of a new era in the judiciary. State and local governments have continued to enact laws and regulations placing restrictions on their citizenry. Sometimes such laws, policies, or regulations interfere with or come into conflict with the religious beliefs and practices of certain individuals and groups; however, such government involvement is subject to federal judicial review, providing a variety of instances and circumstances in which both clauses of the First Amendment are considered. As a result, the courts have decided numerous cases relating to religious matters after *Cantwell* and *Everson*.

Free Exercise Clause: Post-Cantwell

As discussed, the doctrine by which the Court determined there was a distinction between religious belief and action was determined in the *Reynolds* and *Davis* cases and reaffirmed in *Cantwell*. The Court firmly acknowledged the right of citizens to believe any religious doctrine, no matter how preposterous such beliefs may appear to others. However, the Court also recognized that the right to engage in a particular religious practice is not, in and of itself, a blanket guarantee of the free exercise clause. The Court also affirmed the importance and necessity of government regulation through criminal penal codes and other regulatory statutes to govern the behavior of the citizenry. In line with the *Reynolds*, *Davis*, and *Cantwell* decisions, the Court continues to balance the rights of free exercise against the appropriateness of various ordinances and laws and their implementation or enforcement.

Three basic elements have been considered in the adjudication of free exercise claims. First, the Court forbids outright prohibitions and prior restraint on religious expression. Second, regulations that are deemed discriminatory in nature were also forbidden; however, third, the Court also affirmed that general regulations that ultimately served to protect the safety of the public were legitimate (Witte, 2000).

The following five cases from the 1940s further illustrate the ideology of the Court in developing its doctrinal distinction between belief and action. Each examines statutes and ordinances in terms of their impact on or appropriateness to the free exercise of religion, balancing the legislation against the specific actions and circumstances involved. Each case involves citizens who had violated the law while pursuing a particular religious activity. These cases may not be considered landmark religious liberty cases, yet the Court opinions are instructive and reflective of the views of the Court at the time.

Prince v. Commonwealth of Massachusetts (1944)

This case involves the criminal conviction of Sarah Prince, who was found to be in violation of Massachusetts child labor laws. The state laws in question made it illegal for boys under the age of twelve and girls under the age of eighteen to sell or offer to sell articles of merchandise. It also provided sanctions for any parent, guardian, or custodian who permitted such a minor to work in violation of the law. The Massachusetts statute, like other state child labor laws, was established to protect children from exploitation and servitude, which had been common practice during the Industrial Revolution. Sarah Prince was the aunt and custodian of nine-year-old Betty Simmons and the mother of two young boys. Ms. Prince and the children were Jehovah's Witnesses and, on the night in question, were performing their religious duty by attempting to sell copies of the *Watchtower* and *Consolation* on a street in Brockton. Ms. Prince was subsequently convicted of being in violation of the state child labor laws.

Ms. Prince brought her case to the U.S. Supreme Court under two principles in reference to the First and Fourteenth Amendments. She argued that the Massachusetts law violated her right to parent Betty and teach her the tenets and practices of her faith. She also argued that the law violated Betty's right to practice her religion, which in this case meant preaching the gospel by public distribution of pamphlets. In addition, she argued that the public street is in fact the church of Jehovah's Witnesses; therefore, she and her children had a right to preach in this particular manner. In its review of the case, the U.S. Supreme Court considered the gravity of the state's interest in protecting children. In a 5 to 4 decision, the Court affirmed the criminal conviction of Ms. Prince. Justice Rutledge delivered the opinion of the Court:

> [N]either rights of religion nor rights of parenthood are beyond limitation. Acting to guard the general interest in youth's well being, the state as parens patriae may restrict the parent's control by requiring school attendance, regulating or prohibiting the child's labor, and in many other ways … the power of the state to control the conduct of children reaches beyond the scope of its authority over adults, as is true in the case of other freedoms, and the rightful boundary of its power has been crossed in this case …
>
> However Jehovah Witnesses may conceive them, the public highways have not become their religious property merely by their assertion. And there is no denial of equal protection in excluding their children from doing what no other children may do.

Justice Rutledge went on to state:

> Our ruling does not extend beyond the facts the case presents. We neither lay the foundation "for any (that is, every) state intervention in the indoctrination and participation of children in religion" which may be done "in the name of their health and welfare" nor give warrant for "every limitation on their religious training and activities."

United States v. Ballard (1944)

A few months after the *Prince* decision was rendered, the Court considered *U.S. v. Ballard*. On appeal, the U.S. Supreme Court considered the appropriateness of the charge given to the jury during the criminal trial of three defendants, Guy W. Ballard (deceased at the time), Edna Ballard, and Donald Ballard. The Ballards had been arrested and tried on twelve counts of using and conspiring to use the mail to defraud. They were charged with scheming to defraud by organizing and promoting the "I Am" movement and using the mail to distribute and sell movement literature and memberships on the basis of false pretenses. They were charged with falsely representing themselves as spiritual healers who could cure people with both curable and medically incurable diseases and as having cured hundreds of people.

During the charge to the jury, the District Court firmly instructed the jury not to be concerned with the actual religious beliefs of the defendants but to consider only whether the defendants' actions were conducted honestly and in good faith. The jury was instructed to consider whether the defendants knew their actions were based on false pretenses. The Ballards were convicted of the federal charges related to religious fraud and, on appeal to the Circuit Court of Appeals, argued that the instructions to jury were in error. The Circuit Court of Appeals agreed and reversed the convictions. In a 5 to 4 vote, the U.S. Supreme Court reversed the judgment of the Circuit Court of Appeals and remanded the case to the Circuit Court of Appeals for further processing. Justice Douglas delivered the opinion of the Court:

> Men may believe what they cannot prove. They may not be put to the proof of their religious doctrines or beliefs. Religious experiences which are as real as life to some may be incomprehensible to others ... If one could be sent to jail because a jury in a hostile environment found those teachings false, little indeed would be left of religious freedom ... So we conclude that the District Court ruled properly when it withheld from the jury all questions concerning the truth or falsity of the religious beliefs or doctrines of respondents.

Cleveland et al. v. U.S. (1946)

Cleveland et al. v. U.S. involved a challenge to the Mann Act of 1910 (18 U.S.C. 398), which prohibited the transportation of women or girls across state lines for immoral sexual purposes. The act, often referred to as the "White-Slave Traffic Act," was enacted to prevent men from utilizing interstate commerce for the purpose of engaging in commercial sexual acts. The act mainly targeted prostitution; however, the language of the act also included transportation for any other "immoral" purpose. The act was passed in response to concerns over the growing prostitution trade in the United States and abroad.

In this case, the petitioners were members of the Fundamentalist Mormon sect and, with the exception of one petitioner, had more than one wife. Each of the petitioners had transported or assisted in the transportation of plural wives across state lines for the purpose of engaging in plural marriage. They had been convicted under the Mann Act. Having already upheld the Mann Act, the Court did not dispute the act itself but rather interpreted its applicability to the circumstance of polygamy. The U.S. Supreme Court ultimately affirmed the convictions of the petitioners. Justice Douglas delivered the opinion of the Court:

> The establishment or maintenance of polygamous households is a notorious example of promiscuity … We could conclude that Congress excluded these practices from the Act only if it were clear that the Act is confined to commercialized sexual vice. Since we cannot say it is, we see no way by which the present transgressions can be excluded. These polygamous practices have long been branded as immoral in the law. Though they have different ramifications, they are in the same genus as the other immoral practices covered by the Act.

Marsh v. State of Alabama (1946)

In *Marsh v. State of Alabama*, the Court considered whether the State of Alabama could impose a criminal sanction on an individual engaged in proselytizing on the grounds of a town owned by a private company. Gulf Shipbuilding Corporation, owner of the property in a town named Chickasaw, posted a notice that clearly prohibited solicitation of any kind without permission. Ms. Marsh attempted to distribute religious literature in the company-owned town and was subsequently arrested when she refused to leave the grounds. Ms. Marsh, a Jehovah's Witness, was convicted of violating an Alabama law prohibiting individuals from remaining on private property after being warned to leave. Ms. Marsh argued that the state statute was inapplicable to her specific circumstance since her acts were religious in nature. The U.S. Supreme Court agreed and reversed her conviction.

A number of different cases have come before the Court involving the specific actions of Jehovah's Witnesses and their practice of proselytizing. The *Marsh* case is of particular interest because it deals with such actions on private property owned by a corporation. Like many other communities in the United States, Chickasaw was a town that was chiefly built and owned by Gulf Shipbuilding Corporation. The town functioned very much like any other town, with its area freely accessible to the public. The Court reasoned that to deprive an individual of the free exercise of religion in such circumstance would be to deny constitutionally protected rights. Justice Black delivered the opinion of the Court:

> As we have stated before, the right to exercise the liberties safeguarded by the First Amendment "lies at the foundation of free government by free men" and

we must in all cases "weigh the circumstances and appraise ... the reasons ... in support of the regulation of (those) rights." *Schneider v. State,* 308 U.S. 147, 161, 60 S. Ct. 146, 151. In our view the circumstance that the property rights to the premises where the deprivation of liberty, here involved, took place, were held by others than the public, is not sufficient to justify the State's permitting a corporation to govern a community of citizens so as to restrict their fundamental liberties and the enforcement of such restraint by the application of a State statute.

Tucker v. State of Texas (1946)

In a similar case, *Tucker v. State of Texas,* decided in the same year, the Justices examined a Texas law that prohibited individuals from peddling goods or merchandise. Mr. Tucker, also a Jehovah's Witness, claimed he was not a peddler of goods but a minister transmitting religious views and literature. He was arrested in the Hondo Navigation Village, a village owned by the federal government. The Court determined, as they did in *Marsh v. Alabama,* that a town owned by the government could not prohibit the actions of Mr. Tucker, which were protected under the First and Fourteenth Amendments. Justice Black again delivered the opinion of the Court:

> True, under certain circumstances it might be proper for security reasons to isolate the inhabitants of a settlement, such as Hondo Village, which houses workers engaged in producing war materials. But no such necessity and no such intention on the part of Congress or the Public Housing Authority are shown here.

Free Exercise Clause: Compelling Interest Test

As these five cases indicate, the Court continued to distinguish between belief and action, recognizing that not all religious action would be theoretically protected by the First and Fourteenth Amendments. For the next twenty years or so, the Court continued to reason free exercise cases in a similar manner. In the 1960s the Court began to utilize a more definitive test that scrutinized government regulation to a higher degree. The compelling interest test, as it is referred to, involves the examination of specific legislation or regulations to determine whether there exists a compelling state interest for their existence when they interfere with the practice of religion for specific individuals. Here I explore three key U.S. Supreme Court cases that illustrate the developing shift in the reasoning of free exercise cases toward a more definitive balanced examination of the benefits of particular secular laws against the pursuit of free exercise of religion. The *Braunfeld, Sherbert,* and *Yoder* cases, often cited by scholars as being the pinnacle cases in this regard, also illustrate the careful approach the Court has taken toward examining the beliefs, actions, and needs of specific religious groups.

Braunfeld et al. v. Brown (1961)

In *Braunfeld,* the Court considered a 1959 Pennsylvania criminal law that prohibited businesses from opening on Sunday. The Pennsylvania law was a typical "blue law." Blue laws regulate public and private conduct by restricting on at least one day a week the types of activities citizens can engage in. Blue laws were originally enacted in the Puritan colonies of New England in an effort to control morality. It is believed they were called blue laws because of the color of paper the laws were printed on. Although most communities have repealed such laws, some blue laws still exist in the United States today, especially in communities heavily populated with religious fundamentalists. For example, one of the most prevalent blue laws still in operation today restricts the sale of alcohol on Sundays.

The 1959 law in question in *Braunfeld* made it especially difficult for the appellants, who were Orthodox Jews and observed the Sabbath, to take the entire weekend as rest. They argued that since they had to refrain from working from Friday evening until Saturday evening, they would be unfairly economically disadvantaged by not being able to open their place of business on Sunday as well. The appellants argued that the statute, in effect, established a religion and violated the equal protection clause of the Fourteenth Amendment. The appellants also argued that the statute prohibited their ability to exercise their religion freely. The U.S. Supreme Court immediately dismissed the first two arguments since they had previously ruled on such issues in a case that dealt with the same state statute. The Court had determined in *Two Guys from Harrison-Allentown, Inc. v. McGinley* (1961) that the Pennsylvania statute did not establish a religion, nor did it violate the equal protection clause. Thus, the Court in *Braunfeld* considered only whether the statute interfered with the appellants' ability to practice their religion freely.

The opinion of the Justices in *Braunfeld* reflected a shift in their test by more clearly scrutinizing whether a particular criminal statute interfered with religious practice. In *Braunfeld,* the Court examined whether the state policy placed a burden on the exercise of religion for specific individuals or for a whole religious group, the extent of that burden, and whether the state directly or only indirectly burdened religious practice with the establishment of its law. Upholding the Pennsylvania statute, Chief Justice Warren wrote the opinion for the majority:

> To strike down, without the most critical scrutiny, legislation which imposes only an indirect burden on the exercise of religion ... would radically restrict the operating latitude of the legislature ... Of course, to hold unassailable all Legislation regulating the conduct which imposes solely an indirect burden on the observance of religion would be a gross oversimplification. If the purpose or effect of a law is to impede the observance of one or all religions or is to discriminate invidiously between religions, that law is constitutionally invalid even though the burden may be characterized as being only indirect.

Chief Justice Warren also wrote:

> the Sunday law simply regulates a secular activity and, as applied to appellants, operates so as to make the practice of their religious beliefs more expensive ... Fully recognizing that the alternatives open to appellants and others similarly situated—retaining their present occupations and incurring economic disadvantage or engaging in some other commercial activity which does not call for either Saturday or Sunday labor—may well result in some financial sacrifice in order to observe their religious beliefs, still the option is wholly different than when the legislation attempts to make a religious practice itself unlawful.

Sherbert v. Verner (1963)

A couple of years later, the Court decided *Sherbert v. Verner* (1963), in which they continued to build upon the reasoning established in *Braunfeld*. In this landmark case, Adeil Sherbert, a member of the Seventh-day Adventist Church, was fired from her job after she refused to work on Saturday, the Sabbath day of her faith. Unable to find employment that did not require her to work on Saturdays, she applied for unemployment benefits to the South Carolina Employment Security Commission. She was denied unemployment benefits because she had failed to provide good cause why she could not accept work. She argued that she was willing to work but wanted to find employment that was consistent with her schedule to observe the Sabbath. The Supreme Court Justices ruled in her favor, finding that the rejection of unemployment benefits was a burden on her free exercise of religion. Also, the Justices ruled that unlike in the *Braunfeld* case, the state could not demonstrate a compelling state interest in denying unemployment benefits or making her ineligible for such benefits.

The *Sherbert* case was the first time the Court engaged in setting such a strict standard of review or scrutiny regarding the relationship between legislation and its restriction on or interference with religious practice. Under this compelling interest test, legislation that interferes with the practice of religion must serve a larger, more compelling state interest if the legislation is to be constitutionally sound. The State of South Carolina could not establish such a compelling state interest in this case. However, the Court did not go so far as to declare the state policy unconstitutional. Justice Brennan, writing the majority opinion, stated:

> Nor do we, by our decision today, declare the existence of a constitutional right to unemployment benefits on the part of all persons whose religious convictions are the cause of their unemployment. This is a not a case in which an employee's religious convictions serve to make him a nonproductive member of society.

The compelling state interest test utilized in *Sherbert* has also come to be known as the *Sherbert* test. Witte (2000, p. 123) notes that the Court has used this strict scrutiny test in only ten cases since *Sherbert*, ruling in favor of the religious claimant in six cases and in favor of the government in four cases. One such case was *Wisconsin v. Yoder*, which the Court heard in December 1971.

Wisconsin v. Yoder (1972)

This case involved a review of the conviction of Jonas Yoder and Wallace Miller, both members of the Old Order Amish religion, and Adin Yutzy, a member of the Conservative Amish Mennonite Church. As residents of Green County, Wisconsin, they were tried and convicted of violating the state's compulsory education law, which required children to attend public or private school until age sixteen. In keeping with the tradition of Amish communities, they had pulled their children from school after the completion of eight grades. They argued that the compulsory school attendance law violated their right to exercise their religious beliefs freely and was in conflict with the Amish way of life. Central to the Amish belief system is the desire to live a simple life, one that is closely in accord with nature, without the trappings of material goods. Their children are raised to "reject the competitive spirit and seek to insulate themselves from the modern world" (Fisher, 2002, p. 23). Members are required to live off the land and to adopt a more communal approach to living. Children engage in continued vocational education whereby they are prepared specifically for the obligations of Amish life. Mr. Yoder, Mr. Miller, and Mr. Yutzy further argued that traditional public education, past the eighth grade, is in direct conflict with, if not hostile to, Amish beliefs.

The *Yoder* case was not the first of its kind. Amish bishops had issued a statement in 1950 that clearly spelled out the Amish justification for not attending public schools beyond the eighth grade. The bishops declared that after the eighth grade, Amish children were to be educated under the supervision of their parents so they could be properly instructed in the scriptures, particularly in German. Home schooling of this kind would also ensure that young people would continue to marry within the faith to maintain the Amish way of life. Before the *Yoder* case, Amish parents were often fined and jailed for their refusal to abide by compulsory attendance laws and often lost their court battles (Gaustad, 2003).

In *Yoder*, the Court also considered the long and vibrant history of the Amish and their ability to remain true to their religious convictions and way of life for centuries. This, despite the rapid growth and evolution of the modern world, provided evidence to the Justices that compulsory formal education "would gravely endanger if not destroy the free exercise of respondents' religious beliefs."

The U.S. Supreme Court continued to utilize the compelling state interest test, or the *Sherbert* test, as its core rationale in deciding cases in the 1970s and 1980s. A reading of the written opinions of the *Braunfeld*, *Sherbert*, and *Yoder* cases also illustrates the careful approach the Court has taken toward gaining an understanding of the specific beliefs, actions, and needs of the religious litigants before them. Even a cursory review of the language used by the Justices in their opinions in the cases noted here illustrates a growing trend toward a more detailed analysis by the Court of the legal and religious issues at stake in regard to the First and Fourteenth Amendments.

Supreme Court decision making regarding free exercise claims has begun to be quantified by researchers. In a study of state and federal judicial court decisions regarding the free exercise clause, Way and Burt (1983) reviewed the litigation of 66 free exercise clause cases from 1946 to 1956 and compared these cases to a set of 384 cases decided from 1970 to 1980. Of particular interest in this study was to determine the extent to which modern courts had supported the practices of marginal religious groups compared with those of more mainstream religious groups. Religious marginality generally refers to groups whose religious beliefs or practices depart from the mainstream. Way and Burt assigned religious groups to the marginal category if more than half of the litigation involved conflicts with officials regarding public evangelism or challenges to specific secular laws on the basis of religious belief. Religious litigants identified as mainstream Protestant, Roman Catholic, or Jewish were considered dominant religious groups. Way and Burt note that the free exercise cases presented to the state and federal judiciary during these periods involved more religious groups defined as marginal than mainstream religious groups. This is probably not so surprising, considering that mainstream religions, by definition, may have more consistent agreement with or accommodation to secular society. Challenges to secular laws from mainstream religious groups were centered on laws or regulations involving zoning, taxes, religious schools, and judicial authority, whereas marginal religious groups' actions were focused on litigation that involved the religious rights of prisoners, proselytizing, employment, education, family law, medical care, and unusual practices. I explore some of these issues, especially those pertaining to conflicts between criminal law and religious practice, in detail in the next chapter.

Way and Burt's (1983) findings indicate that although the majority of all claimants lost their cases, marginal religious groups fared much better than mainstream religious groups. In addition, there was a significant increase in the number of cases presented to the courts involving fringe religious groups, and those groups won a much greater percentage of their cases during 1970–1980. Way and Burt argue that the decisions in *Sherbert* and *Yoder* may be largely responsible for the successes marginal religious groups began to enjoy during this time period.

In a different study, Ignagni (1993) developed eleven hypotheses regarding U.S. Supreme Court decision making in free exercise cases. In a review of fifty-seven U.S. Supreme Court decisions spanning the Warren, Burger, and Rehnquist Courts, he created a model of Supreme Court decision making that includes eleven independent variables to predict the Court's decision making on the free exercise claims presented to them. Several of his hypotheses tested the conclusions of Way and Burt's (1983) study. Ignagni examined the issue of marginality and found significant evidence that when "a marginal religious group was involved in a dispute, the Court was more likely to uphold its claims" (1993, p. 523). His results also confirmed that when a case involves employment rights or education, the Court is more likely to side with the free exercise claimants and that it is more likely not to support the free exercise claims when the case involves tax laws.

Free Exercise Clause: The *Smith* Case

The most recent era of legal doctrine regarding free exercise of religion is marked by the 1990 landmark decision in *Employment Division, Department of Human Resources of Oregon v. Smith*, in which the U.S. Supreme Court appeared to have shifted its doctrine again, only to return to a more conservative reading of free exercise of religion. The *Smith* case involved Alfred Smith and Galen Black, both members of the Native American Church. The Native American Church considers the use of peyote, a substance with hallucinogenic properties, a means to communicate with the spirits and with nature. Church members also believe peyote possesses healing powers. Peyote, and its psychoactive ingredient mescaline, have been used by Native Americans and Aztec Indians in religious ceremonies throughout history. Peyote is derived from the peyote cactus in a process by which it is dried and then ground into a powder, although mescaline can also be produced synthetically (Abadinsky, 2001). It is taken orally. Peyote is a hallucinogen categorized by the Federal Controlled Substances Act of 1970 as a Schedule I drug, meaning it has no accepted medical use, cannot be used safely, and has a high potential of abuse. Other Schedule I drugs include marijuana, heroin, LSD, methaqualone, and hashish. Possession of a Schedule I drug is a felony-level crime. Peyote is also outlawed in the state of Oregon.

Alfred Smith and Galen Black were both counselors at a private drug and alcohol treatment facility in Oregon and were dismissed from their employment when it was revealed that they used peyote during the religious ceremonies of their church. Smith and Galen applied to the Employment Division of the Department of Human Resources of Oregon for unemployment benefits. The Employment Division declined to approve their unemployment benefits on the grounds that they were fired for misconduct related to their employment. Smith and Galen filed an appeal of the decision with the Oregon Court of Appeals, which agreed with their claim that the denial of unemployment benefits violated their free exercise rights under the First Amendment. The Employment Division then appealed to the Oregon Supreme Court, arguing that their denial of benefits was allowable because the use of peyote was illegal. The Oregon Supreme Court decided in favor of Smith and Galen, ultimately reasoning that a burden had been placed on their religious practice. The Employment Division appealed to the U.S. Supreme Court in 1987, in a case that is referred to as Smith I. In Smith I, the U.S. Supreme Court agreed with the Employment Division, reasoning that if the state had not violated the First Amendment in its criminal law regarding peyote use, then it could apply the lesser burden of denying unemployment benefits to those individuals who violate the criminal law. The Court vacated the decision of the Oregon Supreme Court and remanded the case for further processing. The Oregon Supreme Court considered the constitutional arguments and reaffirmed its original decision.

In 1989, the U.S. Supreme Court once again granted certiorari to the *Employment Division (Smith II)* to consider the constitutionality of prohibiting the use of peyote under the free exercise clause. The Court upheld the denial of unemployment benefits to Smith and Galen. Justice Anthony Scalia delivered the opinion of the Court: "We have never held that an individual's religious beliefs excuse him from compliance with an otherwise valid law prohibiting conduct that the State is free to regulate." Oral arguments in the case included testimony regarding the dangers of peyote as a hallucinogenic drug. The attorney for Smith and Galen, Craig J. Dorsey, argued that there is no evidence that the manner in which church members use peyote is harmful or has led to any particular law enforcement issues (Irons, 1997). In a dissenting opinion, Justice Blackmun implied that the criminal law in this case was purely symbolic in nature, since "Oregon has never sought to prosecute respondents, and does not claim that it has made significant enforcement efforts against other religious users of peyote." He also argued that "[t]he State cannot plausibly assert that unbending application of a criminal prohibition is essential to fulfill any compelling interest, if it does not, in fact, attempt to enforce the prohibition."

Since the law in this case was neutral with respect to religion and, therefore, one that had applicability to the general population, it was ultimately considered valid. In contrast to the criminal law in question in the *Smith* case, the Court found that a local ordinance in the City of Hialeah, Florida, violated the free exercise of religion for members of the Santeria religion. The case, *Church of the Lukumi Babalu Aye, Inc. and Ernesto Pichardo v. City of Hialeah* (1993), involved the enactment of city ordinances that specifically prohibited animal sacrifice in the manner in which the Santerias practiced it. In a 9 to 0 vote (although four separate opinions were issued) the Court found that the ordinances were in conflict with the principle that laws should be neutral and have general applicability if they are to burden individual religious practices. In this case, they found the ordinances to be a specific burden to the Santerias and thus in violation of the First Amendment. Yet the *Church of the Lukumi Babalu Aye* decision was overshadowed by the debate sparked by the ruling in *Smith*.

Legal scholars, politicians, and religious groups were surprised by the decision rendered by the U.S. Supreme Court in *Smith*. Perhaps many thought that the compelling interest test established in *Sherbert* and *Yoder* at long last provided an appropriate legal framework in which to view free exercise cases and, therefore, did not imagine the Court would once again shift gears and return to the legal principles adopted in previous Courts. Carmella (1993) refers to the *Smith* decision as one "that has been widely criticized as the virtual repeal of the free exercise clause of the First Amendment" (p. 275). Yet Ignagni (1993) notes that the Court has continually drawn criticism for its decisions regarding free exercise cases, even during the period between *Sherbert* and *Smith*. It is important to note that many of the decisions discussed here were arrived at with a slim majority vote, indicating that the Justices themselves were not in agreement regarding the various legal arguments being applied in these cases. Yet it is also possible that the case was reasoned in this way on the heels of a national war on drugs and the fact that this case involved the specific use of a dangerous Schedule I drug. After all, the decision in *Smith* was consistent with other decisions rendered in cases involving religious practices that violated general criminal laws that related to health and safety. Ultimately, members of the Native American Church were successful at finding legislative relief through 42 U.S.C. 1996a, which provides an exemption for the bona fide ceremonial use of peyote.

In any case, the *Smith* decision ignited a storm of controversy that culminated in the passage of the Religious Freedom Restoration Act of 1993 (RFRA) (P.L. 103-141) by Congress, which was signed by President Clinton in November 1993. The RFRA specifically prohibited any agency, department, or official of the U.S. government or a state government from burdening an individual's exercise of religion, even in cases involving a rule of general applicability. The law specifies that the government may burden an individual's exercise of religion if it can demonstrate a compelling governmental interest and uses the least restrictive means to advance that compelling interest. Members of 103rd Congress declared the purpose of this act was to "restore" the compelling interest test set forth in *Sherbert* and *Yoder*, noting that such a test was a reasonable approach to balancing the needs of individuals against the needs of the government. The RFRA was unique in that it was enacted in response to a specific U.S. Supreme Court decision, in what appeared to be an attempt to undermine the Court's ability to interpret the First Amendment.

Lower courts also responded to *Smith*, rendering decisions consistent with *Smith* and/or consistent with their own state constitutional language, even if that language departs from *Smith*. For example, Carmella (1993) notes that the supreme courts of Minnesota, Maine, Massachusetts, and Washington decided cases consistent with the strict scrutiny language of their state constitutions. In a study of U.S. Court of Appeals responses to *Smith* and the RFRA, Brent (1999) found some evidence that the U.S. Court of Appeals responded to the RFRA with decisions that were more consistent with U.S. Supreme Court decisions made before *Smith*. He found that religious claimants won approximately 32 percent of the cases in the three years before the *Smith* decision, only 20 percent after the *Smith* decision, rebounding to 32 percent in the three years after the passage of the RFRA. He concluded that the lower courts appeared to have accepted both the *Smith* ruling and the RFRA to guide their decision making.

In 1997, the U.S. Supreme Court struck down the RFRA, finding it unconstitutional in the case of the *City of Boerne v. Flores, Archbishop of San Antonio, et al.* This case involved Patrick Flores, the archbishop of San Antonio, Texas, who sought a building permit to enlarge St. Peter Catholic Church, originally built in 1923. The City of Boerne denied his application on the basis of a local ordinance protecting the historic district of the city, arguing that the church was situated in this preservation district. The archbishop filed suit, seeking relief under the RFRA. The Supreme Court reversed the decision of the Court of Appeals, reasoning that Congress had overstepped its authority in creating the RFRA and that "the scope and reach of the RFRA distinguishes it" from other legislation passed by Congress. In the words of Justice Kennedy, writing the opinion of the Court, "Broad as the power of Congress is under the Enforcement Clause of the Fourteenth Amendment, RFRA contradicts vital principles necessary to maintain separation of powers and the federal balance." Justice Stevens believed that the RFRA was a law regarding the establishment of a religion and therefore found that it violated the First Amendment of the Constitution. Concurring with the majority, he wrote:

> If the historic landmark on the hill in Boerne happened to be a museum or an art gallery owned by an atheist, it would not be eligible for an exemption from the city ordinances that forbid an enlargement of the structure. Because the landmark is owned by the Catholic Church, it is claimed that RFRA gives its owner a federal statutory entitlement to an exemption from a generally applicable, neutral civil law.

The *Boerne* decision asserted the Court's authority over Congress and all matters of constitutionality specifically related to free exercise litigation. In a study of U.S. Courts of Appeals decisions after the *Boerne* ruling, Brent (2003) found that support for free exercise claimants in the Court of Appeals declined. Brent asserts that "the Supreme Court apparently succeeded in reestablishing itself as the relevant principal in free exercise cases" (p. 557).

Despite the finding that the RFRA was unconstitutional, Congress continued to craft similar legislation with the blessing of numerous religious advocacy groups. The 105th Congress responded with the Religious Liberty Protection Act (RLPA), which was essentially a revamped RFRA. The RLPA, however, encountered problems. Opposition was raised by civil rights groups such as the American Civil Liberties Union (ACLU) and advocacy groups such as the American Academy of Pediatrics (AAP). The ACLU (1999) raised concerns over the effect such legislation would have on local civil rights by creating a new defense against civil rights claims. The AAP (1999) raised concerns regarding the impact such a policy would have on the health and safety of children whose parents chose to withhold critical medical care from them or engaged in abusive acts as a result of various religious practices.

The RLPA ultimately lost its appeal, only to be replaced by the Religious Land Use and Institutionalized Persons Act (RLUIP) of 2000 (P.L. 106-274), which was signed into law by President Clinton. The RLUIP prohibits land use regulations that impose a burden on free exercise unless the government can demonstrate a compelling interest and the regulation represents the least restrictive means of reaching the goal of the government. The act also works to protect the religious rights of individuals confined to institutions that receive federal funding under the same compelling interest standard. The RLUIP has also been criticized (Geller, 2003), and lawsuits advancing protection under it have advanced in the courts. At the time of writing, it is too soon to predict how the RLUIP and its language will fare in the courts. The Becket Fund for Religious Liberty, a public interest law firm that specializes in zoning laws and religious groups, sponsors a webpage at www. RLUIPA.org to track recent litigation regarding the RLUIP act.

Although cases continue to enter the courts regarding the free exercise of religion, a post-*Smith* jurisprudence is difficult to predict. As new Justices joined the U.S. Supreme Court in 2005 and 2006, it is likely that the new Court will explore new dimensions to even the oldest of legal arguments. It is clear, however, that litigation regarding the free exercise of religion, or freedom from religion, is far from any final determination. This is probably most true in situations that involve religious practices that conflict with state or federal criminal statutes. As these cases demonstrate, the Court has been reluctant to dismiss criminal statutes that are neutral, generally applied, and concern the overall health and safety of individuals.

The U.S. Constitution was crafted with the knowledge that religion was especially important in the lives of U.S. citizens and thus worthy of recognition and special protection. Religious groups, whether considered mainstream or marginal, have sought relief under the First Amendment and will continue to bring forth their legal arguments to the courts for resolution in the future. One thing is certain: conflicts between religious individuals or groups and the government will continue to erupt, and criminal laws are likely to be violated.

Part II
Theologically Based Crimes

Crimes against Children

On August 22, 2003, Terrance Cottrell Jr., an eight-year-old boy with autism from Milwaukee, Wisconsin, was brought to the Faith Temple Church of the Apostolic Faith by his mother for a faith-healing service. The minister, Ray A. Hemphill, who had conducted several previous services to rid the child of the evil spirits of autism, performed what many would describe as an exorcism on this fateful night. Over the course of several hours, Patricia Cooper, Terrance's mother, and two other women aided Hemphill in holding down the child while Hemphill lay across his chest. Eventually, Terrance died. The medical examiner's office found bruising to the back of his neck and ruled that he died of suffocation as a result of compression (Nunnally, 2004). Hemphill was convicted in a Milwaukee County Court of felony child abuse and sentenced to two-and-a-half years in prison and another seven-and-a-half years under state supervision (Reynolds, 2004).

Terrance Cottrell died as a result of a religious practice that was intended to heal him. Exorcism itself is not illegal; however, the manner in which the minister conducted the service caused Terrance's death and led to the minister's arrest. In fact, Terrance Cottrell's own mother was an active participant in the events that resulted in her son's death. Perhaps she participated on the premise that her son's behavior was caused by demons, and she firmly believed that the religious ritual would save her son. Or perhaps her inability to manage her son's behavior wore her down to the point where she was willing to consider any intervention her minister suggested. Regardless of the intentions of the parties involved, this healing service ended in tragedy.

This case raises a number of interesting theological, legal, and moral questions. What is acceptable religious practice and what is criminal? How do we create secular laws that also preserve religious liberty? At what point is the preservation of religious freedom a potentially dangerous enterprise? How do we determine what is a bona fide religion or religious practice and thus worthy of special dispensation or relief from secular laws? How do we simultaneously protect religious liberty and the safety of vulnerable populations, especially children? How can law enforcement officials broker such conflicts? Answering such questions is a daunting task indeed. As noted in Chapter 3, the U.S. Supreme Court continues to grapple with the legal dimensions of such questions on a case-by-case basis. The Court has acknowledged that it is important to protect the principle of religious freedom; however, it is clear that legal boundaries do exist.

This chapter explores the theological, legal, and moral concerns raised by crimes like the one committed against Terrance Cottrell—crimes committed as a result of, or in association with, a particular religious practice. As you recall, I have labeled this category of religion-related crime "theologically based." In some instances, crimes are committed within a context in which secular law differs in some substantial way from theological principles. Or, as in the case of Terrance Cottrell, crimes may be committed as a direct result of a particular religious belief or practice. Criminal intent is lacking in many cases; however, it is not always clear whether religion is truly the core feature of the criminal behavior in question. In some cases, religion may be used as a convenient justification for certain behaviors or to mask underlying psychological issues. In either case, as a class, theologically based religion-related crimes do arise frequently enough to warrant the attention of criminal justice practitioners and human service professionals. Given that theology in some way underlies the commission of these crimes, it is important that legal, medical, and behavioral health professionals understand the complex nature of religious ideology and how it can affect the behavior and decision making of otherwise law-abiding citizens.

Family members, particularly women and children, are most likely to be the victims of theologically based religion-related crimes (see Chapter 5 on violence against women). Social scientists have begun to unravel the complex and dynamic relationship between religion and different forms of family violence. Religion obviously plays a critical role in family life, so it should be no surprise that religious tenets that condone or encourage violence within the family unit are likely to result in abuse or neglect. In some cases, religious doctrine creates an environment in which the basic needs of children—medical care, proper nutrition, education—are jeopardized. Because of their size, age, cognitive abilities, and lack of social power, children are particularly vulnerable to abuse when the religious ideals of their parents or caregivers are inconsistent with the law. I borrow Mildred Pagelow's (1984) definition of family violence because it clearly articulates the types of family crimes described in this text:

> Family violence includes any act of commission or omission by family members, and any condition resulting from such acts or inaction, which deprive other family members of equal rights and liberties, and/or interfere with their optimal development and freedom of choice. (p. 21)

Children are equally at risk of victimization from other forms of religion-related crime. For example, elsewhere we explore the victimization of children by clergy, within communal "cult" environments, and among fundamentalist Mormons in their practice of plural marriage. Our focus here is on cases where religious views or specific religious practices are the central feature of the abuse or neglect of children, with specific attention to medical neglect, physical or sexual abuse, and nonpayment of child support.

Child Abuse and Neglect

The maltreatment of children, whether physical, sexual, or emotional, is a significant social problem that warrants governmental concern and intervention. Children who experience maltreatment at the hands of their parents or caregivers suffer numerous short-term and long-term consequences that can affect their cognitive, affective, and physical development. In the most tragic cases, children are killed as a result of abuse or neglect. In 2004, an estimated 872,000 children in the United States were found to have been victims of child abuse or neglect, and an estimated 1,490 children died as result (USDHHS, 2006). These statistics likely represent only the tip of the iceberg, since they count cases that have come to the attention of child welfare officials. Other research has estimated that 2 million children are victimized each year (Sedlak & Broadhurst, 1996).

Children are particularly vulnerable to theologically based crimes, since their overall well-being is dependent upon their parents or caregivers. Also, since these crimes involve the belief systems of the parents or caregivers, it is especially challenging for child welfare and law enforcement officials to intervene using traditional approaches. Parents who abuse or neglect their children on the basis of specific religious ideals mainly do so because they believe a higher power has commanded it. Parental belief systems guide child-rearing practices, educational choices, decisions about medical care and disease prevention, and, in some cases, marriage and sexual relations. It is important to note that our current methods of measurement cannot accurately quantify the extent to which children are abused or neglected within a particular religious context. Yet child welfare officials, therapists, medical providers, law enforcement officers, and court professionals confront such issues.

Medical Neglect

Medical neglect occurs when a parent or caregiver withholds necessary medical care from a child. In 2004, a total of 14,791 children suffered from medical neglect, as reported by forty-five states (USDHHS, 2006). As with all forms of child neglect, the reasons for medical neglect are complex. Many children who suffer from medical neglect are from impoverished families who simply cannot afford medical care or whose access to medical treatment is limited because of geography or transportation problems. In some cases, parents are unaware of the potential seriousness of health problems and are uneducated about what medical providers can offer. In other cases, parents or caregivers suffer from their own mental or physical impairments, which impede their ability to attend to their children's medical needs.

Here we are concerned with parents or caregivers who withhold necessary medical care from their children on the basis of religious belief—usually with the best of intentions rather than because they are neglectful of their children's needs in general. The current data collection methods do not allow us to determine how many of the nearly 15,000 children who suffered from medical neglect in 2004 did so because of religion. In addition, it is impossible to estimate the degree to which other members of the community were exposed to communicable disease as a result.

Religious leaders, child welfare advocates, and public health professionals are embroiled in a bitter debate regarding medical neglect on religious grounds. The issue raises not only medical concerns, but moral, ethical, and legal ones as well. It is a complex problem involving not only the provision of medical treatments once a child has taken ill, but also prevention measures such as immunizations and diagnostic tests. The issue is also complicated by the fact that not all illnesses can be reliably cured with medical treatment, nor do all illnesses necessarily warrant medical attention. In the case of communicable diseases, the concern grows to include the community at large. Some argue it is the right of parents to determine whether their child should receive medical care consistent with religious doctrine. Others, such as the American Academy of Pediatrics (AAP) and Children's Healthcare Is a Legal Duty (CHILD), vehemently argue such considerations are irresponsible and dangerous to both children and the community. Leading the charge for the second group is Rita Swan PhD, president of CHILD. She and her husband,

Douglas, were devout Christian Scientists in 1977 when they lost their only son to untreated h-flu meningitis, an illness that can be treated with antibiotics. After the death of their son, they left the church and have since founded the advocacy organization (Swan, 2000).

A number of religious groups refuse to permit medical or preventive health treatments or diagnostic measures on religious grounds. Some faiths refuse all medical interventions, while others object only to specific procedures or treatments. For example, Jehovah's Witnesses do not permit blood transfusions on the basis of specific verses from the Apostolic Commands, Book of Acts (Heller, 1998). Other religious groups are more interested in using prayer as a healing mechanism. In particular, front and center in the debate are members of the First Church of Christ, Scientist (commonly referred to as Christian Scientists), who choose spiritual healing over traditional medical treatment. According to the Web site of the Mother Church, located in Boston, Massachusetts, "Christian Science, as discovered by Mary Baker Eddy, refers to the universal, practical system of spiritual, prayer-based healing … A means of spiritual care through which individuals have found better emotional and physical health, answers to life's deepest issues and progress on their spiritual journeys." In addition, the Web site states, "Healthcare decisions are always a matter of individual choice." Furthermore, Christian Scientists believe that it is hypocritical to use both spiritual healing and medical treatment at the same time. They do often call on specialized practitioners to provide "spiritual reassurance and skillful, non-medical physical care for anyone relying on Christian Science for healing" (First Church of Christ, Scientist, 2006). Rita Swan (2000) states, "Christian Science theology had trained us to believe that physicians don't really heal—at best, they only relieve symptoms; the underlying cause of the disease remains a moral problem that God alone can solve" (p. 11).

Many different denominations choose faith or spiritual healing over traditional medical treatment. In their landmark study of religious-related child fatalities in 1998, Asser and Swan (1998) identified more than twenty-three different denominations, from thirty-four different states, engaged in such practices with tragic results. Eighty-three percent of the cases were associated with five religious groups: the Church of the Firstborn, End of Time Ministries, Faith Assembly, Faith Tabernacle, and Christian Science.

Medical Consequences

As the Asser and Swan (1998) study avers, the concerns of public health professionals should be taken very seriously, since research provides clear evidence that the consequences of medical neglect can be tragic. In fact, the Committee on Bioethics of the AAP (1997) issued a clearly articulated statement in which they assert that "children, regardless of parental religious beliefs, deserve effective medical treatment when such treatment is likely to prevent substantial harm or suffering or death" (p. 279). The AAP goes on to argue that parents who refuse medical treatment for children should face the same legal consequences as other parents who abuse or neglect their children.

Asser and Swan's (1998) study sought to determine whether standard medical treatment would have saved the lives of 172 children who died between 1975 and 1995. Cases were chosen for inclusion in the study if there was evidence that parents withheld medical care because of religious beliefs. Of the 172 deaths, 140 were attributed to medical conditions in which the typical survival rate would have exceeded 90 percent had standard medical treatment been applied. Therefore, it is likely that the lives of these 140 children could have been saved. Eighteen other cases had an expected survival rate greater than 50 percent. In fact, in all but three of the remaining cases, medical treatment would have likely had some benefit. Asser and Swan (1998) conclude: "When faith healing is used to the exclusion of medical treatment, the number of preventable child fatalities and the associated suffering are substantial and warrant public concern" (p. 625).

Of particular concern to public health officials are outbreaks of communicable diseases, especially those that are normally controlled through immunization programs. Since parents in many states can file an exemption from mandatory vaccination regulations on religious grounds, the transmission of communicable disease is a concern not only for unvaccinated children but also for those who have been immunized. According to CHILD, outbreaks of polio, measles, whooping cough, and diphtheria can be traced to religious groups who sought exemptions from state immunization laws. For example, in 1991 there were 492 cases of measles in Philadelphia among children associated with Faith Tabernacle and First Century Gospel Church; six children died. Between 1985 and 1994, four major outbreaks of measles plagued Christian Science schools in the St. Louis area, claiming the lives of three children. The 1994 outbreak resulted in a total of 247 cases and even spread to children in the public schools (CHILD, 2006).

Medical research provides evidence that communicable disease is a potential danger for the entire community. Sonja Hutchins and associates (1996) examined outbreaks of measles in response to a six-to nine-fold increase in reported cases of measles during 1989 and 1990. They defined an outbreak as five or more epidemiologically linked cases. They found 815 outbreaks during the period 1987–1990, which accounted for the majority of cases reported. Both vaccinated and unvaccinated children were affected; therefore, the researchers conclude that full implementation of immunization regulations is necessary to eliminate measles. Feikin and associates (2000) found that religious exemptors placed their children at a 22.2 times greater risk of acquiring measles and a 5.9 times greater risk of pertussis than immunized children. They also found that at least 11 percent of the vaccinated children who contracted measles did so through contact with a child who had not been immunized because of religious exemption. In a similar study, Salmon and associates (1999) found religious exemptors were 35 times more likely to contract measles than were children who were immunized. Novotny and associates (1988) traced the impact of two measles outbreaks among a Christian Scientist college and camp. In these outbreaks, 187 individuals contracted measles and three people died, but the disease was not transmitted into the general population. Novotny and associates found that early reporting, investigation, and quarantine were effective means of disease control in these cases.

Kaunitz and associates (1984) found that members of religious groups in Indiana who refused prenatal care and gave birth at home without trained assistants substantially increased the risk of death for themselves and their babies. Their findings indicated that the perinatal mortality rate was 3 times higher, and the maternal mortality rate was 100 times higher, than statewide rates. In addition, William Simpson (1989, 1991) found evidence that adult Christian Scientists have overall higher mortality rates than the general public.

Medical neglect may also be associated with psychological distress. Bette Bottoms and associates (1995) conducted a survey of 19,272 clinical psychologists, psychiatrists, and clinical social workers and found that these professionals had victims of religion-related child abuse among their caseloads. Specifically, they found evidence of victimization through medical neglect. Interestingly, many of the parents were described by the mental health providers as mentally ill. In addition, some of the children who suffered from medical neglect also suffered from physical, sexual, and/or emotional abuse at the hands of their parents or caregivers.

The faith healing-community is reluctant to submit to scientific inquiry into their claims of success. Members of religious groups are encouraged to document the successes of their spiritual healings through testimonials. Christian Scientists in particular make a practice of giving testimony to their individual experiences of healing. However, these groups consistently resist opportunities to have their practices tested by medical researchers. At this time, there is little verification that members have been properly diagnosed or that medical intervention was necessary for some of the ailments they claim spiritual healing has cured. Since spiritual healing has not been empirically tested, there is little to no evidence to suggest it is remotely close to being as successful as standard medical interventions. Research investigating the potential health benefits of intercessory or distant prayer has been conducted with mixed results (Aviles et al., 2001; O'Laoire, 1997; Sicher, Targ, Moore, & Smith, 1998; Walker et al., 1997). Few dispute the power of the mind or the potential of prayer as a complementary therapy. However, until religious leaders allow faith healing to be scientifically tested with the same vigorous methods used in the testing of conventional medicine, it will be difficult for many public health professionals to support faith healing as the only form of medical intervention in life-threatening situations involving children.

Legal Issues

Because of the inherent danger involved in withholding medical care to children, parents or caregivers who choose to follow religious beliefs may find themselves the subject of civil or criminal litigation for endangering the welfare of their children. Some parents have been arrested under criminal statutes for the crimes of child abuse, child neglect, child endangerment, or manslaughter. Others have been the subject of family court proceedings for child abuse and neglect. Still others have found themselves in a bitter child custody battle when one parent chooses spiritual healing and the other desires conventional medicine.

The courts have generally acknowledged the right of adults to refuse their own medical care on religious grounds. However, the right to withhold treatment for a child on the basis of religious beliefs has put the courts in the precarious position of balancing the free exercise of religion against the responsibility of the state to protect children. As a result, parents have found their decisions regarding medical treatment for their children subject to legal scrutiny.

Religious groups claim the free exercise clause of the First Amendment gives them the right to reject medical treatment for their children. The U.S. Supreme Court grappled with similar issues in 1944 in *Prince v. Massachusetts*, when the Court considered the rights of the government to protect minors against the rights of parents to raise their children consistent with their religious beliefs. As I discussed in Chapter 3, the *Prince* case involved Sarah Prince, a Jehovah's Witness who was found to be in violation of child labor laws in Massachusetts. The Court upheld the child labor laws as important to the overall protection of children. Delivering the opinion of the Court, Justice Rutledge stated: "Parents may be free to become martyrs themselves. But it does not follow they are free in identical circumstances, to make martyrs of their children before they have reached the age of full and legal discretion when they can make that choice for themselves." He goes on to cite other cases: "The right to practice religion freely does not include the liberty to expose the community or child to communicable disease, or the latter to ill health or death."

Despite this ruling from the Supreme Court in 1944, legal arguments remain, spanning policies in the public health, educational, civil and criminal arenas. Both legislators and the courts have struggled to find compromises that balance the right of free exercise of religion and the protection of children. States continue to embed exceptions for a variety of medical treatments or preventive and diagnostic measures in legislative mandates because of political pressure from religious organizations. Exemptions include immunizations, metabolic and hearing testing and prophylactic eye drops for newborns, lead screening, bicycle helmets, vitamin K, and physical medical exams. Today, the legal controversy is centered on three main issues: religious exemption from immunization laws, religious exemption from child abuse and neglect statutes, and the use of religion as a legal defense when criminal charges are laid.

All states have requirements that children be vaccinated for certain diseases before entering school in kindergarten through twelfth grade. Some states require immunization before entrance to day care, Head Start programs, or college. Immunization laws require protection against diphtheria, tetanus, polio, measles, rubella, and in some states mumps, pertussis, hepatitis, and vermicelli. Exceptions exist for children who may be at further risk of illness if they are immunized. Forty-eight states allow exemptions from immunization on religious grounds (Mississippi and West Virginia are the exceptions). Some states require that parents file an exemption as a member of a recognized religion, while others require an affirmation of religious objection (Hinman, Orenstein, Williamson, & Darrington, 2002). One study found the process of claiming exemptions from immunizations requires less effort than fulfilling the immunization requirement itself (Rota et al., 2001).

States have generally supported religious exemptions because the vast majority of children in any community are vaccinated, providing "herd immunity," or the overall protection of a community from a particular disease because the majority of the community has been protected through vaccination and so the risk to nonvaccinated individuals is relatively low (Friedman-Ross & Aspinwall, 1997). However, as the research noted above indicates, both nonvaccinated and vaccinated children can still be at risk, and even die, as a result of communicable diseases that have generally been brought under control through immunization.

Another area of concern is religious exemption from child abuse statutes. The Child Abuse Prevention and Treatment Act (CAPTA), originally enacted in 1974, was amended in 1996 with new language to clarify that CAPTA does not constitute a federal requirement that parents or guardians provide treatment inconsistent with their religious beliefs. CAPTA was reauthorized and amended by the 108th Congress as the Keeping Children and Families Safe Act of 2003 (42 U.S.C. 5101) with no change in this provision, despite protests from many different professional associations and advocacy groups. In 2003, thirty-four states provided some type of exemption in their statutory definitions of child abuse and neglect for parents who choose not to seek medical attention for their children. In other words, parents will not be found to be neglectful if they can demonstrate their religious beliefs exempt them from the law. Some state statutes require that the parent or guardian be a member of a recognized church or denomination or a "bona fide" religious group. Of course, how a court determines one is a member of a bona fide religion is not specified in state statutes. Other state statutes are even vaguer and provide little direction other than that such an exemption exists to protect parents from being labeled negligent. Paula Monopoli (1991) argues that such exemptions are not historically part of American jurisprudence but a result of the lobbying power of religious groups such as the Christian Science Church.

Exemptions do not necessarily preclude the state from ordering medical services for a child in critical need, nor do they preclude the courts from acting in the best interests of the child pursuant to child abuse and neglect statutes (NCCANI, 2003). For example, in the 1968 U.S. Supreme Court case of *Jehovah's Witnesses in the State of Washington et al. v. King County Hospital*, the Court, citing *Prince v. Massachusetts*, affirmed the decision of a lower court that blood transfusions may be administered to a child against the religious objections of the parents. The courts have consistently ruled in favor of the health and safety of the child in life-threatening cases, yet there has been no uniform agreement in the courts when a case involves a non-life-threatening medical condition or an incurable illness (Plastine, 1993).

In addition, exemptions do not preclude the possibility of civil and/or criminal sanctions being applied to such cases. In 1995, a landmark civil judgment was rendered by a jury in Minnesota against a mother and three other Christian Scientists who chose not to seek medical assistance for her eleven-year-old son, who consequently died of untreated diabetes. In *McKown v. Lundman*, a judgment in the amount of $1.5 million was issued, which was reduced from an original award of $14.2 million. The boy's father brought the wrongful death suit against the mother, stepfather, a hired prayer practitioner, and a Christian Science nurse for not seeking medical treatment after three days of prayer, even after the boy slipped into a diabetic coma. The father also sued the church in *Lundman v. First Church of Christ,*

Scientist, in which a jury awarded $9 million in punitive damages; however, a state appellate court overturned the award, finding that the church itself was not liable for the actions of the individuals involved (*National Law Journal*, 1996).

Numerous criminal cases involving medical neglect are reported by the media. The case of Dennis and Lorie Nixon is noteworthy. The Nixons were members of the Faith Tabernacle Congregation in Altoona, Pennsylvania, a church that believes illness can be healed through prayer. The defendants' daughter, Shannon (aged sixteen) became ill and died of complications related to diabetes acidosis. Shannon did not request medical treatment during her illness, nor did her parents. Dennis and Lorie Nixon were arrested on charges of involuntary manslaughter and endangering the welfare of a child. They were convicted and sentenced to two-and-a-half to five years in prison and a $1,000 fine. On appeal, the Nixons argued their daughter was a mature minor and could therefore refuse medical treatment. The Superior Court upheld their convictions, citing past rulings (*Commonwealth v. Cottam* [1992] and *Commonwealth v. Barnhart* [1985]) that a child's religious beliefs did not relieve the parents of their duty to care, especially in life-or-death situations. The Nixons argued that the state's child abuse and neglect statutes allowed exemptions from medical treatment in line with religious tenets. However, appellate judge Del Sole maintained that an action can qualify as involuntary manslaughter even if it does not constitute child abuse; in effect, the Child Protection statute protects the Nixon's against being labeled child abusers but does not relieve them from criminal responsibility (Rodier, 1999). This was not the first time the Nixons had faced criminal charges. A decade earlier, they pled no contest to endangering the welfare of a child and were sentenced to community service. Their son Clayton, aged eight, died from an untreated ear infection (Gibb, 2001).

In another case, several members of the religious sect called The Body, from Attleboro, Massachusetts, drew national media attention when it was discovered that several children had died in their care. The complex case involved Jacques Robidoux, who was convicted of first-degree murder on June 14, 2002, for the death of his infant son, Samuel. Samuel, not quite twelve months old, died in 1999 from starvation. Jacques, following specific dietary instructions from his sister, Michelle Mingo, instructed his wife Karen to drink only almond milk and to feed their baby only breast milk. Karen and Jacques, believing Michelle had orders from God, abided by the regime for fifty-two days, until Samuel died. Karen was charged with second-degree murder and eventually pled guilty to assault and battery charges. Michelle Mingo pled guilty to two counts of being an accessory before the fact of assault and battery on a child. During the investigation, police were led to the burial ground of baby Samuel in Baxter State Park in Maine, only to find the remains of another child, Jeremiah Corneau, next to Samuel's (Ellement, 2004).

Jeremiah was the infant son of Rebecca and David Corneau. Rebecca is the sister of Jacque Robidoux, and their father, Roland Robidoux, was the proclaimed leader of their church. As the case unfolded, child welfare officials were successful in declaring Jacques, Karen, and Michelle unfit parents in Bristol County Juvenile Court, and ultimately their parental rights were severed. The Department of Social Services also sought to protect the other three children of Rebecca and David, and the unborn child Rebecca was carrying at the time. Rebecca refused to discuss her pregnancy with a court-appointed guardian. In September 2000, Judge Kenneth Nasif ordered she be held in a state correctional facility that housed pregnant women until she gave birth. Once Rebecca's daughter was born, she too was taken into custody by the state. In all, fourteen children from this religious sect were removed from their parents' care and custody and cleared for adoption. At least two babies lost their lives. The court determined the parents were unfit because they did not access medical care or send their children to school, and there was evidence they were abusive in their disciplinary practices ("Attleboro sect couple facing jail," 2002).

This case, extreme as it might appear, captures some of the significant concerns criminal justice, child welfare, and health care professionals have regarding the role of religion in child abuse and neglect. Sharing that concern, Massachusetts amended its state criminal laws and civil codes to remove religious exemptions in 1993, paving the way for a legal resolution to this particular case. The children in this case were subjected to dangerous nutritional regimens, lack of proper medical care, educational neglect, and physical abuse. It is likely that most, if not all, of the fourteen children removed from the religious sect will experience cognitive, affective, and/or social developmental impairments as a result. Unfortunately, the boundary between parental rights to rear their children consistent with their religious doctrine and the rights of the child is not always as clear-cut. This leaves law enforcement professionals, child welfare officials, and the courts, in their role as parens patriae, in the precarious position of determining the limits to parental decision making on a case-by-case basis. Religious exemptions in child abuse and neglect statutes make it even more difficult for the state to determine appropriate boundaries to protect children from harm. This prompted the AAP (1988) to assert that "state legislatures and regulatory agencies with interests in children should be urged to remove religious exemptions clauses from statutes and regulations" (p. 170).

Another legal issue is the use of religion as a criminal defense. When a child dies as a result of religion-related medical neglect, states often prosecute one or both parents for criminal homicide, murder, manslaughter, or felony child abuse, depending on state penal codes. Parents often contend that the free exercise clause of the First Amendment protects them against criminal liability, although the courts have consistently ruled against this argument. In other cases, parents have contended that the religious exemptions found in child abuse and neglect statutes protected them against criminal liability, although many courts have either ruled against such arguments or limited the actual application of exemptions (Plastine, 1993). The exemptions, in effect, confuse the issue, leaving parents and church leaders with the impression that their actions are immune to legal scrutiny (Monopoli, 1991).

Physical and Sexual Abuse

Another area of concern is religion-related physical and sexual abuse. Thousands of children are abused by their parents every year, and sometimes the brutality leads to a child's death. Physical abuse is characterized by actions that cause physical injury to a child, including hitting, punching, kicking, biting, burning, and throwing. Depending on the age of the child, severe injury can be caused by shaking or rough handling. Physically abused children suffer from injuries such as burns, welts, bruises, lacerations, abrasions, and fractures. Injuries can cause both short-term and long-term medical problems. Child sexual abuse is characterized by forcing children to engage in or assist in any simulation of sexual acts or conduct. Examples include fondling, sodomy, intercourse, rape, exploitation through prostitution or photography, and exhibitionism.

In addition to physical injury, children can suffer great emotional turmoil as a result of being abused. Since children are often abused during critical times in their physical and emotional development, we cannot underestimate the developmental consequences of abuse. Physical and sexual abuse can affect a child's physical, emotional, and cognitive growth and development (for research summaries see Kurst-Swanger & Petcosky, 2003; USDHHS, 2005). As in the case of medical neglect of children, the reasons for child physical and sexual abuse are many. Etiological factors include a parental personal history of being abused as a child, witnessing partner violence, social isolation, and stressors such as single parenthood, poverty, substance abuse, and mental illness (Gelles, 1997).

Religiosity also can play a role in the abuse of children, although at this time we cannot quantify the extent of the problem. It is unclear whether religion alone can be considered an etiological factor, or whether particular religious views, combined with other parental or social influences, make a parent more at risk for abusing their child. It is probably safe to assume that the latter is true in many cases. For example, in a survey administered to psychologists, psychiatrists, and clinical social workers to identify cases of religion-related abuse, Bottoms and associates (1995) noted that some practitioners were hesitant to label a case of child abuse as religion related because the perpetrator was mentally ill.

Social scientists have just begun to examine the relationship between theological views and practices and child abuse. A number of issues have surfaced that have gained the attention of child welfare practitioners, advocates, and researchers. Cases such as the death of Terrance Cottrell illustrate the abuse some children endure because their parents believe they are possessed by demons. In other cases, strict disciplinary practices, guided by biblical interpretations, can be related to child abuse or children may be abused during ritualistic practices. Here, I examine the relationship between religion and corporal punishment and a phenomenon referred to as "ritual abuse."

Corporal Punishment

Many children are injured as a result of disciplinary practices gone awry. Often referred to as "corporal punishment," the use of physical force as a means of discipline is still a socially accepted child-rearing practice in the United States. It is sanctioned by many parents and institutions that serve children, such as child care programs and schools. Corporal punishment is a general term; it encompasses a wide range of measures, including spanking, hitting, slapping, shaking, and paddling. It can be doled out with a parent's hand or with a belt, stick, rod, or paddle. Regardless of the method, using physical force on a child can and does result in injury and, in some cases, death. Because of the potential risk of both physical and emotional harm, corporal punishment is a highly contested child-rearing technique around the world.

The social debate on whether corporal punishment is an effective means of discipline continues to rage among social scientists. Some researchers have concluded that corporal punishment is beneficial to children (Baumrind, 1996; Larzelere, 1996); others have found that it is not effective in modifying child behavior in the long run and can actually do more harm than good (Cyan, 1997; Straus, 1994; Straus & Paschall, 1998). In an effort to clarify the issues, Elizabeth Thompson Gershoff (2002) analyzed eighty-eight studies of the impact of corporal punishment on children and found that "although it is related with immediate compliance, corporal punishment is associated with 10 undesirable constructs" (p. 549). She found that corporal punishment was associated with both short-term and long-term constructs such as a decrease in the moral internalization of the behavior, increases in both child and adult aggression, increases in delinquent and antisocial behaviors, increases in adult criminal activity and antisocial behavior, decreases in both child and adult mental health, increased risk of abuse, and an increased risk of abusing one's own children or spouse.

Although Gershoff's research should not be considered the final word on the subject, her results underscore the concerns of numerous professional associations and citizens groups that have called for a legal ban on corporal punishment in the United States and elsewhere in the world. Groups such as the American Bar Association, the American Medical Association, the American Public Health Association, the American Psychological Association, the National Parent-Teachers Association, the National Association of School Psychologists, the National Education Association, the National Association of Social Workers, and the National Association of Pediatric Nurse Associates and Practitioners have recommended alternative forms of discipline (Pollard, 2002). Groups such as the National Coalition to Abolish Corporal Punishment in Schools (NCACPS), End Physical Punishment of Children (EPOCH)-USA, and the Center for Effective Discipline (CED) advocate educating the public and lawmakers about the effects of physical punishment and effective disciplinary alternatives. Legal scholars argue that corporal punishment violates children's liberty and is thus unconstitutional (Pollard, 2002). According to the Global Initiative to End All Corporal Punishment of Children (EACPC) (www.endcorporalpunishment.org), a global advocacy initiative of EACPC, eighteen countries have abolished the use of corporal punishment by institutions and families because they want to end all forms of violence against children (EACPC, 2007). Despite the efforts of advocacy groups, it appears as though the United States is still lagging behind, since all states still permit corporal punishment in the home, and many states still allow its use in schools and alternative care settings.

The concern over corporal punishment relates to the connection between corporal punishment and abuse. Parents who spank, paddle, or slap their children as a means of discipline risk crossing the tenuous line between discipline and abuse. In fact, Gershoff (2002) found that the two most dissimilar constructs—immediate compliance and physical abuse—were most closely associated with corporal punishment in the studies she examined. Her results indicate that although corporal punishment appears to be effective in getting children to comply immediately with parental demands, child abuse researchers are justified in their concerns regarding the escalation of corporal punishment into physical abuse.

One reason corporal punishment has continued in the United States is because of social and religious traditions. Some parents believe their religious foundations dictate the use of corporal punishment and allow them to permit others to use it with their children as well. Since religious teachings offer believers guidance on moral and ethical questions, it follows that religious families would seek religious guidance on issues of family life and child rearing. Some consider the use of physical force against their children not only a right but also a religious duty.

Greven (1991) notes that violence against children has been justified through biblical interpretations for more than 2,000 years. The biblical *Book of Proverbs* contains several relevant passages that Christians of various denominations and fundamentalists alike have interpreted in different ways. The most commonly cited phrases are "He that spareth his rod hateth his son: but he that loveth him chasteneth him betimes" (*Proverbs* 13.24), "Withhold not correction from a child: for if thou beatest him with the rod, he shall not die. Thou shalt beat him with the rod, and deliver his soul from hell" (*Proverbs* 23.13–14), "Chasten thy son while there is hope, and let not thy soul spare for his crying" (*Proverbs* 19.18), "Foolishness is bound in the heart of a child; but the rod of correction shall drive it far from him" (*Proverbs* 22.15), and "The rod and reproof give wisdom: but a child left to himself bringeth his mother to shame" (*Proverbs* 29.15).

These proverbs, coupled with belief in the existence of Satan, who inspires sin, and the belief that God is vengeful and will punish sinners through eternal damnation in Hell, convince many believers it is their duty to rid their children of sin through physical force: "it is better that children experience a temporary hell inflicted by loving parents than they burn in an eternal hell" (Bottoms, Shaver, Goodman, & Qin, 1995, p. 86). The New Testament gospels and epistles and the *Book of Revelation* provide what many Christians consider important references to "hell" and eternal banishment to hell for unsaved sinners. Faced with the prospect of eternal punishment, parents are responsible for paving appropriate paths to salvation for their children. As viewed particularly by evangelical and fundamentalist Protestants, that path is one of fear. Fear, instilled through the wrath of a parent, parallels the relationship between Christians and their heavenly father. Corporal punishment and the fear that it evokes are seen as necessary to rid children of self-will (Greven, 1991).

Some Christians construe biblical passages literally, while others are more interested in the symbolic nature of the language. Those who view the Bible as inerrant, or without error, are more likely to interpret the language of the passages in very literal terms and may therefore be more likely to find religious justification for the use of physical violence in child rearing. Conservative Protestants, in particular, have been the focus of research and debate on this issue. A growing body of evidence suggests that they are more likely to have positive attitudes toward corporal punishment and to use it more frequently than other parents (Day, Peterson, & McCraken, 1998; Ellison, Bartkowski, & Segal, 1996; Gershoff, Miller, & Holden, 1999). Yet, even among literalist conservative Protestants, there appear to be differences in readings of the *Book of Proverbs*. For example, Bartkowski (1996) notes that two prominent conservative evangelical parenting specialists, James Dobson and Ross Campell, both of whom contend that the Bible is inerrant, have come to strikingly different conclusions as to the application of these passages to child rearing. Several studies have suggested that although religiously conservative individuals may use corporal punishment more frequently than others do, they do not appear to use corporal punishment to the exclusion of other disciplinary methods (Gershoff, Miller, & Holden, 1999; Jackson et al., 1999). Further research is necessary to determine the dynamics of biblical interpretation within the context of child discipline (Bartkowski, 1996).

From the perspective of many child welfare professionals, corporal punishment, no matter what its form, is a violent approach to discipline. No matter how benign they may seem, all violent actions toward children can be harmful (Greven, 1991; Kurst-Swanger & Petcosky, 2003), and infants and toddlers are at greatest risk of harm by corporal punishment. Even well-meaning, loving parents can physically harm their children during incidents of discipline. Since numerous other effective disciplinary alternatives are available, child welfare professionals argue it is not necessary to utilize a potentially physically and emotionally injurious method.

Social scientists have just begun to explore the relationship between religiosity, corporal punishment, and child abuse. In a study that sought to examine the child, maternal, and family characteristics associated with spanking, Jean Giles-Smith and associates (1995) analyzed data from the 1990 National Longitudinal Survey of Youth (NLSY), which was administered at the Ohio State University Center for Human Resource Research. They compared data on spanking by four different groups: Protestants, Catholics, those with no religious preference, and those with other religious affiliations. They found that Catholics used spanking the least and that Protestants and those with other religious affiliations were more likely to spank their children. Yet, among those who spanked their children, there were no significant differences in the frequency with which they used spanking. Similarly, Gershoff, Miller, and Holden (1999) found that conservative Protestants were more likely to use corporal punishment than other parents were, yet no significant differences based on religion could be associated with other disciplinary techniques.

In a study seeking to predict the abuse proneness of parents by examining parental attitudes and disciplinary practices, Shelly Jackson and associates (1999) considered the role of religion in their analysis. They examined the survey responses of a nationally representative sample of 1,000 parents and found a complex set of variables associated abuse proneness, with religiosity being related in complex ways. For example, the study found that "parents for whom religion was important were more likely to have attitudes that devalue children" and "parents who had attitudes that devalue children were more likely to use physical discipline with their children" (Jackson et al., 1999, p. 25). Conversely, they found that "the less important religion was to parents, the more likely they were to have positive attitudes towards physical discipline" (p. 24).

Bottoms and associates (1995) surveyed psychologists, psychiatrists, and clinical social workers to investigate the extent of religiously based child abuse among the patients they treated. They found that both child and adult victims of religiously motivated physical abuse were present among their caseloads. For example, out of 271 "pure" cases involving religion-related child abuse, 69 cases involved abuse in an attempt to rid a child of evil, and approximately one-half of these involved some form of sexual abuse and three cases involved murder. The majority of incidents involving ridding the child of evil were committed in the home by families with fundamentalist or Protestant religious affiliations. Bottoms and associates also found that in many cases the physical abuse was quite severe.

These studies have only begun to explore the complex relationship between religion and child physical abuse. Yet the results are interesting and suggest further investigation is warranted. Among the difficulties in resolving the debate regarding corporal punishment is the broad use of the term. Further research should distinguish among various forms of corporal punishment, since some forms may present a greater risk of physical and emotional harm to children than others. It is likely that spanking, as a type of corporal punishment, would garner more social support among parents than, say, hitting a child with a rod or a belt.

Ritual Abuse

Another area of concern in reference to religion-related child abuse is ritual abuse, which become a national concern in the 1980s and continues to draw critical attention worldwide. Since the very existence of ritual abuse has been questioned, many therapists, law enforcement officials, and child welfare advocates approach potential cases of ritual abuse with trepidation. Professionals across different disciplines have been polarized by the controversial nature of the issues involved, partly because a coherent definition of ritual abuse has not yet crystallized (Lloyd, 1992). Ritual abuse, sometimes referred to as "satanic ritual abuse," is best described by Finkelhor, Meyer Williams, and Burns (1988) as "[a]buse that occurs in a context linked to some symbols or group activity that have a religious, magical or super-natural connotation, and where the invocation of these symbols or activities, repeated over time, is used to frighten and intimidate children" (p. 59).

This definition is useful because it distinguishes this form of religion-related child abuse from the other forms I have described elsewhere in this text. It is important to note that not all abusive ritualistic behavior is motivated by a religious belief system, nor is all such behavior satanic. Unlike the other theologically based crimes I describe, little is known about the belief system of those engaged in such practices. Ritual abuse is so controversial because despite the detailed descriptions of child and adult survivors of such ritualistic abuses, often in therapy, few cases have been substantiated by law enforcement. Children and adults worldwide recount unspeakable acts such as cannibalism, animal mutilation, murder, baby breeding, blood letting, sexual abuse, cleansing rituals, and torture. These atrocities are often reported as having been committed as part of ceremonial rituals, using symbols, artifacts, chanting, and so on, often with satanic reference. Such abuses have reportedly occurred in secret settings such as secluded wooded areas, structures that resemble churches, day care centers, and private homes. The issue is complicated by the fact that individuals who have never met each other often report the bizarre elements of their experiences similarly. This can be compared to the hundreds of individuals who have reported similar experiences with alien abduction (Lanning, 1991), and researchers have begun to investigate the similarities between the two populations (Bader, 2003).

As Kenneth Lanning (1992), supervisory special agent with the Behavioral Science Unit at the National Center for Analysis of Violent Crime (NCAVC) of the Federal Bureau of Investigation points out, modern forensic techniques should be able to identify trace evidence to support such allegations. However, little evidence of such heinous crimes exists. He has concluded that it is unlikely that any large organized crime conspiracy involving serious violent crime such as human sacrifice exists. However, he does not discount the possibility that ritual activity occurs, some of which may be criminal. He notes that law enforcement officials have investigated crimes linked to ritual activity such as vandalism, defilement of and thefts from churches and cemeteries, gang activity, and teen suicide, although he notes that most of these crimes have involved teenagers (Lanning, 1992).

The involvement of adolescents in satanic activities has raised concern among law enforcement officials, child welfare specialists, and therapists. Struggling with the developmental challenges of adolescence, coupled with persistent psychological problems and histories of victimization, some young people are drawn to groups that identify with satanic themes. Such groups might identify themselves as Satanists, Goths, or vampires. It is unclear what level of organization actually exists in such groups and to what degree actual belief systems play a role in their activities. Teens may identify with their peers in such groups on a purely social basis, rather than a truly religious one. It should be noted that not all such groups engage in criminal ritual activities; however, concern about the emotional and physical well-being of adolescent members is probably warranted. In a study of ten hospitalized youth who proclaimed to be voluntary members of satanic groups, Belitz and Schacht (1992) found that all of the boys had been physically and/or sexually abused by one or both parents and many had witnessed acts of intimate partner violence. They found the boys were drawn to satanic groups to legitimize their feelings of rage and fear with the promise of power and sexual prowess in the future. Another study examined a group of five youth self-identified as members of a vampire cult and charged with first-degree murder for killing the parents of one of the group's members in rural Kentucky. Members of the Vampire Clan had significant psychological problems from enduring physical, sexual, and emotional abuse in childhood. Life-long patterns of psychological troubles, marked by self-mutilation, substance abuse, truancy, and sexual pervasion, were evident: "the attraction to cults and killing are indicative of the rage and distortion of perceptions regarding relationships with others, the lack of caring and love experienced in their lives, and the complete inability for them to attach or bond to a significant other or to society" (Miller et al., 1999, p. 217).

While criminal evidence may be lacking to resolve cases of ritual abuse in a court, the psychiatric evidence appears to be mounting. Although there is little evidence to suggest that "babies are being bred and eaten, that 50,000 missing children are being murdered in human sacrifices, or that Satanists are taking over America's day care centers" (Lanning, 1991, p. 173), psychologists, psychiatrists, and clinical social workers continue to encounter patients who discuss witnessing or enduring such events. Some survivor stories may be a function of distortions, misinformation, emotional confusion, substance use, false memories, or an improper diagnosis. For example, Yeager and Lewis (1997) report a case in which a thirty-nine-year-old female patient, claiming to have been victimized by a satanic cult, found that her memories of such abuse emerged only after she attended a cult abuse survivors support group. They caution clinicians to explore the context in which memories of abuse first surface.

Regardless of the accuracy of every detail of a survivor's narrative or at what point in recovery a survivor discloses abuses, therapists and child welfare specialists should share concern regarding the psychological and physical well-being of survivors. Given the psychiatric symptoms present in these patients, it is very likely that many suffered trauma in their childhoods, even if it was not completely ritualistic in nature. Many patients who disclose ritual abuse suffer from complex emotional problems, often consistent with the types of problems exhibited by others who have experienced substantiated non-ritualistic childhood trauma. Therapists have found that such patients display high degrees of fear; many have been diagnosed with post-traumatic stress disorder, dissociative identity disorder, borderline personality disorders, or depression (Coleman, 1994; Noblitt & Perskin, 2000). Self-harm is also a consistent theme.

Dissociative identity disorder, formerly referred to as multiple personality disorder, is of particular interest, since this diagnosis involves symptoms in which patients experience trances, amnesia and time loss, changes in voice and demeanor, and auditory hallucinations. Patients with dissociative identity disorder who disclose ritual abuse often do so through one of their alter personalities (Noblitt & Perskin, 2000). Canadian psychiatrist George A. Fraser (1990) notes that of his thirty-six patients in 1990 with the diagnosis, eleven had reported memories of ritual abuse. Ten of these patients reported victimization by satanic groups, and one patient experienced horrific sacrifices "for Christ" in a fundamentalist religious group. Lewis and associates (1997) examined twelve individuals convicted of murder who had a diagnosis of dissociative identity disorder and found that all had extensive substantiated histories of being abused physically or sexually during childhood, establishing a strong link between severe child abuse and dissociative identity disorder. They also note that false memory could not be a factor since these murderers could not even remember their childhoods. In fact, they either denied or minimized their early victimization.

Despite the difficulties inherent in substantiating claims of ritual abuse, particularly when the alleged abuses may have occurred years before the disclosure, it is difficult to ignore the voices of survivors who divulge such abuses during therapy. Noblitt and Perskin (2000) suggest that in some cases, heinous acts may have been simulated, rather than performed, to demonstrate the power of the abusers, thereby creating an atmosphere to terrorize and intimidate child victims. Role-playing human sacrifice, bloodletting, and cannibalism can be as harmful, especially for children, who are likely to be unaware of the difference.

It is also difficult to determine, on the basis of such disclosures, how such abuses are related to a specific belief system. Since few offenders have come forward to offer testimony as to the religious basis for ritual abuse, little is known about who is involved in such abusive behavior or why. As we find in other religiously based criminal activity, few have come forward to justify their behavior on religious grounds. It is unlikely, therefore, that we can clump all abusers into one neat category of offenders. It is plausible that no one religious tradition or view is involved but that many different types of religious traditions are expressed ritualistically, some of which might be purely the invention of the individual abusers involved. Some abusers may use rituals involving magic or supernatural connotations to enhance their power, or as a method of grooming to get children to comply, or to grant themselves "permission" to engage in deviant abusive behaviors with children. Still others may be reenacting their own abusive childhoods. Some may be fulfilling deviant sexual fantasies through drama and theatrics, while others may suffer from untreated mental illnesses.

It is also possible that many do engage in ritualistic abuse as a part of a particular belief system. Noblitt and Perskin (2000) remind us that there are religious traditions from around the world in which members seek a trancelike state as a spiritual experience. Survivors treated by Dr. Noblitt reported experiences that resonated with these different religious traditions. For example, Vodou (also referred to as Vodum, Vodun, Voodoo, and Voudou) members communicate with their ancestors, African deities, or Catholic saints via dreams or trance states. Shamans, found in different religious and cultural contexts, are individuals who possess the ability to control spirits via a trance or ecstatic state, often achieved by excluding sensory stimuli through drumming or substance use. Shamans are generally called upon to mediate between the spirit and his or her community (Bowker, 2000). In religious affiliations such as these, the goal is not to exorcise a bad spirit but to possess the spirit within one's own body, through trance; therefore dissociation is desired. This process has been referred to as "adorcism." In some instances, sexual themes can also be identified in the trance and possession rituals of religious and cultural groups around the world (Lewis, 2003).

Sara Scott (2001) interviewed survivors and asked them to describe the religious views of their abusers. She noted that survivors did not reveal one concrete doctrine; rather themes involving power emerged:

> Satan/evil is all powerful, Power is the (ultimate) goal/aim, Rituals bring power, Power is gained by eating flesh/drinking blood, Energy is released by death/sacrifice, They know everything you say/do, You will die if you tell/disobey, Good is evil/evil is good, Pain is pleasure/strength. (p. 86)

Scott received questionnaires from survivors who noted the belief system of their ritual abusers was non-satanic: Mormonism, Roman Catholicism, fundamentalist

Christian, Masonic, neo-Nazi, and Pagan witchcraft. She concluded that although no one coherent doctrine emerged from her interviews with survivors, "beliefs might be usefully regarded not so much as 'mental' convictions but rather as something evidenced within ritual practice and known through embodied experience. They might not necessarily be diminished by ignorance of a formal creed, but rather enhanced by the adornment of secrecy" (p. 102).

In any case, as individuals continue to come forward to describe violent, deviant acts of physical torture and sexual abuse, it is important that therapists and law enforcement officials retain an open mind. It is equally important that social scientists continue to probe this troubling phenomenon.

Refusal to Pay Child Support

It is not uncommon for differences in religious beliefs to be at the center of divorce and child custody proceedings. In some cases, one or both partners may disapprove of divorce on religious grounds, making separation or divorce a difficult legal option. In other cases, child custody battles erupt out of disagreements about what religion children should be brought up in, what religious practices are appropriate for children to participate in, and how to resolve differences when the religious practices of one parent interfere with the visitation rights of another. In such disputes, the courts have had the duty of determining what is in the best interest of the child, while trying to balance the rights of the parents. In some cases, judges have to determine whether abuse or neglect is a factor. Even on a good day, such judicial decisions are difficult. Judges are often presented with a "no-win" situation in which children are clearly caught in the middle.

A related issue is the nonpayment of child support on religious grounds. There is little evidence to suggest this occurs with great frequency; however, cases have been presented to the courts for resolution, and thus are worthy of mention here. In *Hunt v. Hunt* (1994), Eugene Hunt was found in contempt of court for failure to pay child support and appealed to the Supreme Court of Vermont against the court-ordered child support and the contempt of court charges, arguing that his religious beliefs prevented him from making child support payments. Hunt and his wife were members of the Northeast Kingdom Community Church of Island Pond, Vermont, today referred to as the Messianic Communities.

Members of this religious group continue to experience legal problems. They have lost child custody battles owing to their alternative lifestyle. Suspicions of child abuse abound because of their strict disciplinary practices. For example, in 1984, the Island Pond settlement was raided by Vermont state troopers who were working with child protection officials, although all charges were eventually dismissed (Bozeman & Palmer, 1997). Members have also been fined for violations of child labor laws (Lovett, 2001). Members give up their personal possessions and live a communal lifestyle. According to the church Web site (http://www. twelvetribes.com):

> Soon we began to form our own economy based on cottage industry, farming, and traditional crafts, because we wanted to keep this new culture pure, free from greed and selfishness. With conviction, we took our children out of the public school system in order to teach them at home. We realized that everything we did would be in vain if we left our children to be corrupted by the disrespect, independence, and peer pressure of the old culture.

In 1989, Eugene Hunt's wife left him, taking their children with her, and filed for divorce. She was granted custody, and the court ordered Eugene to pay child support, which he did not pay. He argued that his church forbids no-fault divorces and does not permit the financial support of estranged spouses or children who live outside the community. He argued that since he lived communally with other members of the church, he had no personal property and could not work outside the community. He could not seek an income to support his children. Although the Supreme Court of Vermont found that his religious beliefs were sincere, it affirmed the reasoning of the lower court's ruling validating the child support order. The Supreme Court did, however, vacate the contempt order and remanded the case to determine the least restrictive means to enforce his support obligation.

5

Crimes against Women

On February 11, 1815, Abigail Abbot Bailey died at the age of sixty-nine in the home of her son, Asa Bailey, in Bath, New Hampshire. A Congregationalist living in New England in early America, Abigail was a woman of strong faith who raised fourteen children and finally divorced her abusive husband after twenty-six years of marriage. Shortly after her death, her friends saw it fit to publish her memoirs on the assumption that the public had much to learn from her painful experiences of being married to an abusive man, Asa Bailey. Originally published in 1815 by Reverend Ethan Smith and reprinted by religious historian Ann Taves in 1989, Bailey's memoirs provide an intimate glimpse into the pain and suffering endured by many women across the globe and illustrate the strong role religion plays in the life decisions of devout followers.

We continue to draw lessons from her memoirs. Betrayed by the man who swore to love and protect her, Abigail Bailey experienced a marriage filled with violence and psychological abuse. Unfortunately, her story is captivating not because it is unique, but because it is rather ordinary. Even some two hundred years later, women around the world can relate to her experience. It is disheartening to realize that women and children continue to be maltreated in similar ways today. In fact, some may argue little has changed since 1767, when she exchanged marriage vows with Asa Bailey.

Her memoirs are still relevant today on a number of levels. The details of her life provide us an opportunity to explore the firsthand experiences of a woman living in New England during the later eighteenth century. Images of the social, political, and religious life of early Americans are juxtaposed against Abigail's sorrow. More important, her story raises provocative questions about the relationship between religiosity and violence against women and children. As a Congregationalist, her strong religious convictions served as both an asset and a detriment. She relied on her religious convictions to make sense of her husband's cruelty and sought religious meaning in his controlling and violent behavior. In faith she found solace for her pain. She remained committed to an abusive marriage for twenty-six years, in part because of her strong religious values and the belief that God had willed this type of life for her. She submitted to her husband's reign as consistent with the teachings of her faith and the prevailing patriarchal paradigm of early America. She wrote:

> God gave me a heart to resolve never to be obstinate, or disobedient to my husband; but to always be kind, obedient, and obliging in all things not contrary to the word of God. I thought if Mr. B were sometimes unreasonable, I would be reasonable, and would rather suffer wrong than do wrong. (Bailey, p. 57, as cited by Taves, 1989, p. 28)

She decided to petition for divorce only after she learned that her husband was sexually abusing their sixteen-year-old daughter, Phoebe. During this period in American history, acts of incest were considered adulterous and were viewed as a crime against the marriage, not necessarily the child. Many Christians viewed incest as unnatural because it involves sexual acts outside of marriage for purposes other than procreation (Taves, 1989). Although Asa Bailey had been accused of raping another woman and having a sexual relationship with a servant, the sexual abuse of her daughter became Abigail's impetus for change. She finally came to the conclusion that she could not dishonor God by continuing the marriage. Like many of her contemporaries, seeking a divorce and a property settlement from an abusive controlling partner proved to troubling for her. She completes her memoirs with the following passage:

> Thus I have sketched some of the most important events of my life, through which God, in his deep and holy providence, caused me to pass, from the time I entered the family state, A.D. 1767, in the twenty-second year of my age,—till A.D. 1792, when I was in my forty-seventh year. Great trials, and wonderful mercies have been my lot, from the hands of my Heavenly Father. (Cited by Taves, 1989, p. 178)

Abigail Bailey's journey through a troubled marriage underscores the role of religious fervor in domestic violence. Several important themes surface. Her husband's abusive behavior was not necessarily driven by his own theology; rather her religious beliefs prevented her from seeking safety outside the marriage. Like so many other religious women, she looked to her faith for explanation and support.

She accepted her "lot" in life, concluding that it was God's will that she experience such mistreatment.

Nancy Nason-Clark (2004) argues that women of strong faith are more vulnerable when they are abused because their religious views reinforce traditional gender roles, rendering them less likely to seek support outside the religious community and less likely to leave a violent partner. She acknowledges that abused women of strong faith share the same concerns as battered women in the mainstream culture, but she notes that religious women are more likely to have intensified feelings of fear, vulnerability, and isolation. Worldviews that instruct religious followers to forgive the misdeeds of others and the firm belief that marriage is a holy union to be undone only by death bond women to remain in abusive marriages. Religious leaders may inadvertently put women in further danger by encouraging prayer to heal the family or by reinforcing religious doctrine that could place victims in unsafe relationships.

This chapter explores the connection between religion and crimes against women. As you may recall from Chapter 4, women and children are most vulnerable to theologically based crimes because of religious orientations and their influence over family life. Here I explore two specific crime types, domestic violence and plural marriage. Both raise a number of questions about the relationship between religion, crime, and family life. Also, it is important to note that although I have included these examples in a chapter on crimes against women, both domestic violence and plural marriage have significant implications for children as well.

Domestic Violence

Many women across the globe confront personal violence in their daily lives. Some are physically and/or emotionally abused by their intimate partner, and some are stalked and hunted by strangers, while others are violated through sexual assault or genital mutilation. Such violence takes a deadly turn for thousands of women each year. Violence against women appears to be a worldwide phenomenon, victimizing women of different cultural, economic, ethnic, and racial backgrounds, as well as women of different age groups. Even in the United States, one of the world's most influential nations, overtly concerned with human rights, violence against women persists as a social problem. Domestic abuse is a complex phenomenon with enormous consequences for the health and well-being of women and their children.

Women are especially vulnerable to abuses within intimate partner relationships. I have argued elsewhere that I prefer the term "intimate partner violence" over "domestic violence" because I believe it more adequately captures the reality of partner violence. Violence occurs in same-sex relationships, as it does in heterosexual dating relationships, whether or not the partners are co-habiting or married (Kurst-Swanger & Petcosky, 2003). Since states define "domestic abuse" in various ways, and some clearly limit their definition to include only those relationships in which the partners are married or have children in common, it is important that the terminology be clearly articulated. Yet here you will find that I distinctly favor the term "domestic violence." I do so because religion-related partner abuse tends to be especially relevant as a dynamic of marriage. In families of strong faith, marriage is not just a legal or social arrangement but a sacred duty. For many, it is through the sacrament of marriage that one can be true to one's faith. Thus, marriage holds a special significance.

Intimate partner violence in general, and abuse within marriage in particular, is far too common. The actual prevalence of battering is difficult to measure since so many victims do not come forward to report abuses to the authorities. However, when we consider the extent of battering as indicated in household surveys and cases reported to authorities, it is clear that domestic abuse is a social problem that needs intervention. In a 2005 compendium report prepared with data complied from several sources, the Bureau of Justice Statistics (BJS), through the U.S. Department of Justice, examined statistics pertaining to family violence in the United States. Data from the National Crime Victimization Survey (a survey conducted by the BJS), Supplemental Homicide Reports (compiled by the Federal Bureau of Investigation [FBI]), and the National Incident-Based Reporting System (compiled by the FBI) indicate that approximately 3.5 million violent crimes were committed against family members during 1998–2002. Of these, 50 percent (1.73 million) were violent crimes against a spouse. Of the 1.73 million offenses involving spouses, the most frequent crime was simple or aggravated assault (86 percent); however, 4.7 percent of the offenses involved a sexual assault, 8.9 percent involved a robbery, and 0.3 percent involved a homicide. In addition, it is important to note that women represented 84.3 percent of all spouse abuse victims (Durose et al., 2005).

The explanations for domestic violence involve a myriad issues that span micro, meso, and macro dimensions of analysis. In an attempt to explain why violence between domestic partners occurs, social scientists have sought to examine individual, familial, and social constructs. A number of factors have been found to be associated with domestic abuse, including substance abuse, power differentials, isolation, cultural approval of violence, stress, intergenerational transmission of violence, and patriarchy (for a full discussion of theoretical explanations, see Cardarelli, 1997; Eigenberg, 2001; Gelles, 1997; Kurst-Swanger & Petcosky, 2003).

Religion and Domestic Abuse: The Role of Patriarchy

Social scientists have just begun to research the link between religion and domestic abuse. Domestic abuse appears to occur across all religious boundaries; therefore, it is unlikely that religion alone can explain the vast majority of abuse. However, religious views, particularly those that dictate a patriarchal system, may be more amenable to the perpetuation of abuse on both the individual and social level because of the differential impact patriarchal systems have on women. This is especially relevant given that the sanctity of marriage is both religiously and culturally determined. Therefore, a central theme in understanding all violence against women, and in particular battering within intimate relationships, is patriarchy.

I have argued elsewhere that patriarchy alone cannot explain all acts of intimate partner violence, since in some instances women are perpetrators of violence against other women or against men (Kurst-Swanger & Petcosky, 2003). Yet it is difficult to ignore the notion that battering is a form of social control over women that has been legitimized in numerous ways throughout history (Eigenberg, 2001). Battering is, in effect, an extension of the historical and social control men have had over women (Dobash & Dobash, 1979). Examining domestic abuse from a macro level requires that we explore the ways women are exploited and controlled through policies, procedures, and, in this case, religious tenets.

When we consider religion-related domestic abuse, patriarchy is central, because it is a foundational principle by which many religious families live. "Patriarchy" is an anthropological term used to describe societies in which males tend to occupy positions of power. Similarly, the term "matriarchy" is used to describe female–dominated societies. The term "patriarch" also has religious roots. It was an official title given to bishops of Christendom in the Roman Empire, who had authority over the people in their territory, as well as the title given to leaders within independently hierarchical Orthodox churches, churches in union with Rome, Oriental Orthodox churches, and Assyrian churches. In addition, "patriarch" is also the English equivalent of *Soshigata*, which refers to the founder of a Buddhist school and his lineage successors (Bowker, 2000).

Patriarchy, or the notion of male supremacy, is embedded in the core beliefs of many different faiths through the religious and cultural context of marriage. In many faiths, wives are expected to be obedient to their husbands to demonstrate their submission to God. For example, Dena Saadat Hassouneh-Phillips (2001a), in a study of American Muslim abuse survivors, explores domestic violence within the context of religion and culture. She notes the Qur'anic verse that provides guidance on what makes a good wife within marriage:

> Men are the protectors and maintainers of women, because God has given the one more strength than the other, and because they support them from their means. Therefore the righteous women are devoutly obedient, and guard in their husband's absence what God would have guard. (Ali, 1993, p. 195)

Hassouneh-Phillips notes there was no consensus on the practice of obedience in marriage, yet the notion of obedience itself was a culturally common belief among American Muslim women, especially among women who believed obedience was a religious duty. Some of the participants in her study who were victimized reported that they were willing to tolerate submission, subservience, and some level of abuse since the majority of their religious experience was so positive. In the absence of extended family networks and Muslim courts to control abusive husbands, the women had little recourse within their own community.

Many liberal and conservative Christian families abide by a similar patriarchal worldview, and, as in Muslim families, patriarchy is practiced to differing degrees. Bartkowski (1996, 1997) notes that even among conservative, fundamentalist Protestants, different interpretations have been garnered from biblical readings. Some evangelical family commentators take a very traditional, patriarchal approach to gender roles and marriage responsibilities, while others view marriage as mutual submission. *Ephesians* 5.22–24 provides guidance regarding wifely submission:

> Wives, be subject to your husbands, as to the Lord. For the husband is in the head of the wife as Christ is the head of the Church, his body, and is himself its Savior. As the Church is subject to Christ, so let wives also be subject in everything to their husbands.

Such passages, coupled with a belief system that views the Bible as inerrant, have led some scholars to hypothesize that conservative fundamentalist Christian men are more likely than others to abuse their wives. Researchers have begun to study this question; however, to date little evidence has been found to support the hypothesis. For example, Brinkerhoff, Grandin, and Lupri (1992) examined the influence of religious denomination and church attendance on domestic abuse in Canada and found that both religious affiliation and "religious patriarchy" had little, if any, relationship to abuse. Several years later, Ellison, Bartkowski, and Anderson (1999) found similar results in their study of more than 4,000 men and women. They found no evidence that denominational ties or specific theological convictions were related to higher rates of abuse among conservative Protestants. However, there is some evidence to suggest that fundamentalist men and women arrive at sexist attitudes in different ways: whereas for men, sexism is related to their fundamentalist affiliation, for women, sexism is related to their personal belief in the inerrancy of the Bible (Peek, Lowe, & Williams, 1991).

Patriarchy is also embedded in the religious and social culture of many Jewish families. Beverly Horsburgh (1995) notes that gender hierarchy exists in various Jewish sects in which women are treated differently in most aspects of life, including religious rituals, permissible apparel, daily habits (such as bathing rituals), and educational opportunities. It is the religious and cultural oppression of women within many Jewish communities, she argues, that tends to perpetuate domestic violence, although there is no evidence that abuse is more prevalent in the Orthodox community than in other religious communities. However, the toleration of abuse within the rabbinical commentary and the difficulty many women face in initiating divorces under the *halakhah* (Jewish law) have presented many challenges for Jewish women who are battered (Horsburgh, 1995). The *Shulchan Arukh*, which is accepted as the most authoritative code of Jewish law, addresses laws regarding everyday life, including marriage and divorce (Bowker, 2000). This code makes only one reference to the appropriateness of battery under certain circumstances (Rabin, Markus, & Voghere, 1999).

Horsburgh (1995) also argues that many abused Jewish women, particularly Orthodox Jews, are isolated from secular services that could be of assistance. She notes that their religious practices and lack of education may leave many women ill prepared to support themselves. In particular, Hasidic women are brought up to be totally dependent on men and are often not educated to be able to survive on their own. Since Orthodox mores command that women seek the advice of their rabbis instead of calling the police or another secular authority, they are bound by whatever advice their rabbis may give. Horsburgh suggests that rabbis are not necessarily inclined to advise women to seek shelter or restraining orders and that many may tell women to try harder to please their husbands for the sake of *shalom bayit*. In addition, she argues that some women may not disclose abuse since Jewish law forbids gossip or derogatory speech.

Horsburgh (1995) also notes that outside the traditional texts where abuse appears to be condoned, the Orthodox community today does not sanction abusive practices. She acknowledges that many modern Jewish families interpret Jewish law with the understanding that it was written at a time when cultural and social mores and norms were different than today. She notes progress in the Rabbinical Council of America's passing of a resolution in 1994 forbidding domestic abuse and recommending that Orthodox rabbis have a responsibility to protect victims.

Challenges Facing Women of Strong Faith

As mentioned, battered women of strong faith, regardless of religious affiliation, share certain challenges. Let us examine some of them in a little more depth. First and foremost, the notion of patriarchy is so embedded in many religious traditions that acts of violence might be difficult for some women (and men) to define as abuse; therefore it might be difficult to assess the extent of abusive behaviors in some families. Individuals have different degrees of tolerance toward coercive control and physical aggression. For example, some men and women might consider a push or shove as abusive, while others would not define an act as abusive unless it left a visible mark. For some, just the notion of wifely submission might seem abusive. Those who advocate on behalf of victims of domestic violence would consider a wide range of physical aggression as being abusive, including, but not limited to, pushing, shoving, kicking, punching, and pinching. In addition, behaviors that deny a women her autonomy, isolate her from her family and friends, instill fear through intimidation, threats, or manipulation, "punish" her for challenging a husband's authority, or limit her access to financial resources are generally considered to be abusive in nature (Kurst-Swanger & Petcosky, 2003).

Therefore, how one defines concepts such as wifely submission, patriarchy, and abuse is likely to affect how one experiences and defines certain acts or behaviors. Thus, drawing the line between acceptable behavior and abuse within a patriarchal model may be difficult for men and women of strong faith. Patriarchal ideology by its very nature denies that domestic abuse is abuse; thus there may be incongruence between research and reality (Battaglia, 2001). Even if followers define particular behaviors as abusive, many women of strong faith are encouraged to believe the problem is one of spirituality and faith. Thus, further research is needed to explore the prevalence of domestic abuse in religious denominations that support a patriarchal model.

Second, social isolation is a factor in many violent families. Isolation need not be geographic. It can be achieved through a lack of physical or emotional attachment to one's neighborhood, family, or associates. Abuse is more likely to persist in families that are secluded from others, since isolation helps maintain secrecy and minimize interference from others. Gelles (1997) notes that "where privacy is high, the degree of social control will be low" (p. 125).

Many families of strong faith desire social isolation because the broader community does not necessarily share their values. For example, families of strong faith may desire to live in neighborhoods with other members of their faith community. Adherence to certain religious tenets might also restrict a family's interaction with society via the mass media, such as television, movies, newspapers, or radio. Some families choose home or faith-based schooling over other educational options to control the influence of the outside world on their children.

Therefore, battered women may be unaware of the resources at their disposal or the laws governing abusive actions. Some may seek the advice and counsel of their religious leaders. However, many clergy significantly underestimate the problem of domestic violence within their faith communities and often believe it is the result of a spiritual problem that requires spiritual solutions (Nason-Clark, 1997). Some churches reinforce the notion that only church leaders can advise followers about life issues and that followers who seek advice outside the church community are in danger of losing faith (Whipple, 1987). This compounds the difficulty in linking victims with appropriate services to ensure their safety. Also, current domestic violence education/prevention models are unlikely to have an effect on women living in secluded religious communities without outreach and distinct consideration for their belief system or individual needs.

Social science research must continue to examine domestic violence in more isolated religious communities, since much of the research to date has focused on religious communities that are more socially accessible or allow battered women access to some type of social or health service. For example, Jon Krakauer (2004), in his best-selling book *Under the Banner of Heaven: A Story of Violent Faith*, chronicles the lives of isolated fundamentalist Mormons who continue to practice plural marriage. He exposes a dark and chilling religious subculture where violence against women (and children) appears to be the norm, not the exception. Such a portrayal raises provocative questions about the role of religiosity in domestic abuse.

A third challenge facing many battered women is the difficult decision to leave the relationship. There is some evidence to suggest that the greater the wife's dependence on the marriage, the more likely it is she will endure the abuse (Kalmuss & Strauss, 1982). Many women lack the financial resources to leave an abusive marriage or to live on their own. For women in secluded religious communities, this is an especially difficult reality. Under the patriarchal model, women are expected to be cared for by their husbands, and thus there is no need to develop job skills or attain higher levels of education. Consequently, women who are willing to leave their abusive marriages may be prevented from doing so for financial reasons. For women of strong faith, this practical reality is reinforced by religious beliefs that view divorce or separation in a very negative light (Whipple, 1987). Self-identity compounds the problem: Many women of strong faith define their very existence by their roles as wife and mother; leaving these roles would have consequences for self-identity (Horsburgh, 1995).

Another challenge facing battered women of strong faith is the lack of religiously sensitive secular services that can address their specific needs. A vast array of services targeted to assist victims and batterers alike exist in many communities (for a full discussion of available services, see Kurst-Swanger & Petcosky, 2003), including shelters, advocacy services, and specialized courts; however, religious members may not always feel comfortable seeking secular services. This may be especially true for religious women whose dress, dietary restrictions, and religious customs differ from those of the mainstream community. Religious women might be offended by what they experience in domestic violence shelters or counseling groups, particularly when those services serve a diverse population of victims. In many communities, domestic violence services are unable to cater to the special needs of their clientele, and, therefore, women of different cultural, ethnic, and religious backgrounds find it difficult to access such services. Women of strong faith may find the language, exposure to cigarette smoke (Whipple, 1987), contact with television, nonobservance of dietary restrictions, and a lack of religious rituals (Horsburgh, 1995) uncomfortable. Domestic violence services that cannot address the religious needs of these battered women are not likely to be perceived as helpful, nor are they likely to be accessed with any frequency.

Faith-Based Solutions

Given the distinctive needs of battered women of strong faith, the solution to domestic violence is likely to be found within the faith community itself. In September 2004, approximately 150 ministers, laypeople, and victim advocates gathered in Lincoln, Nebraska, to explore how faith communities can better respond to domestic violence. The statewide conference, jointly sponsored by the Nebraska Domestic Violence Sexual Assault Coalition, Interchurch Ministries of Nebraska, and the Family Violence Council of Lincoln–Lancaster County, was developed as part of the Faith Community Outreach Project. The Faith Community Outreach Project received funding from the U.S. Department of Justice, Office of Violence Against Women, to work with faith communities to improve their readiness to respond to domestic violence. The project's work includes training clergy to provide safe responses for victims and perpetrators of violence and encouraging religious leaders and members to speak out against domestic violence (IMN, 2006).

The conference, appropriately titled "Building Bridges to Safety: Faith Community Responses to Domestic Violence," featured Reverend Al Miles, an ordained minister in the Church of God (Anderson, Indiana) and minister at the

Queen's Medical Center in Honolulu, Hawaii. Reverend Miles has taken a unique position among faith leaders by speaking out against intimate partner violence. He has challenged clergy to "confront the misuse of religious beliefs, teachings, traditions, and sacred texts by Christian men who perpetrate domestic violence" (Miles, 2005, p. 1). Clergy from across Nebraska joined in Reverend Miles's charge by signing a statement condemning domestic violence. The statement reads, in part:

> We recognize domestic violence as a crime, as well as a sin. We state clearly that violence inside or outside the home is never justified. We condemn the use of scripture or other religious tenets and traditions to support abusive behavior in any form. We recognize that violence and abuse break the covenant of a marriage, not divorce. We accept our empowering victims to make their own decisions. We recognize the religious communities' role as a resource, not a roadblock for victims … (NDVSAC, 2004, p. 3)

The Faith Community Outreach Project should be applauded for its efforts to change the way faith communities understand the dynamics of intimate partner violence and for exploring opportunities to improve response to families. Domestic violence advocacy organizations and faith communities across the country have teamed up in similar fashion. For example, clergy in Utah have developed a training manual to assist more than 800 clergy in the state to better understand the dynamics of domestic violence, their role in finding solutions, how scriptures are misused to justify acts of violence, and how best to assure the safety of women (Rosetta, 2005). In Philadelphia, the American Muslim community, through the Philadelphia clergy council known as the Majlis Ash'Shura of Philadelphia and the Delaware Valley, adopted a strict policy of public shunning of Muslims who abuse or abandon their spouses. The policy, adopted in May 2005, was intended to send a strong message vilifying domestic violence by placing offenders' names on a "black list" that can be distributed to the local Muslim community (Holmes, 2005).

As these communities have found, the solution to religion-related family violence is likely to be found within the religious community itself. Faith communities can play a critical role in preventing the perpetuation of violence among their membership if religious leaders understand the dynamics of violence within families and how some of their followers may interpret religious teachings to rationalize such behavior. Deeply religious people tend to defer to religious tenets and teachings to guide all aspects of their life, especially their interpersonal relationships and family life. Particularly for those who view their religious writings as inerrant, religious leaders can play an important role in developing assistance for families that is sensitive to their religious teachings and belief systems, while reducing violence in the home.

Plural Marriage

On March 12, 2006, Home Box Office launched its new series *Big Love*, chronicling the trials and tribulations of a polygamous family living in suburban Salt Lake City. Bill Henrickson and his three wives, Barb, Nicki, and Margene, have a total of seven children and live on a property containing three single-family homes with adjoining backyards. As you might imagine, the show's premiere ignited a flurry of controversy in all corners of America and revived the public debate about plural marriage. Although the Henrickson family is fictional, plural marriage is a way of life for an estimated 20,000 to 50,000 Americans. As the show progresses, it will be interesting to see how *Big Love* will portray the religious, social, political, and economic realities of plural marriage and the inherent social conflicts it provokes. Only time will tell whether the general public is ready to embrace such a family, albeit a fictional one, given the subtle aspects of human behavior it is likely to explore.

"Polygamy" is a general term used to describe plural marriage; "polygyny" specifically relates to a man with two or more wives, and "polyandry" refers to a woman with two or more husbands. Approximately 80 percent of cultures in the world practice polygamy, of which about 78 percent practice polygyny and less than 1 percent engage in polyandry. Only 21 percent of the cultures in the world are strictly monogamous (Altman & Ginat, 1996). I use the term "polygamy" and "polygyny" interchangeably, referring specifically to family systems in which a man has two or more wives. In the United States, polygamy is not socially or legally sanctioned and is practiced mainly by secluded fundamentalist Mormons in Utah, Arizona, and British Columbia (Altman & Ginat, 1996; Krakauer, 2004) and by some Muslim Americans (Hassouneh-Phillips, 2001b), although the prevalence among Muslim Americans is largely undetermined.

In the United States, polygamy has been practiced for well over 150 years and continues to flourish as a centerpiece of a fundamentalist belief system despite the fact it is prohibited. Since there is little support for polygamy in the mainstream United States, those engaged in plural marriage often reside in homogeneous, secluded communities where they can live a more communal lifestyle without fear of reprisal from outsiders. Many live in homes and towns owned and operated by their church and church leaders. However, other practicing polygamists reside alongside more mainstream American communities, and members run their families more independently and work for secular businesses or organizations (Altman & Ginat, 1996). Not unlike the fictional Henrickson family, those engaged in plural marriage often keep this aspect of their lives private; thus very little is known about role of plural marriage in contemporary American society. More is known about polygamous practices elsewhere in the world, including the Middle East, Africa, and France (Anderson, 2000; Elbedour, Ornwuegbuzie, Caridine, & Abu-Saad, 2002; Sargent & Cordell, 2002). Much of what is described here relates specifically to the problems raised by the polygyny of fundamentalist Mormons and the political debate their actions have generated. I begin with a brief historical overview of plural marriage in the United States as a religious principle of fundamentalist Mormons, exploring the political and legal challenges it presents. This is followed by a discussion of contemporary concerns.

Historical Perspective

Mormon polygamy, or specifically polygyny, has its roots in early Mormonism. Mormonism was founded in 1830 by Joseph Smith Jr. (1805–1844) in Palmyra, New York. As a teenager Joseph had religious visions in which, he said, God and Jesus Christ were revealed to him. In 1823, at the tender age of eighteen, he was visited by an angel, Moroni, who told Joseph that "gold leaves" or "plates" existed that documented the history of an ancient people who came to North America from the Holy Land during the time of the prophets of the Old Testament. The sacred text, along with materials useful for translating them, were found three years later buried in a hillside by Joseph after another vision from the angel Moroni, the son of the prophet Mormon. Joseph translated the text with the assistance of several others, and the Book of Mormon was published in 1830 (Davies, 2004). The book told that Moroni was the last prophet and that he hid the record of his people "until such time as a righteous man appeared in 'the latter days' to restore the gospel and divinity of Christ" (Altman & Ginat, 1996, p. 23). Shortly after the Book of Mormon was published, Joseph founded the Church of Christ; in 1834 it become the Church of the Latter-Day Saints, and in 1838 it became the Church of Jesus Christ of the Latter-Day Saints. For many followers, the Book of Mormon grounded America as a sacred place in its own right and provided answers to the questions troubling many in the early nineteenth century (Butler, Wacker, & Balmer, 2003).

The Latter-Day Saints experienced a tumultuous and violent beginning. They were persecuted for their religious beliefs and in turn were antagonistic to their neighbors. This sometimes led to bloodshed (Butler, Wacker, & Balmer, 2003;

Krakauer, 2004). Mormons found themselves fleeing to Ohio, Missouri, and Illinois to escape the wrath of their neighbors. As they took hold in each new community, they inserted themselves into the economic dealings and politics of the local community, thereby creating controversy and conflict (Altman & Ginat, 1996). They engaged in bloc voting, formed their own private militia, dealt only with an exclusive list of approved merchants, and participated in aggressive proselytizing (Gordon, 2002). Also, there were accusations that some Mormons participated in illegal activities such as theft, counterfeiting, shady banking land practices (Arrington & Bitton, 1979), and property damage (Krakauer, 2004).

Joseph Smith and his followers found little support from the federal government, since at the time religious freedom was protected by the states. Frustrated by his inability to lead his flock consistently with how he interpreted the U.S. Constitution, Joseph Smith declared his candidacy for the presidency of the United States in 1844 (for a more detailed account of the early history of the Church, see Arrington & Bitton, 1979; Gordon, 2002; Krakauer, 2004). His candidacy was cut short later that year when he and his brother, Hyrum, were murdered. Both had been jailed by law enforcement officials for treason and other crimes. They were killed by an angry mob that stormed the jail. Thus, Mormonism was a mere fourteen years old when its prophet and leader was killed.

Joseph Smith's successor, Brigham Young, guided followers westward, where they eventually settled in the Great Salt Lake Valley in Utah, where many Mormons still live today. Not all of Joseph Smith's faithful followers joined Brigham Young, and new churches were formed, such as the Church of Christ (1845) and the Reorganized Church of Jesus Christ of the Latter-Day Saints (1860) (Davies, 2004).

The doctrine of polygyny evolved about a decade after the publication of the Book of Mormon, although most historians agree that Joseph Smith himself engaged in plural marriage much earlier, in secret (Altman & Ginat, 1996; Gordon, 2002; Krakauer, 2004). The official doctrine came in 1843 after Smith received the "Revelation on Celestial Marriage," in which he acknowledged that because biblical patriarchs such as Abraham and Jacob had practiced polygyny, it must be considered a necessary principle. Some have argued that the revelation came in response to external pressures from his flock and his wife (Newell & Avery, 1984; Van Wagoner, 1989). Jon Krakauer (2004) suggests that the actual written revelation was documented on July 12, 1843, in an effort to appease Emma Smith, Joseph's first wife, who despised his marriages to other women. After reading the document, Emma Smith turned to her friend William Law, who promptly threatened Smith, but Smith refused to withdraw the document. After much conflict between Smith and Law, Law published an editorial in the first and only edition of a newspaper called *The Nauvoo Expositor* exposing Smith's principle. Later, Smith was charged with burning the printing press to the ground (Krakauer, 2004).

Polygyny, or, as it has come to be called, "the Principle," got off to a poor start, since few Mormons engaged in the practice. It was not until 1852, several years after the Mormons had migrated to Utah, that the Church officially declared polygyny to be doctrine. Scholars speculate that church leaders sought to consolidate their settlement in Utah before recognizing and encouraging the practice (Altman & Ginat, 1996). Brigham Young himself is thought to have had at least twenty wives—maybe even as many as fifty-seven—and an estimated fifty-seven children (Krakauer, 2004). The practice appeared to flourish after the Church's pronouncement, although not all Mormons participated heartily in the doctrine. Church leaders, including Brigham Young, did their best to encourage plural marriage by threatening eternal damnation to those who did not participate (Altman & Ginat, 1996; Krakauer, 2004).

As the practice of polygyny took hold, Mormons continued to see themselves as a persecuted people, for little support was garnered from outsiders. The turmoil and violence that marked the early days of the Church continued into Utah under the leadership of Young. The rest of the nation abhorred the practice of polygyny and became weary of the Mormons' political actions, their growing economic base, attacks against non-Mormons, and their demonstrated defiance of secular law: "the Saints installed a legal system of their own singular design, which very cleverly ensured that whenever the two bodies of law clashed, God's laws would prevail" (Krakauer, 2004, p. 207). Anti-polygamists stepped forth to liken polygyny to slavery, which reverberated in a nation headed toward civil war. Congress and President Lincoln responded with the Morrill Anti-Bigamy Act of 1862, which was intended to outlaw the practice of polygamy in the territories of the United States. In addition to other provisions, the law prohibited any religious organization from owning real estate worth more than $50,000 (Gordon, 2002). However, amid the crisis of the Civil War, President Lincoln did little to enforce the act.

Twenty years later, under the leadership of John Taylor, the Saints cemented their holy principle further, despite the growing opposition of outsiders. During a Sunday assembly, Taylor proclaimed, "Polygamy is a divine institution. It has been handed down direct from God. The United States cannot abolish it ... I defy the United States; I will obey God" (cited by Krakauer, 2004, p. 253). Yet Congress passed the Edmunds Act of 1882, which prohibited men from cohabitating with more than one woman as a wife and excluded polygamists from jury service, political positions, or elected office. Legal loopholes were closed with the

Edmunds/Tucker Act of 1887, which required that all marriages be registered with the territorial probate court and all men who wished to vote take an oath swearing that they did not practice or encourage others to practice plural marriage (Altman & Ginat, 1996).

These and other pieces of legislation, coupled with U.S. Supreme Court cases such as *Reynolds v. U.S.* (1879) and *Davis v. Beason* (1890) and the death of the Mormons' president, John Taylor, in 1887, set in motion the erosion of the Saints' political and economic power and their polygamist practices as well. The crushing blow came with the U.S. Supreme Court decision in *Church of Jesus Christ of Latter-Day Saints v. U.S.* in 1890. In this case, the Court considered whether Congress had the power to dissolve the charter of the Church and confiscate all church property not in use for religious purposes. The Church had real estate holdings valued at $2 million and personal property valued at approximately $1 million, which was in violation of law. Of particular concern to the Justices was the intended use of the Church's funds for the promotion of polygamy. The Court upheld the revocation of the Church's charter and confiscation of property. Justice Joseph Bradley delivered the opinion of the Court:

> Notwithstanding the stringent laws which have been passed by Congress,—not-withstanding all the efforts made to suppress this barbarous practice,—the sect or community composing the Church of Jesus Christ of Latter-Day Saints per-severes, in defiance of law, in preaching, upholding, promoting and defending it …The organization of a community for the spread and practice of polygamy is, in a measure, a return to barbarism … Whatever persecutions they may have suffered in the early part of their history, in Missouri and Illinois, they have no excuse for their persistent defiance of law under the government of the United States.

Defeated, President Wilford Woodruff of the Church of Jesus Christ of the Latter-Day Saints issued a "manifesto" declaring that Mormons should abandon the practice and abide by the laws of the land. The manifesto came as a surprise to followers who had invested so much in living the doctrine. Krakauer (2004) notes that polygamy was not abandoned altogether but rather was driven underground among a group of followers. Scandals eventually erupted, and by the 1920s most Saints were against polygamy and supported the prosecution of those who violated the law. Eventually, members of the Church who continued to support plural marriage were sanctioned by church leaders and some were excommunicated.

Despite the mounting pressure to abandon the principle from Mormons themselves, a small group of hard-core polygamists refused to give up such a core doctrine of their faith. Referring to themselves as fundamentalists, under the leadership of John Y. Barlow, they established in the 1930s their own communities in Salt Lake City, Utah, and in Short Creek (now called Hildale), a small town on the border between Utah and Arizona, where they could continue to follow the principle without the watchful eye of government officials or the Latter-Day Saints (referred to today as the LDS). Although the early fundamentalist movement enjoyed growth in membership, it also suffered numerous legal setbacks. By 1935 polygamy or cohabitation was considered a felony in Utah, and law enforcement officials were successful in prosecuting both men and women in Utah and Arizona. The most notable law enforcement raids on polygamist communities took place in 1935 and 1944 (Altman & Ginat, 1996; Gordon, 2002; Krakauer, 2004).

Since the 1940s the Fundamentalist Latter-Day Saints (FLDS) have enjoyed a growing membership, and until recently they continued to practice polygamy in secret, without much interference from law enforcement officials. The vast majority of practicing polygamists reside in communities spread across the states of Utah and Arizona; in Bountiful, British Columbia, in Canada; and in Mexico. Although splinter groups have formed and conflict continues, the FLDS Church survives. It should be noted that the LDS, on the other hand, has approximately 11 million members, many of whom reside outside of the United States (Davies, 2004). Today, the LDS, which is generally viewed as a mainstream religious organization, adamantly rejects the principle and does not recognize the FLDS as part of the Church.

Recent Controversy

Recently the veil of secrecy protecting practicing polygamists has begun to be lifted, mainly because of scrutiny from the media, anti-polygamy activists, and law enforcement. At the center of the storm are fundamentalist Mormons, specifically members of the FLDS, whose beliefs and actions have drawn the attention of the authorities. The media have gained access to women and men from fundamentalist communities who have come forward to tell their story. Most recently, the announcement of the HBO series *Big Love* attracted the attention of both practicing polygamists and former members. Several practicing polygamists have gone public to tell their story and to promote the virtues of polygamy, while others who have left polygamous marriages engage in a vibrant anti-polygamy campaign to expose the danger to women and children. Documentaries have been filmed portraying the plural marriage lifestyle. Pro- and anti-polygamy propaganda is readily available on the Internet, although one has to sift carefully through some material to grasp which argument is being made. Interestingly, writer Jon Krakauer (2004), social psychologist Irwin Altman, and anthropologist Joseph Ginat (1996) gained access to numerous individuals who openly agreed to be interviewed or observed.

Anti-polygamists and women's rights activists continue to draw attention to the issue and in some instances have put pressure on law enforcement officials to bring polygamists to justice. Some organizations, such as Tapestry Against Polygamy (http://www.polygamy.org), seek to assist women and girls who want to flee the bonds of plural marriage. In general, anti-polygamy activists are concerned about the institutional practice of plural marriage itself because it subjugates women, placing them at great risk for physical and emotional harm. The strict adherence to male domination within the family and within the church relegates women to a powerless position. Some activists even liken plural marriage to slavery. Activists are also concerned about the impact such arrangements have on children, particularly when young girls are forced to marry men within their own compound or within their own family or to transfer to a different jurisdiction to be married. The financial burden of providing for multiple wives and numerous children often leaves children in poverty. Also, activists are concerned when children are not provided with appropriate levels of education. Since many of the most active advocates against polygamy are women who have successfully left a plural marriage, they have witnessed firsthand the variety of abuse inherent in such an institution as plural marriage and therefore are actively working to expose the hidden secrets of this lifestyle.

Attention to polygamy has also been garnered as a result of the arrest and imprisonment of several polygamous men from Utah, including David Ortell Kingston and his brother, John Daniel Kingston, and Tom Green. Their arrest and subsequent punishment have drawn attention to the types of abuse that have occurred in polygamous communities. These men were convicted of crimes against children, underscoring the concerns anti-polygamous groups have about the safety of women and children in such living arrangements. Other cases have illustrated how a commitment to the principle, coupled with religious extremism, can have tragic consequences. For example, in 1984, brothers Dan and Ron Lafferty killed their sister-in-law Brenda Lafferty and their infant niece Erica (Krakauer, 2004). In another case, in January 1988, polygamist Addam Swapp of Fairview, Sanpete County, Utah, broke into the Kamas LDS Stake Center, set explosive devices, and blew up the building, causing approximately $1.5 million worth of damage. This resulted in an eleven-day siege with law enforcement officials, in which Department of Corrections officer Fred House was shot dead by Timothy Singer. The Swapp/Singer family intended to "resurrect" their father, John Singer, and to force officials to atone for his death in 1979 (Department of Public Safety,

2006). Also, the kidnapping on June 5, 2002, of fourteen-year-old Elizabeth Smart by Brian David Mitchell brought attention to the issue of polygamy. Mitchell abducted Elizabeth from her bedroom, held her for nine months, and forced her to live as his second wife. Mitchell and his first wife, Wanda Barzee, face numerous criminal charges, and determination of their mental state remains a challenge for the courts. Mitchell and Barzee have been declared incompetent to stand trial and are currently being held in a psychiatric facility (AP, 2005; Hunt, 2005). Both Mitchell and Barzee have refused to take the medicine prescribed to them, which has created an additional legal battle. Barzee was given a Sell hearing (a hearing to determine whether the court can force someone to take medication), and the court ruled that Barzee could be involuntarily medicated. Similar legal issues are present for Mitchell and at this writing have not been resolved (Reavy, 2007).

At the time of writing, Warren Jeffs, the leader/prophet of the FLDS, is awaiting trial on several criminal charges. He was indicted by a grand jury in June 2005 on charges related to the sexual abuse of minors and his role in performing spiritual marriages between adult men and young girls and ordering them to procreate. In July 2005, the grand jury indicted him on five additional felony charges, but Jeffs fled prosecution. In May 2006 he was added to the FBI's Most Wanted List in Arizona, and the Arizona Attorney General's Office offered a $10,000 reward for information leading to his capture. He was captured in August 2006 by a Nevada Highway Patrol officer during a routine traffic stop. Items found in the vehicle Jeffs was riding in included thousands of dollars in cash, fourteen cellular phones, a radar detector, two global positioning systems, two female wigs, several knives, multiple credit cards, and seven sets of keys (Adams & Manson, 2006). Jeff's defense attorney challenged the search of the vehicle; however, the Fifth District judge ruled that the evidence collected after Jeffs was detained during the traffic stop was admissible (AP, 2007).

Jeffs also faces civil suits. Several of the boys raised in Colorado City and Hildale have filed lawsuits against Warren Jeffs and several others from the FLDS. Brent Jeff, now twenty-one, disclosed that Warren Jeffs and two of his brothers regularly sexually assaulted young boys in the basement of the FLDS school. Brent decided to disclose the details of the abuses after his brother Clayne, also a victim, committed suicide. Another suit against Jeffs charges that he and other FLDS leaders expelled young men from the community to reduce the competition for wives. The boys, labeled "the lost boys" by the popular media, were expelled from Warren Jeffs' community on a number of different pretexts. According to reporter Stephen Speckman (2004) from the *Deseret Morning News*, about 400 boys have been banished from their homes. Leading the charge on their behalf is former member of the FLDS Dan Fischer, a dentist from Salt Lake City. He has founded a nonprofit group that has reached out to the public and the state to ask for help on behalf of these homeless boys. A press conference in late July 2004 on the steps of the Utah state capitol brought the issue to public attention. Two boys spoke out against Warren Jeffs and told of their personal experiences of being excommunicated from not only their church but also their family and community.

These charges come amid concerns that Jeffs engaged in shady practices in his management of the United Effort Plan trust, which controls more than $100 million in businesses and real estate in Colorado City, Hildale, and Crestone, British Columbia (Dougherty, 2005).

As these examples illustrate, law enforcement officials' concern regarding polygamy extends beyond the appropriateness of plural marriage as an institution to focus on the specific criminal activity and abuses that can occur within such communities. Of greatest concern are crimes of domestic violence, sexual assault and incest, and child abuse and neglect. Officials are also concerned about weapons violations, tax evasion, and welfare fraud.

Domestic Abuse

In *Under the Banner of Heaven*, Jon Krakauer (2004) presents the history of the Mormon Church and the fundamentalist movement as one of violence and crime. An important theme throughout the text is the seemingly commonplace occurrence of violence against women and children within the context of a strong patriarchal belief system. Anti-polygamy activists, particularly those who have successfully fled abusive spouses, argue that domestic abuse is endemic to polygamous communities (see http://www.childpro.org, http://www.polygamy.org), while others who support plural marriage claim domestic violence is a misuse of the principle (see http://www.anti-polygamy.org, http://www.truthbearer.org, http://www.principlevoices.org). Since many polygamous families live in seclusion, it is difficult to determine the prevalence of domestic violence within these families, although criminal justice officials and domestic violence advocacy organizations suspect the rates are high. As I argued above, women of strong faith, particularly those living in homogeneous, secluded religious communities, are less likely to seek assistance from secular services. This is very likely to be true for polygamous women who know their lifestyle is illegal and thus not accepted by outsiders. Thus, law enforcement officials and domestic violence advocates, along with anti-polygamy advocates, have had to work together to begin to penetrate communities to ensure that women have access to services if they want them.

Recognizing the specific needs of battered women from plural marriages, the attorney generals of Utah (Mark Shurtleff) and Arizona (Terry Goddard) embarked on a collaboration in 2003 to improve the law enforcement and human service response to domestic violence in the secluded twin cities of Hildale, Utah, and Colorado City, Arizona. The partnership involves law enforcement officials, state and local social service professionals, and advocacy groups, which convene to discuss the special requirements for serving a geographically isolated population who have ongoing disputes with the government, transportation barriers, and a lack of access to services or information about services (Goddard & Shurtleff, 2006). One challenge facing authorities is getting information to women who do not have access to the media. One approach of the Safety Net program has been to erect large billboards that can provide information to women (and children) who might need assistance or want to talk with someone (Thiessen, 2004).

In addition, the U.S. Department of Justice, Office of Violence Against Women, granted the State of Utah approximately $700,000 in 2004 to fund the Safe Passage program to assist victims of domestic violence in the twin cities. The program coordinates law enforcement, legal, housing, and transportation services and expands the existing domestic violence hotline. In addition, resources for police protection and shelter services were increased.

In the past, victims have been reluctant to come forward to authorities and testify against their husbands, despite the alarming claims of former polygamist wives that beatings, incest, and forced marriage of underage girls are commonplace. Some women are fighting back with civil law suits. For example, Lenore and Milton Holm successfully sued the United Effort Plan (UEP) when the church attempted to evict them from their home after Lenore refused to let her fifteen-year-old daughter marry an older man, as arranged by church leaders (Nichols, 2003).

Financial Issues

The economic demands of caring for a plural family can be overwhelming. The large number of children, the scarcity of high-paying jobs, and the lack of education all contribute to the financial difficulties of the plural family. Complicating matters is the fact that followers of the FLDS are required to pay into the UEP, which is the financial trust that owns all of the FLDS Church's assets, including much of the land. This transfers income from families into the hands of a small number of church leaders who control the trust fund. The UEP is valued at more than $100 million in real estate holdings (Dougherty, 2005), yet the two towns of Hildale and Colorado City (population 6,000) are heavily subsidized by various types of state and federal aid, including forms of public assistance (Brooke, 1998). Since husbands can legally marry only one wife, celestial wives are considered single parents under current welfare laws and are eligible for benefits.

Financial troubles have recently begun to beset the UEP, since Attorney General Terry Goddard made allegations that the Colorado City Unified School District, which is connected to the UEP, has mismanaged its funds. The attorney general alleges that the school district prepaid multiyear leases on the buildings owned by the UEP, allowing the UEP to keep nearly $200,000 in overpayments on buildings that were not leased, for a private school run by the FLDS (Kossan, 2005). Warren Jeffs has ordered his followers to stop paying their property taxes or face banishment from the sect. Although he has been stripped of his financial control over the UEP, it is clear from news reports that he still is very much in control of his followers (Kossan, 2006).

Health Issues

The concern over physical health is centered on both communicable diseases and genetic disorders resulting from inbreeding. In cultures where polygamy is more commonplace, the practice has raised significant health concerns, especially in regard to sexually transmitted diseases such as gonorrhea, syphilis, genital herpes, chancroid, candidiasis, trichomoniasis, and HIV/AIDS (Dada-Adegbola, 2004; Mhalu & Lyamuya, 1996; Toppo, Tiwari, Dixit, & Nandeshwar, 2004).

Specifically, among the FLDS polygamous community, recent news has focused on the twin communities of Hildale, Utah, and Colorado City, Arizona, where twenty cases of a rare birth defect have been identified. Dr. Theodore Tarby, an Arizona neurologist, told news sources that scientists have identified only thirteen other cases worldwide of fumarase deficiency, an enzyme irregularity that causes severe mental retardation, epileptic seizures, and related problems. Transmission of this recessive genetic disorder is likely to have been driven by an early founder of the community who had numerous children and passed the gene on to his children and grandchildren. The commonplace practice of marriage between close relatives has facilitated the alarming rate of transmission of this devastating genetic disorder (Adams, 2006; AP, 2006; Hollenhorst, 2006).

Linda Walker, founder of the Child Protection Project, a Web site focused on exposing institutionalized incest and child abuse (http://www.childpro.org), and a descendant of polygamy, relays her own experience of being part of family that has inherited a form of nephritis known as Alport syndrome. Alport syndrome is a hereditary disease which affects the kidneys and can be associated with hearing loss, eye disorders, immunologic abnormality of the skin, and blood disorders. It is often fatal and is treatable only by dialysis or through kidney transplants. She recalls being part of a large research study conducted by the University of Utah in the 1950s that sought to investigate this rare, life-threatening genetic condition (Walker, 1999). Dr. Gerald T. Perkoff and Dr. Frank H. Tyler initiated the research study after a request was made to investigate the deaths of four male relatives. Dr. Curtis L. Atkins from the University of Utah continued their research until his death in January 2000. Dr. Atkins himself had been diagnosed with Alport syndrome, along with sixty-five of his relatives (Atkins, 1999).

In her essay "Fatal Inheritance: Mormon Eugenics," Linda Walker argues that polygamy is to blame for the passing on of genetic disorders such as Alport syndrome. She argues that endogamous polygamy, or breeding from within, is the culprit and claims the early Mormons practiced this form of polygamy. She argues that other cultures that practice polygamy generally breed from outside the group, and thus reduce their risk of transmitting recessive genes linked to disease (Walker, 1999).

6

Illicit Drugs

In July 1995, Joe and Connie McBride were arrested by members of the Topeka Police Department in violation of laws pertaining to the cultivation of marijuana and possession of drug paraphernalia as well as for failure to affix a tax stamp. Their arrest came after Topeka police officers arrived at their public housing development to check on the status of an apartment in the duplex in which they lived and observed marijuana plants growing in plain sight. Police officers came to their apartment complex to follow up on reports that claimed Joe McBride had given a key to the east dwelling to operate it as a tenant center. Investigating the complaint, officers arrived at the complex, with one officer positioning himself in the front of the building and another in the back. While at the back door, Officer Gilchrist observed numerous marijuana plants growing amid a vegetable garden and in other areas behind the duplex.

Once they had been charged, Connie and Joe McBride moved to dismiss the charges on the basis of the First Amendment's free exercise clause. Both argued they were members of the Rastafarian faith and the use of marijuana was critical to the practice of their religion. Both testified they had been Rastafarians for more than fifteen years and that the plants in their garden were grown solely for religious purposes. Since eighty-six plants weighing 6.5 pounds were found on their property, the district court judge concluded that the sheer quantity of marijuana suggested that they were cultivating the plants with the intent to distribute or sell, and thus he denied their motion to dismiss. Prosecutors filed a motion in limine to prohibit the McBrides from using a free exercise of religion argument at their trial. A motion in limine is a pretrial motion designed to obtain judicial approval in advance for evidence that might be considered prejudicial or inflammatory. The judge ruled in favor of the state's motion on the day of the trial, stating that this case was about cultivation of marijuana with the intent to distribute and nothing suggested to the court that the religious practices of the Rastafarians included cultivation or distribution. The trial court found the McBrides guilty of cultivation and of tax stamp violations but acquitted them of the paraphernalia charges. Both were sentenced to twenty-four months on probation (*McBride v. Shawnee County*, 1999).

On appeal, the McBrides argued that the court had wrongly prohibited their free exercise defense and that the Religious Freedom Restoration Act (RFRA) of 1993 required the state to demonstrate that the Kansas laws regarding cultivation of marijuana and tax stamps constituted a compelling state interest in the absence of less restrictive alternatives. They argued that the district had not required the state to demonstrate this compelling interest. The McBrides did not consider the decision in *City of Boerne v. Flores* (1997), in which the Court struck down the RFRA of 1993; thus the appellant court found their argument regarding the RFRA moot. However, the McBrides also argued that the state was in error for prosecuting them because it allows members of the Native American Church (NAC) to use peyote for religious purposes. The McBrides argued that the state granted the NAC a religious exemption under its controlled substances laws and that by not granting the same exemption to Rastafarians, the state was in violation of both the establishment and equal protection clauses of the U.S. Constitution.

The Kansas Court of Appeals affirmed their convictions on the basis of three main principles. First, the Court found that the McBrides, as Rastafarians, are not "similarly situated" to members of the NAC and thus are not eligible for the same exemption under Kansas state drug laws. The Court reasoned this by virtue of the fact that Rastafarians (as Joe McBride's own testimony indicated) use marijuana indiscriminately, with no rule as to when or how much marijuana is to be consumed. In contrast, members of the NAC use peyote in controlled quantities during very specific ceremonies, and thus very little peyote is actually consumed. Second, the Court considered the level at which marijuana is abused in society and could not fathom how the Drug Enforcement Administration could regulate such an exemption for a religious group that has a belief in the unlimited use of marijuana. Third, the appellate court considered the state and federal drug law exemptions afforded to members of the NAC to be part of broader public policy consistent with the federal trust responsibility to preserve the cultural and political heritage of Native American tribes.

The Court also cited other cases in which the courts consistently ruled against Rastafarians who sought relief from state or federal drug laws. For example, in *Olsen v. Drug Enforcement Administration* (1989), Olsen submitted a proposal for the Court's consideration that intended to accommodate members of the Rastafarian faith while providing a measure of governmental regulation. The DC Circuit Court, however, was not persuaded. Then DC Circuit Court of Appeals judge Ruth Bader Ginsburg spelled out the Court's reasoning in the majority opinion. I include a lengthy quote from her opinion to illustrate the views of the court in this matter:

> The pivotal issue, therefore, is whether marijuana usage by Olsen and other members of his church can be accommodated without undue interference with the government's interest in controlling the drug. Three circuits have so far considered pleas for religious exemption from the marijuana laws; each has rejected the argument that accommodation to sacramental use of the drug is feasible [citation omitted] ... We have no reason to doubt that these courts have accurately gauged the Highest Court's pathmarks in this area ... Even if the government is not required to accommodate to the extent of allowing a broad religious exemption, he argues, it can and must accommodate to the time-and place-specific use he has proposed. Because the tenets of the Ethiopian Zion Coptic Church endorse marijuana use every day throughout the day, however, Olsen's proposal for confined use would not be self-enforcing. It is hardly unreasonable to forecast a large monitoring burden in light of evidence that in years past, the church's "[c]hecks on distribution of cannabis to nonbelievers in the faith [were] minimal," there was "easy access to cannabis for a child who had absolutely no interest in learning the religion," and "[m]embers [partook] of cannabis anywhere, not just within the confines of a church facility." (*Town v. State ex rel. Reno, 377 So.2d at 649, 651*) Critically, Olsen's proposal would require the government to make supplies of marijuana available to Olsen's church on a regular basis ... We are unaware of any "free exercise" precedent for compelling government accommodation of religious practices when that accommodation requires burdensome and constant official supervision and management.

In the *McBride* and *Olsen* cases, and others like them, the courts have generally concluded that the religious use of some substances, particularly cannabis, cannot be accommodated by the government in a reasonable fashion and thus have found that the free exercise clause does not oblige the Drug Enforcement Administration (DEA) to make exemptions regarding religious use of controlled substances. (See *U.S. v. Rush* (1984), *Olsen v. Iowa* (1986), *and Town v. State ex rel. Reno* (1979)).

This, of course, raises interesting questions about drug use in religious practices amid a national war on drugs. You might be surprised to learn that many religious groups, their members and leaders use various chemical substances to enhance their religious experience. For example, Saunders (1995) interviewed four religious teachers: a Benedictine monk, a rabbi, a Rinzai Zen monk, and a Soto Zen monk regarding their experiences with MDMA, more commonly known as ecstasy. Each had used MDMA numerous times to achieve a heightened spiritual experience. Yet each had kept his views and use of MDMA private, except in the company of like-minded religious teachers and students, because of the illegal status of the drug.

Given the fervor of the "war on drugs" in the United States, the courts have had to examine carefully and balance the health and safety of the public against the religious needs of certain groups. As the *McBride* and *Olsen* cases illustrate, the courts have traditionally upheld the convictions of religious drug users. The NAC enjoys special exemptions for the use of peyote under U.S. drug laws, and followers of other religions continue to seek similar legal exemptions for their individual or group use of controlled substances. The religious use of illegal drugs has raised debate among lawmakers, law enforcement officials, and religious groups.

Change may be on the horizon. In February 2006 the U.S. Supreme Court affirmed a preliminary injunction preventing federal agents from banning the use of a sacramental hallucinogenic tea by O Centro Espirita Beneficente Uniao Do Vegetal, a Brazilian Church. This case may eventually change the landscape of religious exemptions from U.S. drugs laws. For now, other religions that use controlled substances in their practice are subject to state and federal criminal statutes that govern the cultivation, manufacture, possession, or distribution of such drugs.

This chapter explores this theologically based crime in detail. We first examine the use of controlled substances in religious practices. When they are used for religious rituals, hallucinogenic drugs are often referred to as entheogens. Several such drugs are described. Second, I provide a brief overview of U.S. drug policy to place even the ritual use of certain substances in the proper political context. The war on drugs has become an epic crime control effort, and thus religious users are subject to strict scrutiny.

The third and final section of the chapter addresses the legal right of members of the NAC to use peyote as part of their religious ceremony. In fact, specific peyote dealers are licensed by the DEA for to procure peyote for members of the NAC for religious use. It is important to understand the cultural, political, and religious factors behind the exemption. Thus, I discuss the evolution of this policy in detail and examine why the courts have generally not found other religious groups to be "similarly situated" to the NAC.

Entheogens

Entheogens are mood-altering substances that are taken sacramentally. They are psychoactive substances that induce alterations of consciousness and induce enlightening spiritual or mystical experiences. Technically known as hallucinogens (they are also referred to as psychedelics), cannabis, or dissociatives, these substances are taken not for recreation but for spiritual or religious fulfillment or healing therapy. Some scholars prefer the term "entheogens" (Ruck et al., 1979) because the drugs are "thought to engender a sense of 'god within'" (Partridge, 2004, p. 370). Also, the term "entheogens" serves to distinguish such substances and their specific use from the mainstream recreational or social use of other psychotropic drugs. Religious followers who use entheogens generally do so within ceremonial rituals. As Benny Shanon (2002) notes in reference to the use of *ayahuasca*, "consumption is never alone, never for fun, always within a ritual grounded in a tradition" (p. 92).

Entheology is a branch of theology that explores the ritual use of psychoactive substances. Aline Lucas (1995) argues that entheology "addresses the experience and/or knowledge of the divine, and of the revelation of the divine, through the agency of psychoactive substances (used as sacraments), be it a revelation of the divine with and/or without the individual" (p. 294).

Entheogens and other hallucinogens are generally derived from botanical sources from around the world. Some hallucinogens can be manufactured synthetically as well. It is likely that approximately 6,000 different species of plants have some hallucinogenic properties, and researchers have isolated about 100 different hallucinogenic compounds (Doweiko, 2002). They have been used by various cultures for medicinal or religious purposes for thousands of years. Archaeologists have found evidence that psychoactive substances were used by prehistoric and ancient civilizations in Mesopotamia, India, Persia, Egypt, Africa, China, Japan, Europe, and Pre-Columbian America (MacRae, 1998). There is also some suggestion that the Judaic and Christian traditions may make reference to the use of entheogenic substances (Shanon, 2002).

Like hallucinogens such as LSD and PCP, these drugs impact the user's central nervous system and distort perception, thought, and mood—creating visual or auditory hallucinations or illusions. The effects are caused by changes in the interaction between nerve cells and neurotransmitters in the brain. Many plants contain chemical compounds similar to serotonin that interrupt the normal functioning of the serotonin system in users (NIDA, 2001). Some hallucinogens, such as mescaline, are related to the neurotransmitters dopamine and norepinephrine (Doweiko, 2002). Hallucinogens have different, and unpredictable, effects on different people according to the individual taking the drug and the setting (social context) (NIDA, 2001; Zinberg, 1984).

Regardless of the known biological or pharmacological pathways of entheogens, users report "mystical" experiences. Some psychologists who study religion use the term "mystical" to characterize a state of awareness beyond the self where individuals are exposed to visions of the divine (Richards, 2005). Put another way, mysticism is the direct intuition or experience of God (Bowker, 2000). Some scholars and religious followers believe that entheogens are "sacred molecules provided by the Creator to contribute to personal and spiritual growth" (Richards, 2005, p. 383).

Timothy Leary, a researcher at Harvard University in the 1960s, had a particularly illuminating experience ingesting "sacred mushrooms" while visiting Mexico during the summer of 1960. His journey with mescaline was, in his words, "without question the deepest religious experience of my life" and prompted him to study hallucinogens and their "revelatory potentialities of the human nervous system" (Leary, 1964, p. 324). His research drew on more than fifty scientists and scholars and more than one thousand participants from various religious backgrounds; he found that between 40 and 90 percent of his subjects experienced intense religious experiences after ingesting entheogens. Leary become a legendary figure in American culture because of his research with and personal use of psychedelic drugs; however, his continued interest in drugs eventually caused him to be removed from his position at Harvard and ultimately landed him in prison, serving time for drug possession. Yet his research sparked the interest of many others who continue to pursue the possibility that certain substances can and do lead to profound religious experiences. Philosopher and religious scholar Huston Smith (2003) argues that research literature suggests approximately one-fourth to one-third of the general population would have religious experiences by ingesting entheogens under the right conditions. Furthermore, he argues that three-fourths of those who have strong faith are likely to define their experience as religious.

As an embedded practice in both ancient and contemporary societies, the use of such organic substances was historically contained to the parts of the globe where the plants are grown. However, the expansion of the global economy and the Internet mean that both religious followers and nonreligious drug users in the United States now have greater access to these hallucinogenic substances. For example, intelligence briefs published by the DEA report that individuals in possession of *Psychotria viridis* and *Salvia divinorum* have likely purchased the substances over the Internet (Blackledge & Taylor, 2003; Pasterchick, 2002). Although such substances may have their place in a religious setting, many violate state and federal drug laws in the United States and therefore are considered illegal, regardless of the set and setting of their use.

Many species of plants are used specifically for religious or spiritual purposes; however, their hallucinogenic properties have attracted the attention of law enforcement and health officials because of the abuse of such substances by nonreligious users, especially adolescents, and because researchers know very little about them. In fact, in recent years the National Institute of Drug Abuse, Office of Dietary

Supplements and the National Institute of Mental Health have made research applications to characterize the chemistry, psychopharmacology, and toxicology of acute and chronic exposure to natural psychoactive products, particularly those plant-derived compounds that affect the central nervous system. Several examples of substances of concern commonly used as entheogens by various religious and cultural groups around the world are provided here. Additional substances (peyote, mescaline, and psilocybin) will be discussed in the next section.

Psychotria viridis

Psychotria viridis is a botanical source of dimethyltryptamine (DMT) that grows naturally in wet lowland tropical forests in Cuba and parts of Central and South America. This plant and other plant species that contain DMT, such as the *Bannisteriopsis caapi* vine, are combined to make a narcotic drink that is often called *ayahuasca, caapi, hoasca, daime, yage, vegetal,* or *holy* tea (Blackledge & Taylor, 2003).

Two religious groups are well known for their use of *ayahuasca*: Santo Daime and Uniao do Vegetal, both originating in Brazil. Religious followers often refer to these plants as "teacher plants" or the "vine of the spirits." They are ingested in a controlled and ritualistic fashion to gain access to the spirit world and to communicate directly with God. Concern over the growing population of religious followers using *ayahuasca* and increased attention to their use by the media led the Brazilian Ministry of Health to declare *ayahuasca* a prohibited drug. The Uniao do Vegetal Church lobbied the Federal Narcotics Council to change public policy. The council responded by establishing a task force to examine the issue. The task force, made up of a multidisciplinary team of professionals, determined that the decades-old controlled ritualistic use of *ayahuasca* posed no significant social harm. The council considered the recommendations of the task force and legalized the use of *ayahuasca* in Brazil (MacRae, 1998).

Although use is now legal in Brazil, religious followers who reside in the United States and use products made with *Psychotria viridis* or other botanicals with DMT are likely to encounter legal problems. Since DMT is a Schedule I drug under the Controlled Substances Act (to be discussed later), it is of serious concern to law enforcement officials. For example, in 1999 in New Mexico federal agents seized three drums of *hoasca* tea from a church member of the Brazil-based church O Centro Espirita Beneficente Uniao Do Vegetal. The Church sued the U.S. attorney general, arguing that federal drug laws prohibiting the religious use of their tea were a violation of the RFRA. The government argued that it has a compelling interest in the uniform enforcement of the Controlled Substances Act.

In 2006 the U.S. Supreme Court made a ruling on this case, perhaps setting a new legal course for the use of entheogens in the United States. In this case, *Gonzales v. O Centro Espirita Beneficente Uniao Do Vegetal*, the government argued that the Controlled Substances Act was the least restrictive means by which to advance a compelling government interest in protecting religious members' health and safety and preventing the use of *hoasca* by recreational drug users (*New Jersey Law Journal*, 2006). Two lower federal courts had prevented law enforcement agents from seizing the tea on the basis of the RFRA of 1993, and the U.S. Department of Justice appealed the federal court injunction. As you may remember from Chapter 3, the U.S. Supreme Court, in *City of Boerne v. Flores*, ruled that the RFRA did not apply to states and local governments; however, it remained applicable to the federal government. In February 2006 the U.S. Supreme Court upheld the injunction barring federal agents from seizing the entheogenic tea. Chief Justice Roberts, newly appointed to the Court, delivered the opinion of the Court, in which he articulated how the Court regards the similarities between the use of *hoasca* and the use of peyote in some Native American religions:

> if any Schedule I substance is in fact always highly dangerous in any amount no matter how used, what about the unique relationship with the Tribes justifies allowing their use of peyote? Nothing about the unique political status of the Tribes makes their members immune from the health risks the Government asserts accompany any use of a Schedule I substance.

Although this ruling is not the final word on this case, many see this as a victory for religious liberty (Hudson, 2006), and it is likely to ignite the interest of other religious groups seeking exemptions under U.S. drug laws.

Salvia divinorum

Salvia divinorum is a perennial herb native to the Oaxaca, Mexico, area. It is a member of the mint family and similar to sage. It is also known as Maria Pastora, Magic Mint, or Sally D. The active compound in *Salvia divinorum* is salvinorin A, and it is generally smoked to release its hallucinogenic properties, although it can also be chewed, inhaled, or made into a tea. Salvinorin A is the most potent naturally occurring hallucinogen currently known (Sheffler & Roth, 2003). Yet it is not listed as a controlled substance under the federal guidelines, and religious followers, spiritual seekers, and others, particularly young people, have been able to access it directly via the Internet (Pasterchick, 2002). It is also available for sale in some "head shops" and is touted as a legal alternative to other hallucinogens, although some businesses have been issued warnings by the U.S. Food and Drug Administration regarding their marketing of such street drug alternatives (USFDA, 2003).

Salvia divinorum has been used for centuries by Mazatec Indians in Mexico in their healing ceremonies. The Mazatecs believe it allows them to visit with God and the saints about divination, the diagnosis of illnesses, and healing. The Mazatecs consume the fresh leaves of the plant, although others tend to use dried leaves, which retain the hallucinogenic properties. The drug is often ritually used in the training of new shamans (Valdes, 1994).

Although currently not listed in the federal schedule, the herb has begun to attract the attention of some policymakers and is likely to be a drug of concern in the future. Valdes (1994) argues widespread use is likely once its effects become known. In 2005, both Louisiana and Missouri included it in their state drug statutes, and other states are considering similar amendments. In March 2006 *Salvia divinorum* made headlines on National Public Radio when reporter David Schaper appeared on the popular show *All Things Considered* to report on this substance. As part of his report, he featured Ms. Kathy Chistister, from Wilmington, Delaware, who believes the use of *Salvia* led to the suicide of her seventeen-year-old son, Brett. She says that Brett had written an essay on *Salvia* in which he described how "tripping on salvia allowed him to give up his senses and wander into the inter-dimensional time and space … and he discovered the secrets to the universe" (Schaper, Siegel, & Block, 2006).

Datura

Plants of the genus *Datura* also possess hallucinogenic properties. The genus is native to tropical climates but has been used around the world. The name *Datura* comes from the liturgical language of Hinduism and means "divine inebriation." It is commonly known as Jimson weed or angel trumpet in the United States. *Datura* and its various species have been considered visionary plants, and they have been used to induce visionary dreams, to communicate with the Gods, as an aid in healing, and to see the future. *Datura* has a rich history of use by native religions, shamans, and in witchcraft as a way to reach altered states of consciousness (Busia & Heckels, 2006).

The alkaloid compounds scopolamine, atropine, and hyoscyamine are present in these plants. According to a report by the DEA (2004), the abuse of *Datura* species is of interest because it has led to numerous deaths and injuries. For example, in Jacksonville, Florida, an eighteen-year-old was arrested for possession of a controlled substance for brewing a tea from the flowers of a species of

Datura in October 2005. The tea sent one of his friends to the emergency room, suffering from tremors, profuse sweating, and incoherence (Scanlan, 2005). In Sarasota, Florida, a woman was convicted of poisoning her boyfriend with angel trumpet seeds she had purchased on eBay. She added water-soaked seeds to her boyfriend's beer, which led him to be hospitalized with stroke-like symptoms. She was sentenced to fifteen years in prison, followed by a five-year term of proba-tion (Scarcella, 2005). The Centers for Disease Control and Prevention, in the *Morbidity and Mortality Weekly Report*, have also noted cases in which individuals have gotten very ill after ingesting seeds from a *Datura* species or tea brewed with the seeds (CDC, 1984, 2003). Because of the psychoactive properties of the vari-ous species of *Datura*, religious followers around the world have regarded them as "plants of the gods" (Fuller, 2000, p. 32).

Cannabis

Cannabis, more commonly known as marijuana, is the most widely used illicit drug in the United States. According to the National Survey on Drug Use and Health 2004, marijuana has about 14.6 million active users (meaning they have used marijuana in the past thirty days). In addition, of drug users of other illicit substances, roughly 76.4 percent also use marijuana. According to the survey, an estimated 56.8 percent of current illicit drug users had used only marijuana, 19.7 percent had used marijuana and another illicit drug, and the remaining 23.6 percent had used only an illicit drug other than marijuana in the past month (SAMHSA, 2005).

Marijuana remains a Schedule I drug despite advocacy efforts by groups such as the National Organization for the Reform of Marijuana Laws (NORML) to reform legislation. Although states have begun to decriminalize simple possession of marijuana, those engaged in the trafficking of marijuana are more likely to expe-rience greater difficulty with the law. This is not without reason. Concerns over public safety continue to dominate the government's legislative agenda in regard to marijuana. There is mounting scientific evidence to suggest that marijuana is a damaging substance; therefore, it is unlikely any major reforms will occur in the near future. For example, researchers have found that marijuana use impairs cognitive functions (Block & Ghoneim, 1993; Herkenham et al., 1990; Pope & Yurgelun-Todd, 1996), impairs driving performance (NHTSA, 2000), damages lung function (it appears to be at least as damaging as the regular use of tobacco: Roth et al., 1998; Tashkin, 1990; Wu, Tashkin, Djahed, & Rose, 1988), and is related to a variety of mental health concerns, including depression and suicide (Brook, Cohen, & Brook, 1998; Green & Ritter, 2000).

Rastafarians are the religious group most closely associated with touting the entheogenic benefits of marijuana. The Farm, a spiritual group committed to a "hippy lifestyle" or doctrine, did encourage its members to use "sacred drugs," including marijuana, for a period of time; however, after the prosecution and imprisonment of its founder, Stephen Gaskin, and others, they abandoned the practice (Partridge, 2004). The Farm continues as a communal living group in Summertown, Tennessee (http://www.thefarm.org).

Many Rastafarians who use marijuana, or "ganga" as they call it, cite biblical passages as their guide—for example, *Revelation* 22.2 ("And the leaves of the tree of life are for the healing of the nations"). Rastafarianism originated as a black liberation movement in Kingston, Jamaica, and today has members around the globe (Partridge, 2004). The religious movement began under the leadership of Marcus Garvey in the 1930s through his "Back to Africa" movement, which identified blacks as the true biblical Jews who had been exiled from Africa as divine punishment (Bowker, 2000). Rastafarianism is inspired by the desire to return to Africa, which is believed to be the promised land where black people can truly flourish without white oppression. It is an apocalyptic, millennial movement that has evolved its own cultural dress, music, dietary guidelines, and hairstyle (dreadlocks). Smoking ganga is consistent with Rastafarians' belief about living in accordance with the laws of nature and allowing users to relax and tap into the divine—the divine being found within the self (Partridge, 2004).

American Rastafarians have had a particularly difficult time finding legal remedies for their sacramental use of ganga. A couple of cases merit mentioning here. Not unlike in the *McBride* and *Olsen* cases described earlier, Rastafarians have had the most legal difficulty when large quantities of marijuana have been seized by law enforcement officials. In *U.S. v. Bauer et al.*, twenty-six people were indicted in 1992 on a number of drug charges, including conspiracy to manufacture and distribute marijuana, money laundering, use of firearms in relation to drug trafficking, and possession with the intent to distribute. The twenty-six defendants in the case moved for severance, and four different trials were held. The appellants in *U.S. v. Bauer et al.* were tried together and appealed their convictions to the U.S. Court of Appeals for the Ninth Circuit. Their appeal was based on a number of legal arguments, and three of the defendants, Bauer, Treiber, and Meeks, used a religious use defense under the RFRA. The U.S. Court of Appeals found that the RFRA was relevant to the charges of simple possession of marijuana, and thus the defendants could be retried on the possession counts; however, upon retrial, the court may conduct a preliminary hearing in which the defendants must present evidence that they are practicing Rastafarians and that the use of marijuana is a part of their religious ceremony. Judges Farris and Noonan stated in the opinion of the Court: "It is not enough in order to enjoy the protections of the Religious Freedom Restoration Act to claim the name of a religion as a protective cloak. Neither the government nor the court has to accept the defendant's mere say-so." However, in reference to the charges of conspiracy to distribute, possession with intent to distribute, and money laundering, the Court found that the religious freedom of the defendants was not limited, since no evidence demonstrated that Rastafarianism requires followers to distribute large quantities of marijuana.

In another case, *People v. Gregory Peck*, the Court of Appeals of California affirmed the conviction and sentence of Gregory Peck, president and a priest of the Israel Zion Coptic Church. The Church, an offshoot of the Rastafarian faith, has more than 200 members who use marijuana, generally three times per day, to make themselves aware of their sins. Peck, who had previously been convicted of growing marijuana for the Church in 1988, was arrested for possessing about 40 pounds of marijuana for sale. He had traveled to California from Wisconsin to buy the marijuana because it was cheaper there; since church members had "chipped in" to help defray his costs and because of the quantity in his possession, he was convicted of possessing marijuana for sale. He was sentenced to five years on probation. As a condition of probation, like most probationers, Peck was to refrain from using or possessing any controlled substance and had to submit to drug tests. The Appellant Court upheld his conviction and sentence, reasoning that there was no evidence to suggest that his religion required him to transport large quantities of marijuana. Nor were the probation conditions considered unreasonable by the Court, since Peck instructed the Court that he smoked marijuana several times a day, while continuing to drive and operate motorized equipment, and his own expert witness testified that church members use the drug to bring about "some effect" (Ofgang, 1997).

U.S. Drug Control Policy

As you are most likely aware, the United States has been embroiled in a determined war against drugs for the past few decades. The drug war has been waged for years and has continued to place religious users of controlled substances in a precarious legal position. Thus, with the exception of members of the NAC, religious followers in possession of various psychoactive substances may find themselves committing theological religion-related crimes. To understand why law enforcement and the courts have typically taken such a hard line on drug-using religious groups, it is important to understand the context in which those decisions are made. In addition to the inherent political and social dynamics of this type of theologically based crime, religious groups have had to demonstrate their overall worthiness, fitness, or legitimacy as viable religious organizations to justify their use of entheogens. As the other theologically based crimes described in this text illustrate, these cases are complex. The use of illicit drugs for purposes of religious fulfillment is certainly no different.

First and foremost, the concern over drug abuse in the United States is multi-faceted. Drug abuse affects all segments of society. Losses to the economy, health care costs, family dysfunction, transmission of infectious disease, chronic illness, public safety issues, and social disorder top the list of concerns. Thus, controlling use and abuse of drugs has resulted in different policies that serve to regulate and monitor the sale of legal drugs and precursor chemicals, as well as policies designed to eliminate the cultivation, manufacture, and trafficking of illicit drugs. Policies cover a spectrum of substances, including legal over-the-counter products that are used as inhalants or to manufacture other drugs, pharmaceutical or prescription drugs, alcohol, tobacco, and illicit drugs. We are also likely to see more policies related to hallucinogenic botanicals in the future.

Policy continues to focus on crime control, mainly because the relationship between drugs and crime is of great concern. Drugs and crime are connected in a number of ways. First, the possession, cultivation, or sale of controlled substances is likely to violate anti-drug statutes; therefore anyone engaging in such activities may be committing a criminal act. Second, some drug users commit additional crimes, such as burglary, robbery, or theft, to obtain more drugs. Sometimes additional crimes, such as assault, robbery, or murder, are committed during the buying or selling of illegal drugs. Third, because psychotropic drugs tend to impair judgment and perception, some drug users commit crime while under the influence of drugs, including driving while impaired. Fourth, organized criminal activity to support the drug trade is tied to a number of additional crimes such as racketeering, money laundering, and tax evasion. Fifth, the illegal possession or sale of legal drugs, such as prescription drugs, alcohol, or tobacco, creates additional crime problems. Finally, the drug-use subculture often places family members and drug users themselves in danger, since drug abuse can leave users and family members vulnerable to victimization. For example, children are at great risk of abuse or neglect when being cared for by a drug-using caretaker.

The war on drugs is not a new phenomenon. Governmental measures to control the use of drugs actually date back as far as the 1800s (Lyman & Potter, 2003), and since the passage of the Harrison Act in 1914, numerous waves of federal policy have been aimed at controlling drug use. The Harrison Act is often cited as the first attempt by the U.S. government to regulate substances, although it was designed as a tax act to garner revenue for the federal government. The act required legitimate sellers of drugs to register their drug sales with the government and to pay taxes on those sales. The enforcement of the act was left to a special unit of the Bureau of Internal Revenue of the Treasury Department, which later became the Federal Bureau of Narcotics (Meier, 1994). Since the Federal Bureau of Narcotics was established in the 1930s, the federal government has played a substantial role in the regulation and control of substances in the United States.

A central policy of the war on drugs is the Controlled Substances Act (CSA) (21 U.S.C. 13), Title II and III of the Comprehensive Drug Abuse Prevention and Control Act of 1970. The CSA categorizes all substances that are subject to regulation under federal law into five schedules. Substances to be regulated are assigned a schedule on the basis of their medicinal value, potential for abuse, and overall potential for harm. Substances assigned to Schedule I are considered the most dangerous and have no accepted medicinal purpose; those with a Schedule V designation are considered least dangerous. Schedule I drugs include heroin, LSD, mescaline, peyote, methaqualone, psilocybin, and marijuana. Also included in Schedule I is dimethyltryptamine, commonly known as DMT.

A mechanism is also provided in the CSA to evaluate the schedule of a particular substance and to add other substances to the schedule categories. The DEA and the Department of Health and Human Services (HHS), as well as any other interested party, can petition the DEA to investigate the possible addition, deletion, or change of schedule of any substance. Once a petition is made, the DEA requests a scientific and medical evaluation of the substance by the HHS, which results in a recommendation on whether a substance should be controlled. This system allows the DEA the flexibility to respond to emerging drug abuse problems in the country. Certainly, the main determinant of whether a particular substance should be scheduled is the potential for abuse. This includes an examination of the historical and current patterns of use by various populations in an attempt to determine the scope, duration, and significance of abuse and what risks there are to public health. The available scientific evidence regarding the pharmacological effects of a particular substance is also important. In addition, in 1984 the CSA was amended by the Comprehensive Crime Control Act to allow the DEA to place a particular substance temporarily in Schedule I if an emergency situation arises and there is no accepted medical use of the substance (DEA, 2005).

In addition to the scheduling of substances, the DEA is responsible for registering, regulating and monitoring companies responsible for manufacturing, distributing, or dispensing any of the controlled substances, including precursor chemicals. Precursor chemicals are legal chemicals required in the manufacture of illicit drug products that have other, legitimate uses. This is a closed system of distribution in which companies are certified by the DEA as authorized to handle various controlled substances. Authorized individuals and companies must maintain complete and accurate records of all transactions and the security and storage of all controlled substances. Religious groups seeking exemptions for their sacramental use of a particular substance often seek a remedy through this regulatory system. The NAC has special exemptions and is supplied with its product through firms authorized by the DEA.

Each state also has its own scheduling scheme, and most states have replicated the five-schedule model, although there are some variations in the number of schedules and the schedule assigned for certain substances. For example, since 1996 several states have amended their drug laws to provide specific exemptions for the medical use of marijuana. These medical marijuana exemptions have conflicted directly with federal law, under which marijuana remains a Schedule I drug, thus creating legal controversy. Yet, in June 2005 the U.S. Supreme Court ruled in *Gonzales v. Raich* that the authority granted Congress in the Commerce Clause does include the power to prohibit the local cultivation of marijuana in compliance with California law.

Federal and state laws include a wide range of criminal charges related to drugs. Because each state crafts its own drug law statutes, the language differs from jurisdiction to jurisdiction, but, generally, criminal charges involve the possession, cultivation, manufacture, or distribution of controlled substances. Other criminal charges may involve the possession of drug paraphernalia, endangering the lives of others while manufacturing a substance, conspiracy, engaging in criminal enterprise, money laundering, tax evasion, and employment of children in the drug trade. If children are exposed to controlled substances, additional charges related to child abuse or neglect might also apply.

Drug use, even for religious purposes, can also become a central issue in child custody cases. For example, well-known marijuana activist, user, and practicing Rastafarian Robert Edward Forchion, also known as NJWeedman, has been limited to one supervised visit per week with his daughter as a result of his commitment to marijuana (Reitmeyer & Mathis, 2002). Even the sacramental use of peyote, which was made legal for members of the NAC by the American Indian Religious Freedom Act of 1994, did not deter a family court judge in Michigan from ruling against a father who wished to have his four-year-old son ingest small quantities of peyote in accordance with religious tradition (Halpern, 2004).

As I have mentioned, the United States is substantially invested in drug control policy. The Office of National Drug Control Policy (ONDCP), an executive office of the president, is charged with the task of establishing policies and priorities for federal drug control. The ONDCP was originally established as a part of the Anti-Drug Abuse Act of 1988, although its mission has been expanded by enabling legislation such as the Violent Crime Control and Law Enforcement Act of 1994, the Drug-Free Communities Act of 1997, the Media Campaign Act of 1998, the Office of National Drug Control Policy Re-authorization Act of 1998, and a variety of executive orders. The most important function of the ONDCP is to construct and implement the National Drug Control Strategy to formalize a national anti-drug effort. The strategy includes priorities for drug control, guidelines for coordination among intergovernmental agencies and local communities, and certifying a budget to accomplish the work of the strategy.

The 2008 National Drug Control Strategy (which can be found on the ONDCP's Web site at http://www.whitehousedrugpolicy.gov) included a budget for fiscal year 2008 requesting federal funding in the amount of $12.961 billion. Three key priorities remain: drug use prevention and education, drug treatment (including treatment offered by faith-based organizations), and disrupting the drug market. Drug use prevention and education include efforts at stopping drug use before it starts through education and community action. Approximately 12 percent of the federal drug control budget is reserved for this goal. Drug treatment involves intervening and healing active drug users as well as supporting addiction research and amounts to approximately 24 percent of the federal drug control budget. The biggest investment is made in disrupting the drug market, which involves a substantial investment in law enforcement in the United States and abroad and represents roughly 65 percent of the federal drug control budget. The National Drug Control Strategy involves the funding commitment of many departments including: the departments of Defense, Education, Health and Human Services, Homeland Security, Justice, State, Treasury, and Veterans Affairs. This federal investment represents only the tip of the iceberg, since the national strategy does not include the investments made by each state in anti-drug efforts.

Law enforcement officials have been very successful at bringing drug violators to justice. For example, the DEA, the lead federal law enforcement agency seeking to disrupt the drug market, made 29,451 arrests in 2004 and seized 117,822 kilograms of cocaine, 672 kilograms of heroin, 264,714 kilograms of marijuana, 1,647.5 kilograms of methamphetamine, and more than 2 million dosage units of hallucinogenic drugs. In fact, since 1986, DEA officials have made a total of 568,596 arrests for violations of federal drug laws (DEA, 2006). These arrests represent one agency's law enforcement effort, and it is important to recognize that state and local law enforcement officials have had impressive arrest records as well. Such statistics illustrate the government's overarching commitment to fight drug use and abuse in the United States. Although religious groups are generally not specifically targeted by law enforcement officials, anyone who violates state or federal drug laws and is apprehended by the police is likely to have to face the criminal consequences of his or her choice, even if it is a religious one.

Religious Exemption: Peyote Religion

The sacramental use of peyote is a contemporary religious practice among some Native American religions; the ritual's history can be traced back several thousand years (Saliba, 2004; Stewart, 1987). It is often referred to as "Peyote Religion" or "Peyotism" and is a central practice of the NAC. Peyote is a hallucinogenic derived from a cactus, and the primary psychoactive compound is mescaline. Mescaline is a Schedule I drug. The cactus is native to the Rio Grande Valley from Mexico City to the Texas border. It is also found in some areas of Arizona and California. The top of the peyote cactus is cut off and dried to produce the mescal button that is ingested during religious ceremonies or meetings. For religious users, peyote is both a healing substance and a spiritual aid (Petrullo, 1934); it is worshipped and treated with great respect (Halpern, 2004).

Peyote is typically consumed during an all-night ceremony or meeting that is accompanied by prayer, singing, and meditation (Parker, 2002). Central to the ceremony is the actual process of harvesting the peyote, for which those responsible for its preparation engage in ritual confession and purification. The peyote is prepared and ingested with great care. Religious leaders or road chiefs (or roadmen) guide the ceremony until dawn, and worshipers share a ceremonial meal (Stewart, 1987). Followers pray for fertility and rain while listening to the shaman recite stories. Some scholars have compared the ceremonial use of peyote to the communion bread received by Christians or as a symbol of the Holy Spirit sent by Christ to heal (Saliba, 2004). Central to the use of peyote is a belief system that holds in high regard supernatural powers believed to control illness, health, weather, and so on. Peyote provides a special connection to the supernatural world, allowing users to access the spirits and powers of the supernatural, generally for the good of the whole group (Fuller, 2000). Nonreligious use of peyote is considered sacrilegious by followers.

Established in 1918 (Saliba, 2004), the NAC is the largest religious denomination among Native Americans, with a membership of about 300,000, many of whom legally consume peyote buttons each year (Halpern, 2004). However, the name Native American Church can be misleading, since there is no hierarchical organization with one central church to dictate church policies. Rather, the NAC is a group of loosely coupled organizations, congregations, or chapters that are responsible for establishing their own policies, although their teachings remain relatively consistent (Stewart, 1987). This has led to some confusion in the courts as they attempt to dispose of cases related to the NAC (Parker, 2002). The theology of the Church integrates some Christian teachings with more traditional Native American beliefs, and the use of peyote is held to allow members to communicate directly with God (*People v. Woody*, 1964).

Most members of the NAC who use peyote do so regularly throughout their life. Most abstain from taking alcohol or other drugs, as is prescribed by their beliefs (Halpern et al., 2005); however, the ritual use of peyote may actually be a beneficial part of the treatment for alcoholism among the NAC population (Albaugh & Anderson, 1974; Pascarosa & Futterman, 1976; Pascarosa, Futterman, & Halsweig, 1976). Peyote is revered for its healing power and for its ability to offer users the opportunity for self-realization, which can serve as a healing mechanism for drug and alcohol problems (Garrity, 2000). Researchers have found that the ritual use of peyote as practiced by Native Americans has no adverse side effects in terms of psychological or cognitive deficits (Halpern et al., 2005). Such evidence helps to confirm the appropriateness of governmental exemptions for members of the NAC and may open the door for future research into the entheogenic benefits of other controlled substances.

The legality of peyote remains contentious, despite legislative efforts to legitimize its use by religious followers and various religious freedom cases that have challenged the courts. Like general drug laws, legislation related to peyote involves statutes and administrative policies at the federal, state, and reservation level. Early in U.S. history, many states crafted legislation outlawing peyote use, although in reality such legislation had little influence over Native Americans living on reservations where state governments had no jurisdiction. Religious users, however, could be arrested and convicted for violation of state laws on state property or highways. Much of the legal conflict regarding peyote use was instigated by white officials who believed that the religious use of peyote only helped to preserve native cultural norms, thereby preventing Native Americans from integrating into white America (Fuller, 2000). Stewart (1993) argues that nearly all the arrests for violations of state laws were test cases intended to challenge anti-peyote laws.

For example, in 1924, Big Sheep, a Crow Indian, was arrested in effect to challenge an anti-peyote law passed in Montana in the previous year. Although the court in *State v. Big Sheep* upheld the state anti-peyote law, it did reverse the conviction of Big Sheep and order a new trial. Peyotists continued to advocate for exemption; however, they were not successful until 1957 (Stewart, 1993).

Some tribal leaders even opposed the use of peyote. For example, the Navajo Tribal Council outlawed the sale, use, or possession of peyote, claiming that its use was not consistent with the Navajo way of life (Fisher, 2002). In 1959, this tribal policy prompted members of the NAC to bring a case against the Navajos to the Tenth Circuit Court after Navajos arrested members of the NAC during a religious ritual. In this case, *Native American Church v. Navajo Tribal Council*, the NAC argued that the tribal council policy was a violation of the U.S. Constitution; however, the Court held that since no policy existed that made the Bill of Rights applicable to Native American nations, the federal courts had no jurisdiction over such a policy (Fisher, 2002).

In 1964 the California Supreme Court decided *People v. Woody* and overturned the convictions of members of the NAC who had been arrested and convicted of violating California laws regarding peyote. In the majority opinion, Justice Tobriner stated:

> We have weighed the competing values represented in this case on symbolic scale of constitutionality. One the one side we have placed the weight of freedom of religions as protected by the First Amendment; on the other, the weight of the state's compelling interest. Since the use of peyote incorporates the essence of the religious expression, the first weight is heavy. Yet the use of peyote presents only slight danger to the state and to the enforcement of its laws; the second weight is relatively light. The scale tips in favor of the constitutional protection.

In addition to legitimizing the ceremonial use of peyote by members of the NAC, *People v. Woody* also considered the First Amendment protection of Native Americans practicing their religion outside of the reservation. Since all Native Americans are considered U.S. citizens (even though some consider themselves citizens of their tribe), this case was important in distinguishing their right to religious liberty under the U.S. Constitution; however, this case did not completely clarify the situation (Deloria & Lytle, 1983). Several other cases were presented to state courts over the years regarding bona fide members of the NAC who had been convicted of violating state laws regarding peyote. Many of these cases were decided in favor of the member of the NAC (Fisher, 2002).

The year following the *Woody* decision, Congress passed a drug abuse act in which it delegated power for legal exemptions to the act as an administrative duty, instead of embedding language in the legislation to specify the exemption for members of the NAC. The exemption is found in the Controlled Substances Act (21 U.S.C. 13) through federal regulation 1307.31, which states:

> The listing of peyote as a controlled substance in Schedule I does not apply to the non-drug use of peyote in bona fide religious ceremonies of the Native American Church, and members of the Native American Church so using peyote are exempt from registration. Any person who manufactures peyote for or distributes peyote to the Native American Church, however, is required to obtain registration annually and to comply with all other requirements of law.

As you might suspect, the DEA soon found it difficult to distinguish bona fide religious users from others who might take advantage of the exemption (Fisher, 2002). For example, in 1990, Robert Boyll, a non–Native American member of the NAC, was indicted by a federal grand jury for importing peyote through the mail and possessing peyote with the intent to distribute. Boyll used the U.S. mail to transport peyote from Mexico to his home in San Cristobal, New Mexico. Consistent with a racially bound reading of the federal exemption, only those with at least 25 percent Native American blood are considered bona fide members of the NAC. Since Boyll was not 25 percent Native American, his case proceeded in federal criminal court. He moved to dismiss the three-count indictment against him on the basis of his active membership in the Church, which is exempted from the Controlled Substance Act. In *U.S. v. Boyll*, the District Court had to determine whether the federal exemption includes non–Native American members of the Church. The Court ruled in favor of Boyll, finding that the federal exemption applies to all members of the NAC, regardless of race. However, as Parker (2002) notes, not all cases involving members of the peyote religion have been resolved in a similar manner. The inability to delineate clearly how the exemption applies to the specific circumstances of religious followers, coupled with the fact that not all states adjusted their drug policies to include such an exemption, resulted in a lack of uniform legal protection for the ritual use of peyote, despite legislative efforts and court rulings. In fact, Congress determined that only twenty-eight states had enacted laws consistent with the federal exemption, thus creating a hardship for religious users (42 U.S.C. 1996a).

Why have other religious groups historically not been able to secure similar legal protection? As mentioned above, other religious organizations have attempted to seek similar exemptions from state and federal drug laws with little to no avail, especially in cases where the use of other drugs, such as marijuana, is at issue—that is, until the 2006 ruling in *Gonzales et al. v. O Centro Espirita Beneficente Uniao Do Vegetal*, which may open the door to other religious groups seeking exemption from U.S. drug laws. Although there is no simple way to answer this question, it is important to acknowledge the desire of the U.S. government to preserve, and thus protect, the diversity of Native American culture. In fact, the U.S. government has a responsibility to do so, and thus the courts have often "allowed preferential treatment of Native Americans whenever that treatment bears a corresponding rational relationship" (Parker, 2002, p. 111). In this vein, Congress passed the American Indian Religious Freedom Act (AIRFAA) in 1978 (PL 95-341) to protect the inherent right to believe, express, and exercise the traditional religions of Native Americans, including their right to access religious sites, use and possession of sacred objects, and the freedom to worship. However, "the act was only a resolution—not a statute with specific rights and duties set forth" (Witte, 2000, p. 146). Amendments (42 U.S.C 1996 and 1996a) included specific language to establish a concrete policy regarding the ceremonial use of peyote to counteract the lack of uniformity across state laws and as a response to the U.S. Supreme Court decision in *Employment Division v. Smith* in 1990. As you may recall from Chapter 3, the *Smith* decision had a chilling effect on American religious freedom jurisprudence, creating uncertainty regarding the legality of peyote use, especially given the fact that the *Smith* case involved two individuals who used peyote sacramentally.

The AIRFAA was intended to provide a nationwide exemption from prosecution under drug laws specifically for members of Native American tribes. The act was clear that the federal exemption applied only to those who belonged to a federally recognized tribe, which is consistent with Congress's interest in preserving Native American culture (Parker, 2002). This, however, continues to leave non–Native American peyote worshippers in legal limbo. For example, in February 2006, federal prosecutors ended the battle between the government and a Utah couple who were indicted on thirteen counts each of conspiracy to possess peyote with the intent to distribute. James "Flaming Eagle" Mooney, a member of a Seminole tribe that is not recognized by the federal government and a member of the Oklevucha Earthwalks Church, and his wife Linda Mooney were found with 12,000 peyote buttons after a police raid on their church. Federal prosecutors agreed to drop the charges against the Mooneys if they agreed to stop using and distributing peyote (Manson, 2006). Thus, it might be argued that this special exemption from U.S. drug laws for Native Americans is more about preserving culture among recognized tribes than it is about religious liberty.

Part III
Reactive/Defensive Crimes

7

Destructive Religious Groups

In November 1978, Americans were shocked to learn the horrific details of a tragedy in which more than 900 American members of the Peoples Temple died in a mass suicide/murder in a remote area of Guyana. Aerial footage from news cameras captured the gruesome scene on film. Viewers around the world became witness to the bodies of hundreds of men, women, and children strewn on the ground of the commune amid the litter of discarded paper cups. The cups contained the deadly brew religious followers agreed, or were forced, to drink on that fateful day. The deaths were orchestrated by their charismatic leader, Jim Warren Jones, who ordered his followers to drink the mixture of cyanide and fruit punch and to prepare for revolutionary death.

Survivor reports suggest that the vast majority of adult followers voluntarily drank the mixture, although Jones had equipped several men with firearms to ensure the success of the revolutionary mass death (Galanter, 1999). Children, of course, had little choice in the matter, and consequently more than 200 children died. Interviews conducted by agents from the Federal Bureau of Investigation (FBI) with defectors from the Peoples Temple indicate that Reverend Jones ordered that a security force patrol the commune. Followers were reassured the armed security force was necessary to ensure their safety from invasion by U.S. officials, including the Central Intelligence Agency (CIA). It was also noted that Jim Jones frequently threatened to use violence against any member of his flock who sought to leave the group (FBI, 1979).

It is likely that the tragedy was spurred in large part by the external pressure perceived by Jim Jones from a visit to the commune by U.S. congressman Leo

Ryan. Congressman Ryan, concerned about the health and safety of members of the Peoples Temple, journeyed to Guyana on November 17 with concerned family members and a news crew from NBC. Congressman Ryan and a few others met with Jim Jones and members of his church on November 17 without incident. But the next day, when Congressman Ryan, accompanied by twenty-eight others, some of whom were defectors, was attempting to leave, he and several others were shot dead by one of Jim Jones's henchmen, Lawrence John Layton. Within hours of the killings, Jim Jones ordered the mass suicide of his followers. Layton was subsequently convicted for the murders (FBI, 1979).

Jim Jones and his church were no strangers to external pressure, including pressure from the U.S. government, since the Internal Revenue Service had denied the temple tax exemption status. This pressure, combined with mounting internal conflicts among followers, prompted Jones to relocate his temple to Guyana from its roots in California (Saliba, 2004). He began to establish the Jonestown commune in 1974 to provide isolated refuge for his flock (Galanter, 1999). Previous members of the Peoples Temple note that Reverend Jones regularly spoke to the need of a revolutionary death such as the one he mandated (FBI, 1979).

The deaths in the Jonestown commune illustrate the potentially tragic consequences of reactive/defensive religion-related crime. Recall the three-pronged framework for religion-related crimes from Chapter 1. A few characteristics of the reactive/defensive type of religion-related crime make such crimes especially noteworthy. First and foremost, they tend to involve more violence, and thus are of particular concern. Understanding the dynamics of these crimes may assist in the prediction or prevention of future violence. Sadly, such violence is often fatal. In some instances, acts of violence may also be properly identified as terrorism.

Second, like the crimes described in Chapters 4–6, these crimes are heavily influenced by theology or belief systems. Reactive/defensive crimes, however, are committed as a reaction to, or defense against, some perceived external force or pressure. The external pressure may be real, imagined, or manufactured by the group leader to meet his own hidden agenda. In any case, followers in charismatic religious groups are likely to do whatever is required of them to protect whatever they believe is being threatened. Criminal activity is thus prompted by the need or desire of believers to protect the belief system and/or other believers, especially when there is a perceived threat to their way of life from nonbelievers. Often those external threats involve government officials or specific social policies. Crimes of this nature are not new. Indeed, many religious movements throughout their history in the United States have experienced problematic periods when violence or other problems resulted (Jenkins, 2000; Krakauer, 2004).

Crimes, particularly violent ones, may target specific individuals or groups in an effort to facilitate some type of social change. In this vein, religious adherents become criminal actors intent on converting secular society to a society better aligned with their theological views. Crimes of this nature may also be characterized as reactionary or revolutionary. Also, since social change often comes with a price tag, religious followers may commit additional crimes to support their intended religious mission.

This chapter explores the defining features of reactive/defensive religion-related crime by examining the elements of "destructive religious groups" (DRGs) that predispose them to committing such crimes. The Jonestown tragedy took the lives of more than 900 Americans, many of whom were children. You might be asking yourself, why? To what end? How could so many people follow the dictates of Jim Jones, knowing that it would lead to their death and the death of their children? You may have equally troubling questions about how it is that otherwise decent citizens can commit the most heinous of crimes, all in the name of religion. Although this chapter is likely to raise more questions than it answers, I hope it will provide a better understanding of the elements that work to place some religious groups at risk for criminal activity.

This chapter begins with a discussion of the terminology that I use in my discussion of this particular type of religion-related crime. For this text, I have adopted the term "destructive religious group" to describe a religious group that engages in criminal activity in reaction to, or defense of, some external stimuli. I explain my reasoning for using this term as an alternative to "cult." Next, I summarize some of the organizational elements of religious groups whose members respond to external pressure through criminal activity. These factors include charismatic leadership and specific belief and social systems. Also, I compare and contrast destructive religious groups with other criminal groups and explore some of the challenges facing law enforcement and human service personnel as they attempt to intervene in potentially dangerous incidents.

What is a Destructive Religious Group?

In the past few decades increasing attention has been paid to new religious movements (NRMs), often referred to as "cults," "fringe religious groups," "alternative religious groups," or "marginalized religious groups." It has been estimated that in recent years approximately 3,000 new alternative religious groups have emerged around the globe (Dawson, 1998). In the U.S., as a direct result of the migration to the West since World War II, many new religious groups have emerged with roots from Eastern and Middle Eastern religions (Partridge, 2004). These groups pursue a wide range of beliefs, practices, and customs, and therefore it is impossible to categorize them into one generalized group (Mayer, 2001). For the most part, NRMs have enjoyed a peaceful co-existence with secular U.S. society, and it is important to note that the vast majority have not participated in any illegal activity. However, some groups have become extremely destructive and have thus gained the attention of researchers, law enforcement officials, and families who seek to understand the psychological, social, and public harm they cause. Why is it that some NRMs, although their beliefs and practices may appear odd, are not harmful, while others have exhibited outright criminal behavior? Yet, some people, particularly those in the anti-cult movement, would argue that all cult-like groups are harmful by design. They would argue that membership in such a group is psychologically damaging for the individual (Bohm & Alison, 2001). Before we explore some of the research related to this issue, it is important that I clarify my terminology.

Of the terms noted above, "cult" still prevails in both popular culture and some of the research literature, although the label generally has a negative connotation. "Cult" is derived from the Latin word *cultus*, meaning "care" or "adoration," which originates from the word *colere*, which means "to cultivate." Originally, the term was coined by scholars studying the sociology of religion to distinguish new religious groups in their research (Richardson, 1993). Within the sociology of religion, the term "cult" is one of four categories used to describe religious groups and their relationship with the broader society. Defined in this way, cults are groups with a unique set of beliefs, practices, and customs and have a high degree of conflict or tension with the mainstream culture (Bowker, 2000). As I mentioned before, all the major religions of the world, including Christianity, Islam, and Buddhism, began as alternative movements considered deviant by the larger society of the time (Zellner & Petrowsky, 1998) and thus would likely be considered cults by this standard definition.

As the deviant activities of some groups become known to the public, the term "cult" came to be associated with such groups. Over time, the term has evolved into a blanket descriptor inappropriately applied to all NRMs whose practices and beliefs are different or not well understood (Richardson, 1993). It has also come to be joined with or become synonymous with derogatory terms such as "extremist," "fanatical," "fatalistic," or "pathological." It is important that we recognize the effect such a pejorative image of cults may have on the objectivity of future research, and thus scholars have provided an eloquent argument for abandoning the term "cult" in scholarly research (Richardson, 1993). Today, many religious scholars prefer to use the term "NRM" in their research.

Barker (1995) describes the competing discourses regarding cultic groups among various segments of society, including cult members and former cult members, mental health professionals, the media, scholars, and various professionals. As Barker so aptly points out, these groups have conflicting perceptions regarding the purpose and intent of NRMs. This makes documenting religious phenomena objectively especially difficult. Both scholarly and popular writing illustrate such debates in which various groups have labeled each other or themselves as anti-cult movements (ACMs), counter-cult movements, cult defenders, or cult apologists. Sociological or psychological inquiry into the beliefs and operations of various religious groups, coupled with media and law enforcement accounts of criminal incidents, has sometimes painted differing views of the same religious groups.

For example, author Dan Brown (2003), in his novel *The Da Vinci Code*, ignited a firestorm of controversy on a number of different levels. One controversy surrounds his dramatic portrayal of a segment of the Catholic Church known as Opus Dei. In Brown's story, a blindly obedient Opus Dei member named Silas commits murder and practices self-mortification. Silas punishes himself for his bad deeds with instruments that draw blood. As a result, members of Opus Dei were called upon by the media to explain their religious organization and to help sort fact from fiction. Most portrayed the "real" Opus Dei in rather benign terms; however, members of the Opus Dei Awareness Network (ODAN) express a very different perspective, suggesting that Opus Dei runs more like a cult. According to its Web site (http://www.odan.org), the Opus Dei Awareness Network was founded in 1991 to provide accurate information about Opus Dei and to provide support for individuals who have been harmed by the religious organization. ODAN argues that Opus Dei implements questionable practices that restrict individual freedom of choice and isolate individuals from their families. This is in stark contrast to the media interviews given by current Opus Dei members, who report that nothing of the sort occurs or say such claims are purely exaggerations of the truth.

Which is the truth? Without personal experience in a group of interest such as Opus Dei, how does one sort the rhetoric from the reality? If the charges made by ODAN are accurate, does that mean a part of Opus Dei could, like other, more notorious groups labeled "cults," be destructive? Is it possible for part of an organization such as Opus Dei to be harmful and other parts to be benign? Does an organization such as Opus Dei fit the definition of "cult"? How does one investigate the potential lethality of a religious group? As you may have gathered from the discussion thus far, I have been in a quandary as to how best to describe the religious organizations analyzed in this chapter. In a previous publication (Kurst-Swanger & Ryniker, 2003), I opted to continue to utilize the term "cult," while recognizing the importance of the arguments of religious scholars for using the term "NRM" instead. Frankly, some religious groups have engaged in heinous criminal acts and deserved a negative label such as "cult."

Since my interest in such religious groups is purely from a criminological point of view, I will utilize a different term, "destructive religious group," to differentiate religious groups with violent propensities or other propensities toward criminal behavior from the general discourse on NRMs, since the vast majority of NRMs have been law abiding. Also, some DRGs are not necessarily "new" movements. Thus, the term "DRG" helps to remove whatever preconceived notions we may have about "cults" or "NRMs" and to create a new definition in which such groups can be examined. In the end, you may come to the conclusion that my definition of a DRG is comparable to your understanding of a cult, but I hope readers will allow me the opportunity to examine more closely the potential destructiveness of various religious groups and to describe the organizational and individual elements that appear to be related to this destructiveness.

The term "DRG" helps to distinguish groups that are held together by shared religious beliefs from other groups that may exhibit destructive/criminal behavior, such as gangs or organized crime networks. Later we explore the unmistakable similarity between DRGs and other destructive/criminal groups. Also, since the term "DRG" is broader in scope, it allows us to examine groups along the church–sect typology that engage in reactive/defensive religion-related crime. For example, we might find that some DRGs are highly organized and structured, while others have more loosely affiliated members. The term "destructive" helps us to differentiate religious groups that are harmless from those that pose a danger to members and society. Kimball (2003) uses the term "corrupt religious group," which is also helpful to distinguish destructive religious groups from other religious groups.

What do I mean by DRG? I return to the sociology of religion typology that I previously discussed in reference to cults. Religious cults are characterized by their novel belief systems, customs, or practices. They tend to be rather small, and because of their theology, lifestyle, and so on, outsiders generally know very little about them; thus, they tend to have tenuous relationships with the broader society. The classic DRG probably fits the general definition of a cult; however, reactive/defensive religion-related crimes can be committed by religious groups that would more appropriately be defined as sects, churches, or denominations and thus are more established within the broader community. In other cases, a DRG is so loosely affiliated that it would be difficult to describe it as a cult, as is the case with the Phineas Priesthood and the Army of God. Neither of these groups is a religious organization by standard definitions; they are more independent and autonomous but have chosen to demonstrate their devotion to their religious principles by committing violent crimes in the name of God. Nor do these groups share the organizational elements of the typical DRG described below; however, such groups warrant the concern of law enforcement officials because of their terroristic methods. These groups will be covered in more detail in the next chapter.

Thus, when religious groups (defined as two or more members) respond to external stimuli with criminal acts such as violence or the destruction of property, they might be labeled DRGs, regardless of whether they are categorized as a cult, sect, church, or a loosely coupled group of individuals who act in concert for faith. This definition helps us to include situations where crimes are committed by small groups of individuals from particular sects or churches. They may commit crime as a response to or in defense of some type of external pressure, but they do not necessarily represent the entire religious organization in which they are members. In this way, my definition of DRGs differs from those of other scholars. Since my purpose is to explore the general phenomenon of religion-related crime, I would argue it is equally important to consider even small groups of religious followers who engage in criminal activity even if the entire religious organization does not participate. My reasoning may become clearer in the next chapter, when we more closely examine other examples of reactive/defensive crimes related to religion.

Put another way, since this text is focused on exploring different kinds of religion-related crime, rather than different types of religious groups, the criminal actions of a particular group are what is of interest here. What defines a religious group as destructive is the danger all or some of the members pose to others or to property and to themselves. Since DRGs tend to engage in reactive/defensive religion-related crimes more frequently, they provide a fitting object of study. This, of course, does not mean a religious group that has engaged in other kinds of crimes would not be considered a DRG. For example, in the previous chapters we have discussed examples of theological religion-related crimes. Some people might consider particular illegal religious practices also to be destructive. In the next few sections attention is focused on the elements, forces, and characteristics of religious groups that are believed to be related to their engagement in destructive criminal behavior.

Organizational Elements

What are the principal forces at work to turn an otherwise benign group of devout religious followers into a group of destructive criminals? Obviously it is difficult to clearly identify which religious movements or groups pose a potential threat.

Social scientists have begun to study the defining features of such religious organizations in an attempt to understand their development and evolution (Bohm & Alison, 2001; Dawson, 1998; Lewis, 1996; Zellner & Petrowsky, 1998). Understanding the complex psychological dynamics of group process, the relationship of a group to its environment, religious conversion, belief systems, and charismatic leadership is critical if law enforcement officials are to evaluate the potential danger of a particular group or to manage incidents successfully as they arise, even if those incidents seem relatively minor at the outset. Evaluation, risk assessment, and proper critical incident management are important to minimize the damage that can result from a reactive or defensive response from a religious group.

It would be impossible to predict the actions and reactions of every religious group perfectly. It would also be difficult to predict what level of external pressure would be necessary for a particular religious group to react in a criminal manner. Much of what we know about DRGs is based on the examination of groups who have previously engaged in large-scale destructive acts, such as mass murder or suicide. Less attention has been paid to groups whose criminal behavior is relatively minor in comparison. To date, researchers have not been able to completely isolate the factors that distinguish destructive groups from more benign ones. Yet there are commonalities among all groups that have demonstrated high levels of destruction. These organizational factors may increase the potential risk of criminal behavior, at least on a grand scale. Galanter (1999) makes a valid point when he argues that our understanding must come from examining the psychology of groups versus the psychology of individuals.

The organizational factors that place a religious group at risk for engaging in reactive/defensive religion-related crimes may include the presence of a single charismatic authority who is capable of exerting coercive control over members; the development of a new social system to accommodate the belief system of the leader, in which isolation from the broader community becomes necessary; and religious beliefs that tend to be apocalyptic or fatalistic in nature, support the use of violence, and involve absolute truth claims. Each of these characteristics, considered alone, is not likely to result in criminal behavior; however, in combination, the potential risk may increase. It must also be understood that these organizational elements should be considered within the context of external and internal factors. Recognizing the important external influences that impinge on a group and how a group views its relationship to the dominant culture is equally important.

Charismatic/Singular Leadership

Charismatic leadership guides the establishment of most NRMs and thus is often a critical feature of DRGs. Leaders are considered to carry charismatic authority when their leadership traits are derived from their personal attributes. Charismatic leaders are regarded as gifted and highly insightful, and people are naturally drawn to them. Such dynamic leadership is often necessary to engage a new community of religious followers and is also often present in emerging political or social movements. In the case of DRGs, such a leader becomes central to the operation of the group and its belief system—so much so, the group would not survive without its leader (Zellner & Petrowsky, 1998).

Although charismatic leadership is generally a positive force and exists within many different types of religious and nonreligious organizations, it is more likely to become destructive when it is singular by design and is used to instill blind obedience, to isolate members from the outside world, or to facilitate coercive control. A single leader who demands total submission from his flock is in a better position to manipulate his followers in whatever direction he chooses if power is concentrated in his hands. The contrast is with other religious organizations that also have charismatic leadership but tend to have power diffused throughout the organization. These organizations may have a hierarchal structure in which many members of the organization have differing roles and responsibilities. Decision making tends to be spread across layers of the organization and not concentrated in the hands of one person. Therefore, members, although observant of the same belief system, move more freely within the religious organization as well as the broader society. For example, democratic governments are less likely to engage in human rights violations than governments controlled by a dictator.

In a DRG, members are encouraged to reject various aspects of the "outside" culture and are focused around a particular belief system, as touted solely by the leader. The group looks to the leader to decipher the meaning of everyday occurrences and the external forces or pressures exerted on the group. Membership in the group, therefore, is dependent upon individual members shedding their individual identity to become group members and true followers of the leader. Obedience to the leader becomes a desired goal toward the realization of religious life. Thus, the concepts of charismatic leadership and conversion are closely linked in that "the authority exercised by charismatic leaders has its roots in their followers' matrix of assumptions about reality" (Balch, 1998, p. 21).

The agenda of the leader becomes central to the future of the group. The group is vulnerable to the demands, wishes, and decisions of the charismatic leader. In the wake of the death and destruction caused by some leaders of DRGs, including Jim Jones and David Koresh, it is often unclear whether they truly believed they were being guided by some higher spiritual vision or consciously manipulated their leadership role to further their own personal agenda or struggled with some form of mental illness. Regardless, what separates problematic groups from other religious organizations is the self-proclaimed supreme power of the leader over the membership and the inherent power differential that is created by such singular leadership.

In addition, leadership grounded solely in charisma is likely to be unstable, setting the stage for volatility (Robbins & Anthony, 1995). Because charismatic authority is not reinforced by institutional supports or contained by institutional restraints, charismatic leaders must deliberately sustain their authority amid internal and external conflict. This may require leaders to find creative solutions to dissent and discord. It may require the leader to punish dissenters, reorganize the membership to destabilize alternative structures within the group, or dictate that members prove their faith by performing a variety of tasks (Robbins & Anthony, 1995). In the case of Jim Jones, internal and external pressure prompted him first to move his flock to an isolated commune in Guyana. It was not until this act of community isolation failed that he insisted on the mass suicide, although he had primed his community that at some point it would likely be necessary. David Koresh responded in a similar fashion in his Branch Davidian compound in Waco, Texas. Warren Jeffs, self-proclaimed prophet of the Fundamentalist Latter-Day Saints of Utah and Arizona, recently captured by the Nevada Highway Patrol, found ways to expel approximately 400 young male members of the FLDS community, forever severing their ties with their families (Speckman, 2004).

Since charismatic leadership is so important to the functioning of the group, it is important that law enforcement officials come to understand the goals, vision, belief system, and issues of the leader. Behavior changes in the leader are very likely to impact the flock. For example, Bohm and Alison (2001) found in their research into twenty-five different cults that seven specific behaviors were most closely correlated with overt acts of destruction (which they defined as mass murder and mass suicide). Of these seven destructive behaviors, several relate very specifically to the leader. Of special concern are leaders who believe in reincarnation, claim to be incarnates, are in preparation for doomsday, collect weapons, and engage in drills.

The importance of the psychology of the relationship between the obedience of a group and the authority of its leader cannot be overestimated. Take, for example, the findings of a famous study published in 1963 by Stanley Milgram. The Milgram experiment, as it has come to be called, examined the extent to which subjects would be obedient to the authority of a scientist even if they were given commands that came into conflict with their moral values. In his study, conducted at Yale University, volunteer subjects were asked to give electric shocks to another study participant, who was really an actor hired to pretend he or she was being shocked. The findings were startling. The majority of the participants administered the final 450-volt shock to what they believed to be a real person, receiving a real electric shock, just because they were told they must for the experiment to continue. Many of the subjects were uncomfortable administering the shocks; however, no participant refused to issue additional shocks before the 300-volt level (Milgram, 1963). The study has been replicated in a number of different settings and experimental designs with similar results. The implications of this body of research are haunting, but it certainly does help to explain how ordinary, law-abiding citizens can be directed to commit crimes, even heinous acts of violence that would normally violate their sensibilities.

Nishida (2001) interviewed members of Aum Shinrikyo (Supreme Truth), a DRG from Japan, and found that members were completely obedient to their leader, resulting in their participation in horrific crimes against the citizens of Tokyo. In 1995, members of the religious group released nerve gas in a Tokyo subway, killing 12 people and hospitalizing 5,000 others. The group was engaged in experiments involving different weapons that could be used to fulfill the leader's apocalyptic beliefs (discussed in the next section). Although the group originally had more peaceful beliefs regarding the apocalypse, the leader, Shoko Asahara, ultimately reacted to external pressures from concerned parents, the police, and other authorities by instructing his members to engage in criminal activities (Wojcik, 2004). He even had a "compassionate" rationale for such violence through the doctrine of poa. The interpretation of this doctrine rationalized "the killing of certain persons in order to prevent them from accumulating more bad karma that would have to be worked out in future lifetimes" (cited by Kimball, 2003, p. 82). The group's criminal activity culminated in the subway attack. Nishida (2001) found in his interviews with members that their obedience to their guru was absolute and that members with a higher status experienced a greater degree of manipulation. Their participation in criminal activity was the result of their obedience to authority and the fear that the, too, would be killed.

Belief Systems

Another driving force behind the criminal behavior of some religious groups is an apocalyptic, millennial, or fatalistic belief system. In this type of belief system, religious adherents are focused on the apocalypse. The apocalypse is the end of the world as we know it. It is considered to be the final battle between good and evil, in which Satan is finally defeated, signaling the second coming of Christ. Judgment day will arrive, and a new heaven and a peaceful and prosperous earth will be created. While some believe that the millennial age of peace can be ushered in only by catastrophe, others believe salvation and peace will come about gradually through human action (Wojcik, 2004).

The terms "apocalypse" and "millennium" appear in the New Testament *Book of Revelation*. Scholars and religious adherents hold various interpretations of the book, and the belief systems of religious groups are informed by their particular interpretation of the *Book of Revelation*.

There is no agreement among Christians as to when the apocalypse will occur; however, many believe the time is fast approaching. To many, the new millennium marks the beginning of the end of days. Believers are preoccupied with the upcoming battle between good and evil and their role in the process. Some believe Armageddon has been initiated by the U.S. government on behalf of Satan, and others believe the U.S. government will act on Satan's behalf in the final battle. This belief has led some religious adherents vehemently to oppose the U.S. government, its laws, and its agents (e.g., law enforcement officials) and to reject the legitimacy of government regulation and the rule of law. Followers may also feel that their beliefs carry a responsibility to fight Satan and all his agents, even if this means fighting agents of the government. This worldview may help to explain why some religious groups believe it is necessary to stockpile weapons and train their membership in military-type drills to ensure they are prepared for the final battle. Viewed through this lens, they may see themselves as soldiers of God. (We discuss this notion in greater detail in the next chapter.) Within such a worldview, themes of conspiracy and paranoia appear to be linked to technological and scientific advancement, government regulation, and the possibility of extraterrestrial life (Stewart & Harding, 1999).

Such notions are not new; in fact, there is evidence to suggest they have been expressed in different ways throughout American history, through popular culture, politics, and the media (Stewart & Harding, 1999). Therefore, apocalyptic and millennial views are not, in and of themselves, a reliable predictor of violence. In fact, many groups actually await the apocalypse with anticipation, assured they will be saved by the grace of God. Therefore, they have no need to prepare for violent conflict (Hall, 1989). Hundreds of groups share this worldview, yet most of them do not condone violence (Richardson, 2001).

Yet it is difficult to ignore the connection between apocalyptic worldviews and criminal behavior, since religious organizations that have experienced violent episodes have been characterized by such worldviews, including groups such as the Branch Davidians, the Peoples Temple, early Mormons, and radical Reformation Protestants such as the early Anabaptists (Robbins & Anthony, 1995). Others engaged in violence—such as the Ruby Ridge group, the Oklahoma City bombers, the Unabomber, and Heaven's Gate—have also embraced such notions.

Although apocalyptic views do not necessarily ignite violence, they may provide a sufficient level of urgency to motivate group members to action (Mayer, 2001). Certainly, sufficient examples of catastrophe exist from which believers can draw evidence that the end of the world is near: the enormity of natural disasters such as the tsunami in Asia and Hurricane Katrina, the threat of nuclear, biological, or chemical warfare, a bird-flu pandemic, all within a post–September 11 climate of anxiety. Such events, coupled with examples of corporate and government collusion, may invoke a sense crisis or emergency (Stewart & Harding, 1999). Contemporary fear and anxiety are likely to resonate with paranoia, giving rise to the type of urgency that is often exhibited by apocalyptic groups before their violence episodes.

Violence may also be associated with concerns that the group or the leader is being persecuted by the government or the broader society. The perception of persecution may result in survivalist behaviors, such as the stockpiling of weapons and supplies or the building of fortress barriers for protection against evil forces. It may also lead to more offensive behaviors such as the initiation of violence. The literature is unclear on whether leaders' expressed persecution is accurate, a manipulative response to internal or external challenges to their authority, or the result of an untreated mental illness. Felt persecution may lead to a redefinition of the group's role in Armageddon or serve as a signal to the leader that the apocalypse has begun. In any case, such behaviors should be a red flag for authorities that some sort of escalation is likely to occur. Both Jim Jones and Shoko Asahara reportedly believed they were being persecuted by outsiders, fueling their acts of destruction.

Belief systems are at the core of all reactive/defensive religion-related crimes. After all, religious traditions, to some extent, rely on and purport to know what the "truth" is, but when the religious organization follows such truth claims rigidly, corruption is more likely to result (Kimball, 2003). In other words, it may not be the belief system that is at issue; instead, groups are at risk of criminal behavior when the belief system becomes absolute. Such "black and white" thinking does not afford the group the ability to function well in "gray" situations, yet it can go a long way toward providing leaders and members the justification they require to engage in criminal behaviors they may otherwise abhor. Absolute truth claims leave little room for negotiation, conciliation, or compromise.

Such worldviews have not gone unnoticed by law enforcement officials. In preparation for the new millennium, the FBI conducted an analysis, referred to as Project Megiddo, to assess the potential for criminal activity by groups with extremist views. Megiddo, which is a hill in northern Israel and the site of many battles, has come to be synonymous with Armageddon, which is the scene of the last battle between good and evil. Project Megiddo resulted in a report that was distributed to law enforcement officials before the new millennium. The report highlights the key elements of apocalyptic religious beliefs, as well as some political beliefs concerning the New World Order conspiracy theory. The goal of the project was to increase awareness among law enforcement officials of the potential threat. Of particular concern are religious groups who view themselves as taking an active role in the end of days and believe violence is necessary. The actions of any group are likely to be predicated on the perceptions and interpretations of external events by group leaders and followers (FBI, 1999). Ordinary events, actions taken against the group by officials or community members, public policy changes, and so on are viewed through the lens of the particular belief system of the group.

The new millennium arrived without much crisis in the United States; however, a tragedy involving an apocalyptic group occurred in Kanungu in southwestern Uganda. More than 900 members of the Movement for the Restoration of the Ten Commandments of God (MRTC) were killed. The leader of the group declared that December 31, 1999, would be the end of the world and those with faith would be saved by God or the Virgin Mary. When the day passed without incident, his followers grew restless and demanded that their monetary and property donations to the movement be returned. Officials believe the leader reacted to the conflict by killing the dissenters and then ending the movement through the mass murder of the membership (Wojcik, 2004).

Group Processes

In addition to charismatic/singular leadership and belief systems, it is important to understand the group processes by which a religious group operates. These include daily living habits, interactions with the external environment, and roles and responsibilities in religious and nonreligious activities. Groups that require members to abandon all familial relationships, live in seclusion from the broader social community, and/or adopt new social norms have gained the most attention (and concern) from outsiders and the media. Many believe that religious groups that require members to shed their previous identities, including the severance of ties with family, are at greatest risk for acts of destruction. Leaders can have a greater hold over followers in a social group that has been isolated from the outside world. Such groups "establish a radical separation between themselves and the established social world, which they regard as hopelessly evil" (Hall, 1989, p. 78).

When conversion requires a "shedding" or "stripping" away of one's previous life and property, maintaining family relationships becomes very difficult. This, of course, is the most frightening aspect for parents and other family members and a critical feature that fuels the anti-cult movement. However, it is difficult to ascertain whether this seclusion from the outside world is considered a "necessary evil" or is desired to achieve ultimate commitment to a particular belief system. As we discussed in Chapter 2, many scholars dismiss the notion that most members are "brainwashed" into shedding their previous social connections; in fact, after twenty years of research there is little scientific evidence to support such claims (Dawson, 1998). Richardson (1994) argued that individuals who join such groups are in search of personal change, and consequently conversion is not coercive. The religious followers in Galanter's (1999) study reported that their emotional state improved after joining a new religious group, whether or not they were seriously distressed before joining. New members were rewarded by the group for their commitment. As Levine (1984) noted, radical departure from a lifestyle is more likely to occur for individuals in late adolescence and early adulthood, because individuals of this age group are generally not fully committed to careers or families of their own. Like the elderly, they are in to position to move freely into or to try out an alternative living environment.

The social system provided by the religious group is one that appears to meet the needs of its members. Some may ask why someone would want to join a group that represents such a radical departure from the dominant culture. Individuals seeking membership in alternative religious groups do so for the same reasons individuals seek membership in more traditional religious organizations. Some find peace and solace in the answers the religious group offers to their core spiritual questions; others are attracted to the rigidity of rules and boundaries set forth by religious authorities; some are inextricably attracted to the charisma of the leader; others benefit from being part of a group that shares their beliefs.

As you will recall from Chapter 2, the process by which someone adopts the principles and goals of a new religion is called conversion. In addition to the features of conversion discussed in Chapter 2, Levine (1984) acknowledged that the conversion of seemingly healthy young people into alternative religious organizations may fulfill a quest for self-identity as one transitions from childhood to adulthood. Wright and Piper (1986) noted that the semblance of a family system is attractive to young recruits who lack meaningful family relationships. Therefore, individuals, often young people, join religious organizations for a variety of reasons and purposes. Research suggests that many members leave such groups within two years of their conversion, running "flatly counter to the assertion of the anti-cult movement that converts are the naive victims of 'brainwashing'" (Dawson, 1998, p. 145).

This is not to dismiss the reality that religious organizations need continuously to recruit new converts for future survival. Groups cannot function without members or financial support. The long-term survival of any group is dependent upon the procurement of financial and human resources, and alternative religious groups are no exception. Many different types of religious organizations put effort into recruiting new members. For example, evangelical clergy minister on television, Mormons engage in "missionary" work, and members of the Jehovah's Witnesses participate in door-to-door proselytizing. Other religious groups encourage families to reproduce.

Leaders must ensure that the flock maintains an appropriate balance of members, and it may be in the best interests of some leaders that members come and go at regular intervals. As we have discussed previously, charismatic authority is difficult to maintain over time, so the rotation of members in and out of a group may in fact serve as a stabilizing factor. Members who appear discontented are likely to be encouraged to leave the group so as not cause any disruption of the leader's authority. For example, Warren Jeffs, self-proclaimed prophet of the FLDS Church, may have rejected 400 male members of his community for such reasons.

Members appear to join alternative religious groups voluntarily, but it is also true that some religious groups engage in focused recruitment practices. Leaders appear to understand the "profile" of likely converts and how to reach out to them. Wright and Piper (1986) noted that young people between the ages of eighteen and twenty-five are likely candidates; however, some evidence suggests that elderly members are targeted for their financial assets (Collins & Frantz, 1994). It should also be noted that in some religious groups, particularly those with longer histories, little outside recruitment is conducted; instead, the religious group relies on its members to marry and reproduce.

The recruitment of new members into the social system of the religious movement is a necessary function of group process. The group becomes a social system in and of itself, not unlike other groups that come together around common goals—for example, sports teams, fraternities and sororities, and social clubs. Not unlike the social systems created within these types of groups (which also have been known to be involved in criminality from time to time), religious movements construct their own "subcultures," evidenced by their dress, language, nutritional habits, daily routines, ground rules for behavior, symbols, and rituals. For communal groups, these defining characteristics are more profound.

Groups with a common belief system and norms for behavior are likely to be cohesive. When group cohesion is strong, joint action is more likely to occur (Galanter, 1999), which may help to explain why, faced with external threats, destructive religious groups have responded by "acting as one." Also, it is normal for humans to categorize the world into "in-groups and out-groups," creating a division or differentiation between "us" and "them" (Staub, 1985). Leaders can take advantage of this tendency by mobilizing an "us versus them" campaign to solidify the group's cohesion by demonizing and devaluing their opponents. This becomes, in effect, a grooming process whereby the leader prepares the group for any eventuality with nonbelievers.

Taking a systems theory approach to charismatic groups, Galanter (1999) eloquently describes such social processes through four functions that are characteristic of systems: transformation, monitoring, feedback, and boundary control. To answer questions regarding the eruption of criminality from groups whose purpose for gathering is spiritual rather than criminal, viewing the group as a system is particularly relevant. Transformation is a system function that involves activities to ensure the stability of the system or, in this case, the group. Membership, conversion, and recruitment are all examples of the function of transformation, where the primary task of the group is to make certain it is prepared to fulfill its mission or to ensure its goals are not disrupted. Self-preservation of the group is important.

The monitoring function of the social system involves the regulation and oversight of group actions and activities. Monitoring becomes important to the group to ensure that its primary task or mission is implemented. Leaders are involved in monitoring the group and thus must make sure that the autonomy of individual members is suppressed. Group members may be pressurized into doing things that are uncomfortable or may endure acts of abuse, but their desire to be committed to the group neutralizes the psychological demands of the "potentially threatening agenda of the leadership" and allows them to "comply with its expectation to achieve emotional relief" (Galanter, 1999, p. 100).

Through feedback, the system has an opportunity to gain information that assists it in evaluating its effectiveness as a system. Since many DRGs have a well-defined system of monitoring through the leadership of the organization, feedback regarding the functioning of the group is at the disposal of the leadership. Negative feedback, particularly the type that surfaces from outsiders, can easily be withheld from the general membership. External pressures, tensions, and interactions with the communities in which they live are an element of feedback that requires careful interpretation and monitoring. Isolation from the broader community can serve as a useful tool. For example, Jim Jones moved his flock to a remote area of Guyana after negative feedback in the United States. In fact, the history of religion in the United States is replete with examples of religious groups responding to feedback through migration and resettlement (Butler, Wacker, & Balmer, 2003; Gaustad, 2003; Jenkins, 2000). Galanter (1999) also notes that active, successful recruitment efforts help to minimize the damage done by negative feedback.

Related to feedback is the function of boundary control. Boundary control functions to protect the system from outside influences that are perceived to be dangerous to the group's mission or functions. The group must, in a sense, draw a line to establish geographic and interpersonal boundaries or safety zones. A fear of outsiders can help a group establish its boundaries, but it can also lead to paranoia. Galanter (1999) notes:

> At times, outright paranoia at the system's boundary may assume sufficient intensity to meet diagnostic criteria for a commonly held delusional system. Such a state is termed a shared paranoid disorder, wherein a delusional state is shared among two or more people so that the pathological perspective of one person in the group is supported by that of the others. (p. 107)

It is at the boundary where problems seem to erupt between outsiders, law enforcement, and the religious group. In some cases, groups define their perimeters with physical structures such as fences, fortresses, or barricades. For Jim Jones and the Peoples Temple, once their "boundary" was perceived to have been irrevocably breached, a mass suicide ensued. In the case of the religious group called MOVE, boundary control was exhibited through a barricade erected in a row house in Philadelphia, which was destroyed when authorities first hosed it with water, followed by explosives and gunfire. Fire eventually razed the building and killed eleven members of the MOVE organization, leaving more than two hundred citizens of Philadelphia homeless. In Waco, Texas, a fifty-one-day siege by law enforcement at the Branch Davidians' compound killed eighty-six Branch Davidians and four law enforcement agents and injured numerous others.

In these situations, maintenance of the boundary becomes a deadly affair for both the religious groups and the law enforcement officials who attempt to penetrate the physical and/or emotional boundary of the group.

Another way to look at the social system of a DRG is to compare it to an abusive family system. Isolation from the broader community and the power differential established by the leader create circumstances in which abuse can occur within the organization. Members establish, in effect, a new family system, and, as is the case in abusive families, isolation and power differentials can fuel physical, emotional, sexual, and financial abuse. The same factors that predispose traditional families to abusive behavior (see Kurst-Swanger & Petcosky, 2003) are likely to be present in any community where individuals live together. Thus, like many families, religious groups that restrict their boundaries may be at risk of abuse.

Women and children are most vulnerable to physical, sexual, and emotional victimization. Women are at particular risk of sexual exploitation (Lalich, 1997), and children are at risk of medical and educational neglect as well as physical, sexual, and emotional abuse (Schwartz & Kaslow, 2001). For example, Sharon Ringe (1992) noted that the patriarchal text of the Bible has been used by many to support oppressive rule over women and justify spousal abuse. As you will recall Chapter 5, this belief system is present in many religious traditions. Thus, leaders may use such interpretations of the Bible as a justification for physical punishment to keep members of their flock in line. In fact, some may even perceive it as their "duty" to "educate" members through emotional, physical, or sexual violence. Leaders may also engage in abusive acts as a result of their own history of victimization, mental illness, or substance abuse; however, little information about the psychosocial histories of DRG leaders is available.

Comparisons with Other Criminal Groups

So far in this chapter we have explored the elements that combine to elicit criminality from religiously oriented groups. Charismatic leadership and specific belief systems, coupled with group processes, can ignite criminality when a group chooses to respond to external stimuli. Of critical importance is the notion of boundary control. Given the influence of these group dynamics, are religious groups that engage in destructive behavior really that different from other groups that commit crime or are considered a threat to the community? It might help briefly to compare and contrast the criminal religious group with other known types of criminal groups to shed some light on how leadership, beliefs, and group processes transform into criminality.

Let us first compare the DRG with a typical street gang. I would agree with George Knox's (1999) assessment that "cult" groups have much in common with "gangs." Both can restrict members' freedom of thought, demand total allegiance to the self-proclaimed leader, and encourage dependence on group identity and estrangement from the larger establishment. Both may employ internal sanctions for disobedience. Both groups rely on their leaders; however, gangs tend not to dissolve when their leaders have been displaced by imprisonment or death, which suggests that gangs are held together by more than just the charismatic qualities of their leaders. In the case of some religious groups, leaders are considered divine, messiahs, or prophets, and their leadership takes on a holy dimension.

In addition, both cults and gangs tend to recruit among those in need of social and personal acceptance. Young people are especially drawn to such groups because they offer a sense of being, belonging, believing, and benevolence (Levine, 1999). In their quest for self-identity, a sense of social belonging, and purpose and meaning for their life, youth can be drawn to groups that appear to provide substantial relief.

Group cohesion is an important feature of gangs as well, even though membership may remain fluid. Shared beliefs are also likely to be present. However, the beliefs of the gang are not likely to resemble religious or spiritual beliefs; rather, gang members may share beliefs about life, family, survival, the law, criminality, and so on. Both groups may rationalize their actions through a belief that the end justifies the means.

Gangs also come into difficulty around issues of boundary control; thus a gang is probably even more likely to escalate its levels of criminality in response to, or in defense of, some type of external threat or pressure. Also, as for a DRG, those external pressures can come from the dominant culture, families, and law enforcement. For gangs, conflicts with rival gangs involve boundaries. For example, in the case of Chinese gangs in New York City, gang wars tend to erupt when boundaries are infringed by other gangs (Kelly, Chin, & Fagen, 1993). Boundaries, or "turf," are important to gangs because they provide a safe haven for gang members and a defined market in which to operate their criminal activities. Thus, in the case of gangs, leadership, beliefs, and group process also function toward criminality.

One critical difference between gangs and DRGs is their overall purpose for assembly. Although both draw members for social and psychological reasons, crime commission is part of the "mission" of a gang and is what distinguishes the group from the dominant culture. Gang members tend to participate in crime as a matter of course or duty, and crime is deliberate and often predatory. Also, gang membership tends to be more homogeneous in terms of race, class, and gender (Levine, 1999).

Destructive religious groups also share some features with organized crime networks. Modern organized crime networks, also known as "criminal enterprises," "criminal organizations," "crime syndicates," or in some cases "crime families," are structured associations of people who conspire to supply illegal goods and services. Groups that operate across national boundaries are labeled "transnational organized crime." Albanese (2000) succinctly defines an organized crime network as "an organization that operates rationally for profit, the use of force, or threats, and the need for corruption to maintain immunity from law enforcement" (p. 411). Criminal activities include prostitution, gambling, loan sharking, drug trafficking, labor racketeering, counterfeiting, selling firearms, money laundering, corruption, coercion, arson, illegal disposal of hazardous waste, human trafficking, and violence. The central purpose of association, and the crimes they commit, is financial profit.

How are destructive religious groups similar to these professional criminal organizations? Obviously, they are dissimilar in purpose. The destructive religious group, for the most part, coalesces around religious ideologies and commits crime as an auxiliary activity. Crime becomes a "sacrifice" necessary to achieve or preserve religious obligations. This is reinforced by the belief that God (however God may be defined) will serve as the final judge and jury for their collective actions. In the case of organized crime, groups function for the exact purpose of committing crime for financial gain with no particular ideology guiding their choices.

This, of course, is not to exclude those crimes that members of religious organizations commit for financial gain. Crimes committed to benefit the religious organization financially may also be considered a type of corporate or organizational crime. The financial gain motive exists for some religious groups, yet the long-term intention is not get rich but to gather the funds necessary to sustain their religious objectives. For example, in 1997 several individuals were sentenced in federal court for a string of bank robberies in the state of Washington. Verne Jay Merrell, Charles Barbee, and Robert S. Berry were apprehended by FBI agents outside a bank in Portland as the men were making preparations to rob the bank. The men, all Christian Identity believers, identified themselves as the Phineas Priesthood. The Phineas Priesthood is not really a church, sect, or cult but rather a small group of self-proclaimed "priests" who see it as their mission to act as vigilantes of Christianity. Bank robberies help to finance their mission, which in this case involved terrorist bombings. We discuss groups such as this in greater detail in Chapter 8.

Like religious organizations, organized crime groups are structured in a variety of ways; some may appear highly structured, while others are more loosely affiliated (Firestone, 1993). Some criminal enterprises may also associate with local street gangs to achieve their goals (Kelly, Chin, & Fagan, 1993). In the case of transnational organized crime groups, similarities can be drawn to political terrorist groups in which loosely organized networks of cells operate to give organizational flexibility and efficacy (Shelley & Picarelli, 2002). Southerland and Potter (1993, p. 264) found that criminal enterprises tend to be small in size, centralized with short hierarchies, with little specialization and unwritten formalization based on socialization. They argue that this type of organizational structure is necessary to achieve criminal goals in an environment in which they may be closely watched by law enforcement officials. Like DRGs, an organized crime group comprises two or more individuals and may not necessarily be part of a larger criminal enterprise. Some organized crime groups are structured along racial, ethnic, or nationality lines, such as La Cosa Nostra, Triads and Tongs, Yakuza, and the Russian Mafia. Others are based on geographic boundaries or common product interests, as is the case in drug trafficking (Albanese, 2000).

Like DRGs, many organized crime groups integrate legitimate activities with illegal ones. Environmental factors influence the frequency and type of criminal activity of organized crime groups. Environment factors include market diversity, complexity and stability, and levels of hostility in interactions with the external environment (Southerland & Potter, 1993). Thus, organized crime groups must also negotiate boundary control issues, which may ultimately result in criminal activities that are reactive or defensive in nature.

Preventing Reactive/Defensive Religion-Related Crimes

Gangs and other organized crime groups appear to have much in common with DRGs. Yet criminological research has rarely considered religious groups in its matrix of structured group criminality, and religious groups have generally not been studied alongside gangs, the mafia, or other criminal enterprises. It may be important to view some religious groups in the same light. Certainly the management of cases involving religiously motivated crime is equally challenging for law enforcement officials. This is especially true within the context of homeland security, international terrorism, and political radicalism.

Preventing reactive or defensive religion-related crime requires an analysis of the relationship between psychology and religion within the context of group function. Being able to predict which groups will ultimately resolve their issues through crime commission is a daunting task. The key appears to lie in developing a greater understanding of the thoughts and behavior patterns of particular religious leaders and their specific behavior in relation to boundary control. Observing what causes changes in the levels of tension or hostility at the border between a religious group and the external community is likely to play a significant role in the prevention of future violence. Since no one factor can fully predict the eruption of violence, it is important to recognize the complex, multidimensional internal and external factors involved. Mayer (2001) presented a schematic tool that is useful to visualize the various internal and external factors associated with violence, which includes organizational elements, environmental influences, and emotional responses to various stimuli.

These red flags can signal to law enforcement officials that trouble may be on the horizon. Yet any monitoring of religious group activity must be undertaken with great care. The theology and ideologies of a group must be not only understood but respected. A delicate balance must be achieved whereby religious values are preserved while the health and well-being of the community at large are safeguarded and protected. Intervention strategies should be aimed at de-escalating the fear, anxiety, and paranoia (Whitsel, 2000) that often exist at the boundaries between religious groups and the broader community. End-of-world concerns or enthusiasm must be tempered against the realities of group process and behavior. Law enforcement officials must listen carefully to the concerns of the leader and the group to discern any subtleties in the negotiation of boundaries, faith, and self-preservation. This may require law enforcement officials to employ specific techniques to fit the psychological dynamics of different religious groups, so that they can avoid the possibility of becoming an "instrument of the prophecy" (Baker, 2001).

For instance, law enforcement intervention with the MOVE organization in Philadelphia and the Branch Davidians in Waco, Texas, ended in complete and utter tragedy. In both cases, law enforcement officials were drawn into a no-win situation, which some critics argue was in part of their own making. In both cases, people lost their lives and property was damaged. Critics have charged that law enforcement officials acted without cause or intervened inappropriately. Some believe that these tragedies have also created a groundswell of antigovernment sentiment that has helped to cement the militia movement (Kaplan, 1997).

The federal assault on the Branch Davidian compound in Waco Texas, which began in February, 1993, resulted in a siege between Branch Davidian followers and federal officials that lasted fifty-one days. The siege ended on April 19 when the complex was destroyed by fire. In the end, almost all of the religious adherents lost their lives, including their charismatic leader, David Koresh. Federal agents also lost their lives on that fateful day, two years to the day later, the FBI building in Oklahoma City was bombed by Timothy McVeigh, killing 168 people in retribution for the acts of the federal government against the Branch Davidians, as well as other incidents.

The MOVE organization, residing in a row house on Osage Street in West Philadelphia, had conflicts with their neighbors and police officers over the course of several years. In 1985, police attempted to serve arrest warrants on four MOVE members. After communications broke down between the group's leader, Conrad Africa, and city officials, the police chief and the mayor decided to make a full-on assault to remove the MOVE members from their residence. MOVE was suspected to have secured weapons in their barricaded row house, and their growing hostility toward the community concerned local officials. Police evacuated about 500 residents from the neighborhood and began applying pressure to group. First, the building was hosed with thousands of gallons of water, which resulted in MOVE members returning gunfire. The incident escalated when officials responded with more than 7,000 rounds of ammunition and dropped an explosive device on top of the building, which ignited a fire in the old structure. Officials purposefully waited about 40 minutes before responding to the fire. This decision ultimately cost the lives of eleven MOVE members and left 250 other neighborhood residents homeless (Galanter, 1999).

Only two members of MOVE survived the ordeal, one of whom was Ramona Africa, who was subsequently sentenced to seven years in prison for her role in the confrontation. Later, civil suits were successfully launched against city officials on behalf of Ramona and other MOVE members. Today, the MOVE organization is headquartered in a Victorian stone house in West Philadelphia. They appear to co-exist peacefully with their neighbors and the police (Hill, 2002). Ramona Africa continues to speak publicly regarding the incident and religious freedom in America.

Like Jonestown, the MOVE and Branch Davidian tragedies have left an indelible mark on American history and have taught law enforcement valuable lessons on how best to approach and manage potentially violent situations involving religious groups. It is important that law enforcement officials understand that the tactic of waiting and watching, without provoking a leader, is a more apt approach to potential confrontation (Galanter, 1999). A process of dialogue will likely yield greater success (Kaplan, 1997).

8

Violence against Abortion Providers

In March 2005, the Bureau of Alcohol, Tobacco, Firearms and Explosives (ATF) and the Olympia Police Department reached out to the public to request information regarding an arson that had severely damaged a women's health clinic in Olympia, Washington. Reward money, in the amount of $5,000, has been offered for any information that leads to the arrest and conviction of the individuals behind the fire, which occurred in January 2005 at the Eastside Women's Health Clinic. The clinic suffered $500,000 worth of damage. Luckily, no one was in the building when the fire was set on the roof. At the time of writing, no arrest has been made.

The structure of building, equipment, and clinic records were damaged. Critical health services for women were interrupted. However, one of the biggest blows came from the insurance company when it came time to rebuild. The clinic's primary insurer cancelled their property and casualty policy, and other insurers offered replacement policies with exorbitant fees attached. The clinic was forced to agree not to provide abortion services to secure an insurance policy that was affordable (Shannon, 2006). This led to the passage of a bill by state lawmakers to protect organizations such as the Eastside Women's Health Clinic from losing insurance coverage if they become victims of malicious conduct such as arson.

Why would insurance companies find the performance of abortions to be a property insurance risk? Well, since the landmark U.S. Supreme Court decision in *Roe v. Wade* on January 22, 1973, there has been great cause for concern. In *Roe v. Wade* the Court struck down state criminal laws that made abortion illegal, reasoning that such laws violated the constitutional rights of women. The ruling provided women and their doctors the opportunity to make decisions regarding abortion in the first trimester of pregnancy. Abortions performed in subsequent months are subject to state statutes. With this decision, women gained the right to make reproductive decisions, and those women who needed to terminate their pregnancy could now do so legally within a medically safe environment. The decision, however, ignited a firestorm of debate that continues today, some thirty years later. The controversy has divided Americans into two camps—"pro-life" or "pro-choice"—although the terms are really misnomers. Blanchard and Prewitt (1993) note:

> The terms *pro-life* and *pro-choice* are political statements by opposing sides in the abortion controversy, and each side resents and protests the name(s) chosen by the other side. Each is seeking to seize the "high ground" of the ethical/moral debate while appealing to as wide a constituency as possible. Those calling themselves pro-lifers hold that pro-choicers are really pro-death, while pro-choicers maintain that the anti-abortionists are really anti-women. (p. 12)

Many Americans may align themselves with one camp or another, although the reality is that there is no clear consensus on what *pro-life* or *pro-choice* really signifies. For example, some pro-lifers support the death penalty or war, while many pro-choicers may personally not chose abortion themselves. They may even make voting or other decisions on the basis of these views.

For some, the fervor of their religious convictions compels them to take a more active role in protesting abortion. Although the vast majority of pro-lifers protest the legality of abortion through legal channels, some are willing to commit the most heinous of criminal acts to defend their principles. These individuals, responding to the legal status of abortion after *Roe v. Wade*, commit reactive/defensive religion-related crimes that not only destroy the physical structures of abortion clinics, as was the case in the fire that damaged the Eastside Women's Health Clinic, but terrorize professionals who work in settings where abortions are performed as well as victimizing women seeking medical services.

The crimes committed are real and have caused immeasurable damage to life, limb, and property. One can understand the stance that a property insurer might take, considering that a total of 41 bombings, 173 arsons, 93 attempted bombings or arsons, and an additional 620 bomb threats specifically targeting facilities where abortions are performed occurred in North America between 1977 and March 2007 (NAF, 2007). Even health clinics that do not perform abortions have been targeted. For instance, in September 2006 David McMenemy of Detroit, who mistakenly thought the Edgerton Women's Health Clinic in Davenport, Iowa, performed abortions, drove his car into the facility, sprayed the first-floor lobby with gasoline, and then ignited it. He was convicted on federal arson charges (AP, 2007). Yet this is only one of many criminal incidents that have been perpetrated against abortion providers since *Roe v. Wade* was decided. According to the National Abortion Federation, a total of 5,622 acts of violence against abortion providers have been reported since 1977, with 1,285 acts of violence reported during 2005–2007 (NAF, 2007). At this point in our history, this crime problem is best described as domestic terrorism. Such criminal acts are widespread, pervasive, and appear to be relentless.

This chapter examines the distinctive features of this type of religion-related crime. Blending politics and religion, abortion-related crime is a function of the status quo. Citizens, frustrated by both the legal and social status of reproductive health in the United States, have responded with a rising degree of violence in what presents as a continued threat requiring close monitoring. First, we explore some of the characteristics of abortion-related crime and present the most up-to-date prevalence data available. The next section illustrates the strong connection such crimes have with religion. Although little is known about the activist groups that have carried out the vast majority of criminal activity, it is clear that religious beliefs are a driving force in their actions. Finally, legal and political responses to the problem are identified.

Defining the Crime Problem

Before *Roe v. Wade* in 1973, women who terminated their pregnancies and any health care provider who assisted in the process were considered criminals. Reproductive politics have been in play throughout American history (Solinger, 2005); thus, it is important to note that women have historically had little control over their own bodies. Just prior to *Roe*, it was even illegal for women to gain access to contraceptives. Anti-contraceptive laws were nullified by the U.S. Supreme Court ruling in *Griswold v. Connecticut* in 1965, which struck down a Connecticut statute that made the use of any drug or article to prevent conception a crime, even for married couples. In 1972, the Court ruled on *Eisenstadt v. Baird*, expanding the right of access to contraceptives to unmarried individuals. Also during this period, women who were raped by their husbands had very little legal protection, since most states embedded exemptions in their rape statutes for marital relationships.

Some women risked criminal prosecution by terminating their pregnancies through illegal, and often dangerous, means. Some initiated abortion themselves, while others found someone else to perform the deed in the dark shadows of a motel room or on a cold kitchen table. To find a willing medical provider, some women were forced to flee the country. Many women traveled to Mexico for help. For example, Patricia Maginnis made a conscious decision to break the law in 1966 in San Francisco when she began referring women to physicians in Mexico and Japan for abortion services. Her defiance of the law led to the development of an organization called the Association to Repeal Abortion Laws (ARAL), the creation of a feminist-based health care agency (Reagan, 2000), and her eventual arrest (Baird-Windle & Bader, 2001). She, and other activists like her, were willing to break the law to ensure that women could make their own reproductive decisions and, when necessary, had access to affordable, safe abortions.

After *Roe*, "the Justices took an enormous step in making women and men equal: for the first time, women had what men had—the right to walk away from an unplanned pregnancy" (Baird-Windle & Bader, 2001, p. 21). Since this landmark decision, the political, religious, and moral debate over abortion and women's right to make reproductive decisions has never subsided. Today, however, the tide has turned, and those who engage in illegal acts against women seeking to terminate their pregnancies or against their health care providers have become the criminals.

It is probably fair to say that both sides have resorted to criminality to further their cause; however, anti-abortionists are responsible for the vast majority of the crime, especially the violent crime, associated with the abortion issue and thus will be the focus here. A report issued by the Life Research Institute claims more violence has been committed against than by pro-lifers (Life Research Institute, 1995); however, it is difficult to determine the validity of their claims on the basis of their methodology. Since the organization has no easily accessible presence on the World Wide Web, it is difficult to evaluate the relevance of their findings. Although the research may be questionable, it is not unlikely that many pro-life activists have felt victimized by police or others as they have engaged in what they refer to as "counseling" or "prayer" when they demonstrate against abortion. My goal here is not to diminish their experience but to point out that the vast majority of criminal activity has been targeted at individuals who perform abortions, their staff, and the facilities that house them. Also, since the crime targeted against the providers has tended to be religiously motivated, it is more appropriate that this text focus on the crimes associated with anti-abortion activism.

Much of the more violent criminality has been widely publicized by the media, so it is likely that you can recall hearing about the murders of abortion doctors in the mid-1990s or the forty-one bombings of clinics since 1977. Law enforcement officials have able to attribute to anti-abortion motives the murders of seven people since 1993, and seventeen more murder attempts were made during the same period (NAF, 2007). Although the media covered these incidents adequately at the time, the crime associated with the anti-abortion movement has been quietly dealt with by abortion providers and the law enforcement agencies that respond to their concerns. The more pervasive, relentless disruption and disturbances have eluded public attention, leaving some with the impression that criminal acts are only episodic or the result of only a handful of misguided religious zealots.

Sadly, the ongoing victimization of reproductive health employees has not been fully acknowledged. Some authors have brought such stories to life in their works. For example, Patricia Baird-Windle and Eleanor J. Bader (2001) eloquently describe the types of crimes committed against abortion workers nationwide in their book *Targets of Hatred: Anti-abortion Terrorism*. Recounting the experiences of 190 reproductive health providers in the United States and Canada, they paint a vivid picture of the day-to-day realities of this profession. Dallas A. Blanchard and Terry J. Prewitt (1993) explore the dynamics of anti-abortion violence through a close examination of the three abortion clinic bombings that occurred in Pensacola, Florida, on Christmas Day in 1984.

Measuring the prevalence of abortion-related crime is an arduous task. Since crime statistics are gathered by the FBI through the Uniform Crime Reporting (UCR) system, crimes associated with anti-abortion activism are counted according to the type of crime that was reported to police (e.g., arson, burglary). Information about the context of these crimes is essentially lost in the UCR method of gathering crime statistics. Recognizing the limitations of the UCR system, the FBI and the Bureau of Justice Statistics are currently rolling out a new method of measurement referred to as the National Incident-Based Reporting System (NIBRS). The new system allows for a record to be developed on each crime reported, giving officials more information on the context in which offenses occur. Thus, in the future we may be able to capture the dynamics of abortion-related crime and track the prevalence on a national scale. However, today, the only source available is the data collected by the National Abortion Federation (NAF), a professional association representing abortion providers in North America. Their data include all incidents reported to them by their members. Obviously, this presents limitations as well, and the NAF claims that the actual number of incidents is likely much higher.

NAF statistics suggest that much of the more violent crime has subsided in recent years, yet the insidious harassment continues. The terror campaign against abortion providers keeps both abortion providers and law enforcement officials vigilant. For example, on June 19, 2006, the U.S. attorney for the district of Maryland, Rod J. Rosenstein, announced in a press release that Robert F. Weiler Jr. (aged twenty-five) had been indicted by a federal grand jury on charges of illegally possessing a firearm, possessing a stolen firearm, and making an unregistered destructive device. Court documents indicate that Weiler was planning to bomb an abortion clinic and to shoot doctors who performed abortions. Law enforcement officials did find a bomb located in the closet of his home and rendered it safe. He pled guilty to the charges in October 2006 (USDOJ, 2006).

It is important that we recognize the reality that anti-abortion criminality is likely to continue in the future. For some anti-abortionists, their criminal activities are meant to "rescue" as many unborn babies as possible on given days of disruption. For others, criminal action is a specific strategy intended to dismantle the industry by terrorizing staff and clients. A more organized criminal conspiracy is still not out of the question. The following examples are meant to draw attention to the types of crimes endured by abortion workers in recent years, particularly those that continue to escape the attention of the media. This discussion does not detail all criminal acts but is meant to illustrate the challenges facing abortion providers and law enforcement officials.

Butyric Acid Threats

Butyric acid is foul-smelling, viscous liquid that is hazardous because it is corrosive and causes irreversible damage to human tissue. Contact with butyric acid can cause severe irritation and burns of the eyes and skin. Breathing it in can irritate the nose, throat, and lungs. It can be easily purchased over the Internet. Anti-abortionists have used butyric acid as a weapon against abortion facilities. The introduction of the substance into clinics has disrupted services, terrorized staff and clients, and caused thousands of dollars' worth of damage. Abortion facilities have had to close and to replace carpeting and furniture (NAF, 2006)—not to mention the emotional toll such an attack takes on staff and clients.

According to the NAF (2007), approximately 100 butyric acid attacks have been made on abortion facilities in the United States and Canada since 1977. Most of the attacks took place between 1992 and 1994, although nineteen attacks were reported in 1998. There have been no reported attacks since then (as of August 2007).

Anthrax Threats

Anthrax is an acute infectious disease caused by the spore-forming bacterium *Bacillus anthracis*. It occurs most commonly in wild animals and in domesticated animals such as cattle, sheep, goats, camels, antelopes, and other herbivores. Humans can also be infected with the disease if they come into contact with infected animals or their products. Anthrax is most common in agricultural regions such as South and Central America, southern and eastern Europe, Asia, Africa, the Caribbean, and the Middle East. Anthrax has occurred in the United States in wild livestock.

Anthrax infection can occur through the skin when the bacterium enters a cut or abrasion. About 20 percent of untreated cases of transmission are fatal. Transmission can also occur through inhalation, which often results in death. The infection can also be transmitted by eating undercooked contaminated meat products. Transmission can occur through contact with contaminated soil or by handling products from infected animals, and between 25 and 60 percent of cases are fatal. Anthrax is not known to be spread by human-to-human contact (CDC, 2005).

Americans became very familiar with anthrax after September 11, 2001, when the threat of bioterrorism became a reality. Abortion providers gained their knowledge of the deadly infection in 1998 when a dozen clinics received letters containing a white powder, threatening anthrax poisoning. The letters, signed by the "Army of God," claimed to contain anthrax spores and that anyone who came in contact with the letter would be infected. Over the course of the next few years, another 643 letters were sent to clinics threatening exposure to anthrax. Of these, 554 letters were attributed to anti-abortionist Clayton Waagner, a self-proclaimed abortion terrorist who capitalized on the national anthrax scare after September 11 by sending out the threatening letters in October and November 2001. He was eventually convicted of fifty-one federal charges, including extortion, threatening to use a weapon of mass destruction, and violating the Freedom of Access to Clinic Entrances Act (FACE, discussed in next section). Waagner was already serving a forty-nine-year sentence for firearms and escape convictions in Illinois and Ohio, and U.S. district judge Anita Brody sentenced him to another nineteen years. Representing himself at trial, he told the jury during closing arguments:

> It's been clearly demonstrated that I am the antiabortion extremist, a terror-ist to the abortion industry. There's no question there that I terrorized these people any way I could ... I did it systematically; I did it over a period of time. I worked as hard as I could to do that (Shiffman, 2005).

Some twenty states have enacted specific legislation to accommodate threats made by letter, such as the ones sent by Clayton Waagner. Federal law protects against interstate threats or harassment using the mail or electronic communication (Miller, 2001).

Stalking

Stalking is a pattern of persistent and repeated unwanted attention or communication, threats, and harassment against an abortion provider, staff member, or patient to induce fear. Stalking and threatening others is considered a very specific problem behavior by forensic mental health experts (Warren, MacKenzie, Mullen, & Ogloff, 2005) and is illegal under criminal statute. Miller (2001) conducted an extensive review of state laws on stalking. He found that state statutes vary in their definitions of stalking, but, as of 1999, all states had enacted criminal laws that address the problem of stalking. All have provisions making stalking a felony crime; however, many vary on what types of stalking behaviors constitute a felony, such as stalking with a weapon, repeat stalking, whether the stalker has to be in the physical presence of the victim, and so on. In some states an overt threat toward the victim must be made for stalking laws to apply; in others, an implied threat is adequate. Federal law provides felony provisions for interstate stalking. Other criminal laws may also apply to the stalking of an abortion provider, such as harassment, terrorist threats, intimidation, and extortion. In addition, twenty-nine states allow for civil protection orders against stalkers, and violation of those orders is a criminal action in many states; however, only ten states have a registry for such protective orders.

Stalking has a significant impact on victims. Research indicates that victims often experience symptoms associated with post-traumatic stress disorder, including anxiety, sleep or appetite disturbances, and other stress reactions (Mullen, Pathe, & Purcell, 2000). In addition, victims often restrict their social activities, make lifestyle changes, and even relocate.

Many occupational groups have endured stalking as a consequence of their jobs, including celebrities, lawmakers, and judges. For example, in June 2004 forty-one-year-old John Mikula was accused of stalking a police lieutenant, a prosecutor, and two town justices who were involved in his previous conviction for stalking a woman in a town near Buffalo, New York. Law enforcement officials found weapons, materials for making a bomb, and evidence he was associated with the Army of God (discussed below) at his residence (Herbeck, 2004). Even psychologists are susceptible to the intrusions of their clients through stalking (Purcell, Powell, & Mullen, 2005). Some abortion workers who are under constant siege from anti-abortionists eventually leave their jobs to relieve the stress and anxiety (Baird-Windle & Bader, 2001).

The NAF (2007) reports that 490 acts of stalking, which they define as the persistent following, threatening, and harassment of an abortion provider, staff member, or patient away from the clinic, occurred between 1993 and

August 2007. The NAF began tabulating the crime of stalking in 1993 and recorded the highest number of stalking offenses in that year, with 188 reported incidents. State law changes in the 1990s may have helped decrease stalking offenses in subsequent years. However, death threats continue. A total of 388 death threats have been documented since 1977, with a total of 23 threats made between 2005 and August 2007 (NAF, 2007).

A Campaign of Harassment and Terror

Harassment is a crime related to stalking. It can be defined as the persistent bothering or annoying of another person. Abortion workers and women seeking to terminate their pregnancies are at risk of being harassed by anti-abortionists. In some instances it is misleading to categorize incidents as simple harassment, since their purpose is often to terrorize. Harassment is generally considered a low-level crime; however, it is one that causes victims great torment and can cause much disruption in the day-to-day operations of a health clinic. The NAF (2007) documented 11,812 incidents of hate mail or harassing phone calls from 1977 to August 2007, with an additional 273 incidents of e-mail or Internet harassment. E-mail and Internet harassment are relatively new phenomena, and these 273 incidents have occurred since 2002. Also, clinics and staff have had to deal with 104 incidents of a hoax device or suspect package and a total of 623 bomb threats. In addition, 378 incidents of invasion, 1,306 incidents of vandalism, 1,727 incidents of trespassing, and 128 burglaries have occurred. Blockades intended to stop women from entering family planning facilities have resulted in 37,715 arrests, with a total of 752 clinic blockades reported (NAF, 2007).

Perhaps the most frightening and potentially dangerous form of harassment and terror has been the "Wanted" posters listing the names and addresses of doctors who performed abortions. The American Coalition of Life Activists (ACLA) marked the anniversary of *Roe v. Wade* in 1995 by presenting the "Deadly Dozen" poster, which declared the doctors guilty of crimes against humanity and offered a $5,000 reward for information leading to their arrest and conviction and the revocation of their medical license. The poster was later published in the *Life Advocate* magazine and distributed at ACLA events. Later, the ACLA unveiled a second poster featuring Dr. Robert Crist that published his home and work address. To mark the 1996 anniversary of *Roe v. Wade*, the ACLA compiled a list of doctors, staff, lawmakers, judges, and other pro-choice supporter, naming the record the "Nuremberg Files," which was then published on the Web. The Web site also included the names of those already victimized by anti-abortionists, with special annotation for those who had already been killed. Neither the posters nor the Web site included any explicit threat of violence; however, the threat was implied.

Since five people had been killed by anti-abortionists in 1993–1994, and the first poster was distributed the next year, the threat was considered real by those affected. In turn, Planned Parenthood and some of the doctors filed a lawsuit against the ACLA and others (*Planned Parenthood of the Columbia/Willamette Inc. v. American Coalition of Life Activists et al. No. 9935320*). They argued the threats violated state and federal laws such as the Freedom of Access to Clinic Entrances Act of 1994 and the Racketeer Influenced and Corrupt Organizations Act (RICO) (both discussed below). The ACLA argued their speech was protected under the First Amendment. A federal jury awarded damages in the amount of $108.5 million to Planned Parenthood and the doctors, which was later lowered to $5 million by the Ninth U.S. Circuit Court of Appeals. Another appeal was filed, which ultimately reduced the judgment to $4.73 million. The District Court also issued an injunction barring the ACLA from making or distributing the posters or the Web page. Remnants of the Nuremberg Files still exist on the Web; however, the Web site has since been removed. The ACLA, in a last appeal attempt, turned to the U.S. Supreme Court. In May 2006 the Court refused to hear their complaint, without comment, ending the ten-year-long case.

A Religion-Related Crime

Anti-abortion crime is characteristic of the reactive/defensive type of religion-related crime. Crimes are committed in reaction to the current legal status of abortion. The sole purpose is to undermine the legal status of reproductive health services; thus, this is also considered a political crime. However, unlike similar crimes committed for political reasons by other terrorist-type organizations, such as animal rights groups or environmental activists, anti-abortion criminality is directly linked to groups who use religious justifications for their actions. In fact, religion appears to plays a prominent role in the criminal activity that has plagued the reproductive health profession since 1973. Anti-abortionist groups claiming responsibility for much of the violence and disruption have chosen names that specifically identify their religious roots, such as the Army of God, the Phineas Priesthood, Lambs of Christ, Advocates for Life Ministries, Missionaries to the Pre Born, and Believers Against Child Killing (BACK). As these names may imply, a variety of biblical passages provide the guidance and justification for criminal action against what they refer to as "merchants of death," "abortion mills," "abortion collaborators," or "abortionists." For example, the following passages are posted on the Web page of the Army of God (http://www.armyofgod.com).

> *Psalm 106:37, 38:* Yea, they sacrificed their sons and their daughters unto devils And shed innocent blood, even the blood of their sons and of their daughters.
>
> *Jeremiah 9:1:* Oh that my head were waters, and mine eyes a fountain of tears, that I might weep day and night for the slain of the daughter of my people!
>
> *Genesis 1:28:* And God blessed them, and God said unto them, Be fruitful, and multiply, and replenish the earth.
>
> *Jeremiah 48:10:* Cursed be he that doeth the work of the LORD deceitfully, and cursed be he that keepeth back his sword from blood.

In fact, the identification with Christian beliefs is also motivating some activists to target Christian churches to remind them of their duty to fight abortion. For example, an organization called the Missionaries to the Unborn is seeking to develop a "list of the apathetic." They are seeking information regarding churches and religious leaders who appear to be apathetic toward abortion (http://www. mttu.com/apathetic/index.htm). According to their Web site, they seek to "expose the shame and hypocrisy of local churches which are supposedly 'Christian' but refuse to lift a finger to help the unborn babies that are dying right outside their doors." They are seeking personal information, including the home phone number and address of the pastor. It is to be hoped that such a list will not result in the type of problems associated with the "Wanted" posters of the past.

Groups such as those mentioned above tend to be varied in their organization. Some are not organized religious groups in the traditional sense but are more loosely assembled advocacy organizations with strong Christian foundations. These groups function much like other advocacy organizations, except they often believe their criminal actions are justified by biblical principles. Other groups define themselves as ministries with specific pro-life goals, rather than as churches or congregations. In some cases, individuals who break the law are members of more established religious traditions, such as Catholics or Baptists. Other groups exist more in a state of "virtual reality," bound only by their beliefs and the Internet. Some break the law as a consequence of a simple protest, while others are involved in a more forthright campaign of criminality to reach their goals. The label destructive religious group (DRG) is befitting of these groups. What makes them different from other DRGs is their central focus on abortion.

There is no denying the commitment those who have broken the law have made to the anti-abortion campaign. Baird-Windle and Bader (2001) found that many people who protest or engage in street counseling or prayer at clinics do so eight to ten hours a day, five to six days a week, leading the authors to question their source of income: "the hardcore group arrayed against us is paid. Domestic terrorism is their job" (p. xiv). Many of the more vocal activists, particularly those who have been arrested numerous times, do appear to have a lot of time on their hands to travel from city to city to attend protests, to organize protest activities, or to maintain Web sites. Therefore, Baird-Windle and Bader (2001) may be on to something with this line of inquiry.

There is certainly no denying that some have dedicated their lives to such activities. For example, Charles Anderson from Savannah, Georgia, known for his many appearances at anti-abortion protests, legally changed his first name to Pro-life in 1987 (AP, 2005). Paul deParrie was a very active anti-abortion activist and was well known for wearing a black beret and carrying a "dead baby sign." As president of BACK, he was described as arguing that violence against doctors who perform abortions is "morally justifiable" (Taylor, 2006). BACK's Web page (http://www.backlife.org) includes the following statement:

> BACK is a political action and lobbying organization dedicated to a no-compromise anti-abortion agenda. In the legislature, BACK's *only* client will be the Unborn. BACK's *only* agenda will be the *complete* protection of their lives.

The Web page also includes a section entitled "Abortion in Light of Scripture," on which about forty biblical passages are quoted. In addition to BACK, Paul deParrie appears as the author of several other Web sites devoted to religious-political activism against abortion. He was also instrumental in crafting the "Wanted" posters described above. In May 2006, at the age of fifty-six, he died of heart failure shortly after giving a speech to other activists in a Denny's restaurant in Wilsonville, Oregon.

His wife, Bonnie deParrie, told reporters that she lost count of how many times he had been arrested and sued for his anti-abortion tactics (Taylor, 2006). For example, on the basis of an anti-stalking law in Oregon, the executive director of All Women's Health Services, Jude Hanzo, received a permanent protective order against him in 1996 after he had stalked and harassed her for more than a year. He had picketed her home, distributed "Wanted" posters with her photo and unlisted home phone number, placed her on a "hit list," and threatened her with phone calls and mail (Feminist Majority Foundation, 1996). To those who work in reproductive health, he was a threat; to his supporters, he was a Christian warrior.

Like Paul deParrie, some anti-abortionists have been arrested over and over again and proudly wear their "rap sheets" like a badge of honor. Some have publicly lent their support for using violence to protect unborn babies. For example, in a Defense Action Statement on the Web site of the Army of God, the co-signatories state:

> We, the undersigned, declare the justice of taking all godly action necessary to defend innocent human life including the use of force. We proclaim that whatever force is legitimate to defend the life of a born child is legitimate to defend the life of an unborn child.

The list of co-signatories of this statement reads much like a "who's who" of those who commit crimes against abortion clinics, since some of those listed have committed heinous crimes and have served, or are serving, time in prison for their actions. For example, Reverend Michael Bray served about four years in a federal prison for the destruction of ten clinics in the Washington DC area. He has also been the subject of several lawsuits and has authored a book titled *A Time to Kill*.

It is important to stress that although most pro-life organizations may share their biblical views on abortion with the likes of Paul deParrie or Michael Bray, most do not advocate the murder of those associated with the provision of abortion services.

Responding to Abortion-Related Crime

Crime associated with the provision of abortion services is multidimensional and thus requires a multilayered response. Police officials must respond to the day-to-day problems as they arise within their communities. Federal law enforcement officials have utilized federal laws to prosecute offenders when appropriate and have also attempted to study the issue in greater detail through a special task force convened by the U.S. attorney general. Federal lawmakers have responded through the Freedom of Access to Clinic Entrances Act (FACE) of 1994, and state legislatures have created buffer zones to protect women. In addition, the courts have been called upon to settle a wide range of legal issues. Like other crime victims, abortion providers have had to find their own ways of coping with the disruption and potential threat.

Law Enforcement Response

Since anti-abortion crime is clustered around clinics that provide abortions, responding to the crime problem has been left to the police agencies with jurisdiction over those locations. Federal, state, and local law enforcement officials have all played a role, although local law enforcement has been responsible for responding to the vast majority of criminal complaints and has been called to maintain order during protests and demonstrations. A national survey of police agencies, conducted by the Kenney and Reuland (2002) for the Police Executive Research Forum, found that two-thirds of the police agencies located in jurisdictions with known abortion providers had reported incidents of abortion-related conflict or violence within their jurisdiction, especially urban police agencies with multiple abortion providers. With a few notable exceptions, the police agencies reported that the severity of violence and conflict appears to have waned in more recent years, resulting in disturbances that they characterized as minor in comparison. Conflicts appeared to have been focused on particular clinics, and police agencies noted that public visibility, access, and location were likely explanations for why certain clinics within a jurisdiction were more apt to experience problems than others. Police agencies also noted that potential for media coverage, number of abortions performed, and the location of religious populations were also probable explanations (Kenney & Reuland, 2002).

Interestingly, in a national survey of police chiefs conducted in 1993, out of a sample of eighty-six urban police chiefs, 50 percent (forty-three) rated anti-abortionists as the group (out of a total of ten groups) most likely to commit a terrorist act in the United States within the next two years. These results suggest that police chiefs, at least those in urban areas, consider the threat of terrorism by anti-abortion groups to be very real (Carlson, 1995). In retrospect, the police chiefs were absolutely on target with their predictions, given the level of violence that occurred in the two years after the survey was completed. For example, in 1994–1995, four people were murdered, nine more murder attempts were made, and a hundred death threats were made. In addition, there were two bombings, seventeen arsons, four attempted bombings/arsons, and fifty-five bomb threats (NAF, 2007).

Federal law enforcement agencies such as the FBI and the ATF have also been involved in the investigation of crimes that violate federal law. In fact, in November 1998, the attorney general, Janet Reno, established the National Task Force on Violence Against Health Care Providers several weeks after Dr. Barnett Slepian was murdered in his home near Buffalo, New York in October. Four other physicians had been attacked in Canada and the United States in November of previous years. The date of Dr. Slepian's murder appears to be significant, because many in the anti-abortion movement have marked Remembrance Day, a November holiday to memorialize Canadian war veterans, "Remember the Unborn Children Day." Providers in Canada and the United States have historically been extra vigilant with security in the weeks before and after the holiday; the NAF had actually sent a fax to Dr. Slepian's workplace and others in the area telling providers to take additional precautions owing to the pattern and timing of the previous shootings, although miscommunication appears to have prevented a proactive police response to the warning (Baird-Windle & Bader, 2001). Eventually, James Kopp, a member of the Army of God, was convicted in 2003 for Dr. Slepian's murder.

The National Task Force on Violence Against Health Care Providers involved representatives from the FBI, ATF, U.S. Postal Inspection Service, U.S. Marshals Service, and Civil Rights and Criminal Divisions of the Department of Justice. It was led by the assistant attorney general for the Civil Rights Division of the Department of Justice. The task force was charged with coordinating the investigation and prosecution of abortion-related incidents, serving as a clearinghouse for information relating to anti-abortion violence, making security recommendations to improve the safety and protection of providers, enhancing law enforcement training, and supporting the work of local working groups and civil litigation. The task force has resulted in numerous federal arrests and convictions, and collaboration with local authorities has resulted in additional arrests and convictions (USDOJ, 2001).

A similar task force, convened in 1994, was charged with investigating the existence of a national conspiracy or conspiracies to commit crimes against reproductive health providers. Although no concrete evidence of a conspiracy was found, the possibility has not been completely ruled out. In fact, at the time of writing the ATF's Web page includes a note that the investigation is still under way (BATF, 2006). The 1994 task force was phased out in 1996, and the coordination of law enforcement responses became the responsibility of the Justice Department's Civil Rights Division. Through the 1994 task force, coupled with the enactment of FACE, the Department of Justice secured the convictions of fifty-six individuals in thirty-seven criminal cases for violations of a variety of federal laws and brought seventeen civil actions against more than a hundred individuals (USDOJ, 2000).

Public Policy

Among the most influential pieces of legislation to combat this form of religion-related crime has been the Freedom of Access to Clinic Entrances Act (18 U.S.C. 248). The act, signed into law by President Clinton in May 1994, was designed to protect those receiving reproductive health care services and those who provide those services. It prohibits "the use of force or threat of force or physical obstruction, to intentionally injure, intimidate or interfere with or attempt to injure, intimidate or interfere with any person or any class of persons from obtaining or providing reproductive health services." It also prohibits the damage or destruction of "property of a facility, or attempts to do so, because such facility provides reproductive health services." The statute created, for the first time, federal jurisdiction to protect reproductive health facilities, staff, and escorts. The penalties associated with FACE violations include fines and imprisonment. For example, first-time offenders who are involved in nonviolent physical obstruction can receive a maximum sentence of six months' incarceration and a $10,000 fine. The statute also provides for civil remedies and allows the courts to impose injunctions, compensatory and punitive damages, and coverage for legal fees (USDOJ, 2001).

The enactment of FACE also attracted attention from lawmakers as they worked to reform bankruptcy laws. Senator Charles Schumer from New York State rallied support for an amendment to the Bankruptcy Abuse Prevention and Consumer Protection Act of 2005 (P.L. 109-8) (as well as previous versions of the act). His proposed amendment would have closed a loophole in the bankruptcy laws to prevent those convicted of illegal anti-abortion activities from using bankruptcy laws to avoid paying their fines. The proposed amendment generated much controversy but was ultimately voted down. According to the Feminist Daily News Wire (2000), several anti-abortion defendants who were court-ordered to pay damages filed for bankruptcy shortly after the court dispositions were rendered.

How effective has FACE been in reducing the crime associated with the anti-abortion movement? For a report prepared by the U.S. General Accounting Office (1998), a survey was distributed to a small sample of clinics, police departments, and U.S. attorney offices that had experienced high levels of incidents before the FACE law came into effect. The purpose of the survey was to determine the effectiveness of FACE as a public policy. The results of the survey indicate that a majority of those surveyed believed FACE was serving as a deterrent, and many of the police departments located in jurisdictions where much of the clinic violence was focused reported that their officers had received specialized training and they had conducted outreach and education with local clinics. Many reported utilizing more proactive policing strategies. Many districts had created abortion violence task forces. In general, clinics reported satisfaction with their relationship with law enforcement officials. As of September 1998, a total of forty-six criminal and civil cases had been either completed or were pending, with the majority of the cases resulting in convictions. Some cases involved challenges to the constitutionality of FACE; however, these challenges have generally been unsuccessful.

In addition to FACE, federal law enforcement officials have utilized other federal laws to prosecute offenders—for example, damage or destruction of property used in interstate commerce (18 U.S.C. 844i), use of a firearm in the commission of a felony (18 U.S.C. 924c), use of the mails or commerce for bomb or fire threats (18 U.S.C. 844c), threats made by use of interstate or foreign commerce (18 U.S.C. 875, 876), interference with commerce by threats or violence (18 U.S.C. 1951), and interstate or foreign travel or transportation to aid in racketeering enterprises (18 U.S.C. 1952). Federal officials must evaluate the specific features of each case to determine which federal laws have been violated.

One complex case is illustrative. In 1986, the National Organization for Women (NOW) and two reproductive health clinics set a precedent by using the civil provisions of the 1970 Racketeer Influenced and Corrupt Organizations Act (18 U.S.C. 1964c), which allow civil claims to be brought by anyone whose business has been affected by acts under the auspices of the RICO statute as well as acts of extortion in violation of the Hobbes Act. The Hobbes Act (18 U.S.C. 1951) prohibits actual or attempted robbery or extortion affecting interstate or foreign commerce. The Hobbes Act was enacted to combat problems of racketeering in labor–management disputes; however, it has been successfully used in cases involving public corruption and corruption involving labor unions. NOW and others filed a class action lawsuit to challenge the actions of the Pro-Life Action League and other anti-abortion activists, such as Operation Rescue, engaged in clinic blockages and other violence toward health care providers. They argued that the anti-abortion activists were seeking to shut down abortion clinics through a pattern of racketeering and extortion. One of the named defendants, Joseph M. Scheidler, is National Director of the Pro-Life Action League, a national pro-life educational and activist organization based in Chicago.

The case, *NOW v. Scheidler*, made its way to the U.S. Supreme Court, which considered whether an economic motive needed to be determined for the RICO statutes to apply. The Court unanimously ruled in favor of NOW and the clinics in 1994, finding that the plain language of the statute does not require an economic motive and thus the case could go to trial. In 1998, the trial jury returned a unanimous verdict finding that the defendants had engaged in a nationwide conspiracy to deny women access to medical facilities. The jury found that Operation Rescue, Joseph Scheidler, PLAN, and their co-defendants were racketeers under RICO and should be held financially liable for damages. The named defendants in this case were further banned by a court injunction from interfering with the right of women to obtain reproductive health services. Scheidler and associates filed an appeal, arguing in part that the injunction interfered with their First Amendment rights of free speech. In *Scheidler et al. v. NOW* (2001), the Seventh Circuit Court of Appeals upheld the injunction against Scheidler and the other defendants, reasoning that the First Amendment does not protect violent conduct. Scheidler and others appealed to the U.S. Supreme Court.

In February 2003, the Supreme Court ruled on *NOW v. Scheidler* that the lower court's injunction could not be justified under the Hobbes Act, which relates to extortion, since the defendants gained no financial benefits from the clinics as a result of the crimes they committed. It sent the case back to the Seventh Circuit Court of Appeals. NOW returned to the Seventh Circuit Court in 2004 and argued that even if the defendants' acts could not be defined as extortion under the federal statutes, their acts and threats of violence do constitute extortion. The Circuit Court sent the case to a trial court to determine whether the defendants could be sued for making threats of violence, whether or not such acts had been committed in conjunction with a robbery or extortion. If so, the injunction could be upheld. The defendants again appealed to the U.S. Supreme Court, seeking relief from the injunction without further action from other courts.

The U.S. Supreme Court agreed to hear their appeal and in February 2006 ended the twenty-year legal battle. The Court ruled that the clinics could not sue under the RICO and Hobbs Acts. The Justices in *Scheidler et al. v. NOW et al.* and *Operation Rescue v. NOW* reasoned that the federal law specifically prohibits the interference in commerce by robbery or extortion and could not be used to block protests. The decision lifted the nationwide injunction; however, clinics have been federally protected since the passage of FACE in 1994, so litigation under RICO or related statutes is no longer necessary.

In addition to federal legislation, states and localities have made public policy changes to better protect women and reproductive health providers. Some states have created floating "bubble zones," which allow several feet of space around a person who is within a specific distance of a clinic and prohibit protesters from violating that personal space without consent. Colorado, Montana, and Massachusetts have established "bubble zone" laws that provide women six to eight feet of protest-free space near the door of a clinic (Guttmacher Institute, 2006). Anti-abortion activists challenged the law in Massachusetts, arguing that the buffer zone infringed on their rights of free speech since it did not equally apply to clinic employees. Massachusetts attorney general Thomas F. Reilly promised to enforce the law neutrally against anyone violating the bubble zone without consent, regardless of their specific views, and thus the First Circuit Court of Appeals upheld the law, ruling that it did not infringe on the First Amendment. Massachusetts crafted the law in response to the December 30, 1994, killing of receptionist Shannon Lowney (aged twenty-five) at a clinic in Brookline and the murder of receptionist Lee Ann Nichols (aged thirty-eight) from another Brookline clinic. Five other people were also injured during this shooting spree by John C. Salvi III. Salvi committed suicide in 1996 in a Massachusetts state prison (Savage, 2005).

Some states have also outlawed specific activities. Legislation covers activities such as the blocking of clinic entrances and exits, threatening or intimidating staff or patients, property damage, telephone harassment, creating excessive noise, possessing a weapon during a protest at a clinic, and releasing a substance that produces noxious odors on the premises of a clinic (Guttmacher Institute, 2006). The prohibition of specific activities is probably indicative of the types of problems clinics in those states have grappled with.

Unfortunately, only a handful of states have taken additional measures such as these to protect women and reproductive health facilities. It is important to note that despite law enforcement and legal successes, reproductive health providers have not always considered law enforcement responses adequate. Baird-Windle and Bader (2001) quote Ellie Smeal, president of the Feminist Majority Foundation: "we believe that both the public and law enforcement are in massive denial about the threat to providers and others" (p. 324). Such frustration is certainly echoed throughout the experiences documented by Baird-Windle and Bader (2001), leading the authors to agree that a culture of denial exists. Carlson (1995) echoes similar concerns by noting the reluctance of the FBI in the past to consider the activities of anti-abortion activists to be terrorism, even though many urban police chiefs consider them to be domestic terrorism threats.

Hate Crimes

One evening in February 1999, Jody-Gaye Bailey, a twenty-year-old Jamaican immigrant and college student, and her white fiancé, Christian Martin, were violently assaulted in their car while driving in Oakland Park, Florida. Before they were both shot with a semi-automatic weapon, the perpetrator, Robert Boltruch, tailed their car yelling racial slurs at them. Ms. Bailey was murdered by Boltruch because of the color of her skin and her interracial relationship. Boltruch made no secret of his intentions that evening; he told several people before the slaying that he wanted to "go out and kill a nigger." Boltruch proclaimed his commitment to the skinhead ideology with the word "skin" tattooed inside his lip, although members of his family claim he was a member of a nonracist skinhead group. A jury convicted Boltruch, and he is serving a life sentence for murder and a consecutive thirty-year sentence for the attempted murder of Mr. Martin.

In 2004, Kurtis William Monschke was convicted of aggravated first-degree murder for the brutal killing of Randall Townsend, a homeless white man. Monschke and three other racist skinheads killed Mr. Townsend in Tacoma, Washington, during a prolonged assault that ended when they "curb stomped" him by placing his open mouth against a railroad tie and jumping on the back of his head. Prosecutors contended that the assault was initiated by Tristain Lynn Frye, who was interested in earning the "right" to wear red shoelaces in her boots to indicate that she had attacked an enemy of the white race. Prosecutors also contended the attack was intended to raise the leadership rank of Monschke in Volksfront, a neo-Nazi group with a white supremacist agenda. After finding no African American target to assault, the crew settled on Mr. Townsend. He was considered a suitable victim because he appeared to be a homeless drug addict.

The Volksfront Web site describes drug dealers as "the lowest form of vermin" (Beirich & Potok, 2004). Monschke was sentenced to life in prison.

In November 2000, Satan worshipper Jay Scott Ballinger pled guilty to numerous federal arson charges related to the twenty-six church fires he had set across the United States. Ballinger, from Yorktown, Indiana, was sentenced to forty-two years and seven months and ordered to pay restitution of more than $3.5 million to the churches he destroyed. As a self-proclaimed "Missionary of Lucifer and a Saint of Hades," he began his criminal rampage of hate against organized Christianity in January 1994 by setting fire to the Concord Church of Christ in Lebanon, Indiana. Over the course of the next five years, he set fire to twenty-five other churches, although he has admitted to setting fifty fires in eleven states. Donald Puckett of Lebanon, Indiana, and his girlfriend Angela Wood also pled guilty for their role in assisting Ballinger (USDOJ, 2000).

Although these three cases are different, Jody-Gaye Bailey and Randall Townsend both lost their lives and numerous churches suffered substantial damage as a result of what are best categorized as hate crimes. The defendants in these cases made no secret of their political and religious views and affiliations. It is clear that hate motivated their actions, and it is likely that religion played a part in fueling their hate. Hate crime is a criminal offense against a person or property motivated in whole or in part by an offender's bias against a race, religion, disability, ethnicity/nationality, or sexual orientation (FBI, 2004).

Hate crimes are committed to intentionally harm, intimidate, or terrify individuals or groups against whom the offender has a specific prejudice. In some instances, community center property or houses of worship are destroyed or vandalized to terrify and threaten. Hate crimes are acts of individualized terrorism. Hate incidents, which involve hostile or hateful speech or other disrespectful or discriminatory behavior, are also of concern, although such acts may not violate criminal law. Hate incidents can easily escalate into dangerous situations in which violence or property destruction result. For this reason, the International Association of Chiefs of Police recommends that police officers actively defuse hate crime by responding to and documenting bias-motivated speech or behavior even when such acts do not rise to the level of a criminal offense (Turner, 2006).

Not all hate crimes have a clearly delineated connection to particular religious beliefs, nor are all organizations that appear to have a hate message involved in criminal activity. Yet the cases described above present an interesting paradox: religion can be both a justification for and a target of hate. As the examples suggest, particular religious views can spur on criminal violence against specific groups, and in other instances a person's religious affiliation may place them at risk of victimization.

This chapter explores the distinct connection between hate crime and religion. Characterizing hate crime as a reactive/defensive type of religion-related crime, this chapter begins with a brief overview of the role of religion in hate crime. Then we explore the prevalence of hate crime in the United States and discuss the measurements used to define the problem. Here we find that our current methods limit our ability to understand the phenomenon. Finally, we investigate the myriad ways citizens, lawmakers, and advocacy groups are working to fight hate crime.

Religion and Hate Crime

Although often shrouded in a political agenda, hate crime is inextricably linked to religion. Specific religious beliefs serve as a catalyst by providing a rationale that such hate is warranted and necessary, especially when these beliefs call for the extermination of gays and lesbians, nonwhites, or specific religious followers. Hate crime is characterized as reactive/defensive religion-related crime because it is as a response to some perceived threat experienced by the offender. As the cases noted above illustrate, Randall Townsend and Jody-Gaye Bailey were murdered because they both represented a threat to the vision of white supremacy held by the offenders, a vision grounded in specific passages from religious texts. Thus, hate crimes with religious overtones can be characterized as reactive/defensive religion-related crimes because of the political and/or social message such acts intend to send.

Of course, not all hate or bias-related crimes can be traced to the religiosity of their perpetrators; however, established hate groups continue to frame their propaganda within religious texts to justify their actions morally. It is clear that religion plays a distinct role, although it is sometimes unclear exactly how much of a role religiosity truly plays amid other psychological or sociological factors, since much hate crime is committed by "lone wolves." In fact, the Federal Bureau of Investigation (FBI) reports through its analysis of the National Incident-Based Reporting System (NIBRS) that during 1997–1999, about three out of four violent hate crimes involved a single offender in a single incident (Strom, 2001).

The fact that much hate crime is committed by "lone wolves" does not diminish the seriousness of these individualized acts of terrorism. It is true that it is difficult to determine, on the basis of current statistical methods, how much hate crime involves individuals affiliated with established hate groups that espouse particular religious justifications for their hate. Legitimate watchdog organizations such the Southern Poverty Law Center and the Anti-Defamation League monitor the activities of hundreds of hate groups nationwide because of the growth of hate propaganda on the Internet and its seemingly intimate connection to hate crime. It is undeniable that the Internet provides a technological pulpit from which hate groups can preach their particular blend of religion and ideology to encourage hate. Many hate groups maintain active Web sites that proudly display the religious, political, and social beliefs of their members. In some instances, hate messages are prominently displayed on the Web sites of groups that appear to be faith-based organizations, such as Kingdom Identity Ministries (http://www.kingidentity.com/doctrine), the Christian Separatist Church Society (http://www.christianseparatist.org/other/welcome), and the Church of True Israel (http://www.churchoftrueisrael.com).

Beliefs, even hateful ones, are fully protected by the U.S. Constitution. It is the reactionary responses that move individuals to act that most concern law enforcement officials and hate crime advocacy groups. Even if a group's active members do not promote the use of violence, the Internet provides a venue where groups can connect to an anonymous audience of supporters who might be incited by such hateful language or see biblical passages as a call to action. As discussed in Chapter 7, apocalyptic/fatalistic belief systems that center on the notion that the end of days is fast approaching may provide a sense of moral urgency to inspire some to act on those beliefs (Mayer, 2001). Also, charismatic leadership and the influence of group processes can combine to ignite violence among adherents, even if those adherents are only loosely tied to a specific group. It is likely that those who create and maintain such Web sites intend to tap into the psychological and emotional turmoil of potential "lone wolves" to subtly encourage them to engage in criminal activity on their behalf. The Internet appears to provide the perfect venue to incite reactionary violence.

Individuals and groups that use an inerrant reading of religious texts to defend their hate are likely to pose the greatest danger. Jacobs (2003–2004) raises provocative questions in his paper entitled "The Last Uncomfortable 'Religious' Question? Monotheistic Exclusivism and Textual Superiority in Judaism, Christianity, and Islam As Sources of Hate and Genocide," a paper he originally presented at the "Conference to Establish the Field of Hate Studies" in Spokane, Washington, in 2004. He argues that each of these religious traditions ascribes superior power to its sacred texts and that since the texts are perceived as coming directly from God or Allah, they are often read literally. In a preliminary examination of some of the texts of the three great monotheistic religious traditions—Judaism, Christianity, and Islam—he concludes:

> Judaism and Christianity and Islam continue to do harm to themselves and to others stemming from their *literal* views of their understandings of God based upon their relationship to their sacred texts … Thus, the very sacred texts of

all three monotheistic religious traditions continue to be used to justify hateful and pre-genocidal acts and behaviors based upon those readings and consequent understandings. (p. 139)

Charles Kimball (2002), in his book *When Religion Becomes Evil,* echoes these concerns. He eloquently argues:

Adhering strictly to particular interpretations of truth claims allows people to feel justified in holding all kinds of attitudes and behaviors, including beliefs and actions that contradict well-known teachings of their religion. When zealous and devout adherents elevate the teachings and beliefs of their tradition to the level of *absolute* truth claims, they open a door to the possibility that their religion will become evil. (p. 44)

Both Kimball (2002) and Jacobs (2003–2004) remind us that history is replete with examples of hatred and intolerance that have resulted in both interpersonal and mass violence—all in the name of religion. Wars have been fought and continue to be fought in reaction to or in defense of some perceived threat to religious principles. The same is true of political conflicts and acts of terrorism that continue to erupt around the globe.

Cultural and religious factors are inextricably linked to both historical and contemporary conflicts. Levin and McDevitt (2002) argue that we are in the midst of a culture of hate that is reflected in popular culture. Bigotry, intolerance, and the reinforcement of negative stereotypes describing various ethnic, racial, and religious groups pervade modern music, comedic humor, and art. This culture of hate ultimately provides social support to those who seek to act on their hateful beliefs. Certainly, we can all agree that Americans are fascinated with violence, since the use of aggression to solve conflicts can be clearly identified in movies, television programming, music, toys, sports, and computer games. Hate and violence are intertwined and inseparable. Popular culture and strong messages of intolerance transmitted by various religious traditions can combine to create powerful social reinforcement for hate crime. This is especially true for young people, who are more likely to respond to their anger and frustration in violent ways.

Woolf and Hulsizer (2002–2003) note that three common patterns appear to exist within groups that engage in mass violence: the use of aggression to solve problems, a perception of the actions of others as threats, and a belief in the superiority of the group. They argue, consistent with the views of Kimball (2002) and Jacobs (2003–2004), that religious groups are susceptible to these patterns and are more likely to adopt a doctrine of hatred when the following characteristics are present: "(1) a culture and history of violence, (2) a theology that identifies itself as the one, true religion, and (3) an orientation that keep it operating as if it were threatened" (Woolf & Hulsizer, 2002–2003, p. 9). In addition, as discussed in previous chapters, religious groups are at greater risk of participating in violence when certain other social-psychological factors are present. This requires that we understand how individuals perceive and interpret information in relation to their membership in a group and that we appreciate the nature of group dynamics. Situational factors, such as external crises that affect the group and its resources, and authoritarian leadership also play a role in religious groups adopting a hate doctrine (Woolf & Hulsizer, 2002–2003). Also important are psychological factors, such as early childhood trauma, distorted cognitions, and emotional techniques that help neutralize or absolve the offender's responsibility and guilt (Sun, 2006). Neutralization techniques, first theorized by Gresham Sykes and David Matza (1957), are rationalizations that allow offenders to commit crime, such as denying the injury they cause, denying the "humanity" of the victim, or appealing to higher loyalties. Certainly, religious doctrine can help fuel psychological problems, providing a blanket of justification for violence.

You might be asking yourself which religious doctrines or religious movements specifically call followers to absorb a hate dogma and why. Although it is beyond the scope of this text to engage in a detailed theological analysis of religious groups and their belief systems, we can take a look at the types of religious rhetoric readily available on the Internet. Here we explore some of the messages currently on the Web sites of a small sampling of organizations that appear to be religiously affiliated. As you review the passages below, a cautionary note is warranted. These passages have been selected to highlight racist and intolerant beliefs and thus may be taken out of context of the full doctrinal belief system of the religious organization. Also, these Web sites may include additional notes that proclaim violence is not supported by the organization; however, such disclaimers are probably lost amid the strong language of the doctrines.

Christian Identity Movement/Kingdom Identity Ministries

The Christian Identity Movement, or the Identity Church movement, has spawned the growth of loosely affiliated churches and organizations, such as the Kingdom Identity Ministries, across the United States since World War II. Identity churches have attracted attention from scholars and law enforcement officials because of the overt proclamation of intolerance in their belief system, their anti-government stance, and the heavy reliance on Identity teachings by other known hate groups, such as the Aryan Nations, the Order, and the Church of Jesus Christ Christian, whose members have long criminal histories.

The origins of the Identity movement lie in the British-Israelism or Anglo-Israelism movement that existed in England in the nineteenth century. Anglo-Israelism refers to the belief that the British are direct descendants of the Ten Lost Tribes of Israel. The movement never culminated in the development of religious sects, nor were members particularly encouraged to reject their traditional religious affiliations. Thus, Anglo-Israelism remained open to the different religious views of its members and created a context in which Christian Identity could later evolve its ideals. What distinguishes Identity from Anglo-Israelism is the Identity tenet that the Jews are the direct descendants of Satan (Barkun, 1997).

In fact, it is probably fair to say that Identity beliefs, although Christian based, differ vastly from those of most other Christian denominations. Identity rejects the doctrine of the rapture, a belief that many Christians share. The rapture is the time when God comes and rescues believers from the seven-year period of Tribulation. Barkun (1997) notes that since Identity views Jews as having satanic origins, the period of Tribulation provides them a welcome opportunity to battle the Jews. Identity also maintains that Jesus was not a Jew, but a descendant of the white peoples of northern Europe. Consequently, they believe "that Blacks and other non-White groups are at the same spiritual level as animals and therefore have no souls" (Levin & McDevitt, 2002, p. 110).

A briefing article entitled "Christian Identity Movement: Right-Wing Terrorism Matters," prepared by the Terrorist Research and Analytical Center (TRAC) of the FBI, chronicles anti-government beliefs as a central cause of concern. For instance, the report notes that Identity contends a Jewish conspiracy has taken over many institutions within the United States, including the government. This conspiracy has led to the passage of laws that have subverted the original intention and design of the U.S. Constitution, making the document invalid and obedience to it unnecessary. Such beliefs have led Identity members to fight government officials and reject tax payments. Identity teachings have been central to the belief systems of many individuals arrested and convicted of bombings, armed robberies, counterfeiting, and the assaults and murders of law enforcement personnel and others (TRAC, 1989).

In fact, some believe that Timothy McVeigh may have identified with Identity teachings. After the bombing of the FBI building in Oklahoma City in April 1995, a review of Timothy McVeigh's activities before the bombing threw up a connection with an Identity settlement in Elohim City in eastern Oklahoma. Apparently, McVeigh made two brief phone calls to the settlement a couple of weeks before the bombing. Some suspect that he was attempting to gain information regarding the fate of Richard Wayne Snell (Barkun, 1997). Snell was closely associated with Robert Millar, the leader of the Identity settlement in Elohim City, and was on death row for murdering a pawnshop owner he thought to be Jewish. Interestingly, Snell was executed on April 19, 1995, the same day as the bombing of the federal building.

Anti-Semitic, anti-government, and white supremacy notions, coupled with the belief that the end of days is near, have provided a sense of urgency for many Identity believers to engage in preparations for the final battle between good and evil. Many Identity followers have migrated to communes (mostly west of the Mississippi River) or settlements, have begun stockpiling weapons, and have engaged in military-type training (Barkun, 1997; Levin & McDevitt, 2002). Given what is currently known about destructive religious groups and the past criminal activities of some Identity believers, concern regarding the potential for crime and violence among Identity followers is warranted. One Identity group, the Kingdom Identity Ministries, proudly displays its beliefs on the World Wide Web. The Kingdom Identity Ministries refers to itself as a "politically incorrect Christian Identity outreach ministry." On their Web site, the following passages appear as part of their doctrinal statement of beliefs:

WE BELIEVE the White, Anglo-Saxon, Germanic and kindred people to be God's true, literal Children of Israel. Only this race fulfills every detail of Biblical Prophecy and World History concerning Israel and continues in these latter days to be heirs and possessors of the Covenants, Prophecies, Promises and Blessings YHVH God made to Israel. This chosen seedline making up the "Christian Nations" (Gen. 35:11; Isa. 62:2; Acts 11:26) of the earth stands far superior to all other peoples in their call as God's servant race (Isa. 41:8, 44:21; Luke 1:54). Only these descendants of the 12 tribes of Israel scattered abroad (James 1:1; Deut. 4:27; Jer. 31:10; John 11:52) have carried God's Word, the Bible, throughout the world (Gen. 28:14; Isa. 43:10–12, 59:21), have used His Laws in the establishment of their civil governments and are the "Christians" opposed by the Satanic Anti-Christ forces of this world who do not recognize the true and living God (John 5:23, 8:19, 16:2–3).

WE BELIEVE in an existing being known as the Devil or Satan and called the Serpent (Gen. 3:1; Rev. 12:9), who has a literal "seed" or posterity in the earth (Gen. 3:15) commonly called Jews today (Rev. 2:9; 3:9; Isa. 65:15). These children of Satan (John 8:44–47; Matt. 13:38; John 8:23) through Cain (I John 2:22, 4:3) who have throughout history always been a curse to true Israel, the Children of God, because of a natural enmity between the two races (Gen. 3:15), because they do the works of their father the Devil (John 8:38–44), and because they please not God, and are contrary to all men (I Thes. 2:14–15), though they often pose as ministers of righteousness (II Cor. 11:13–15). The ultimate end of this evil race whose hands bear the blood of our Savior (Matt. 27:25) and all the righteous slain upon the earth (Matt. 23:35), is Divine judgment (Matt. 13:38–42, 15:13; Zech. 14:21).

WE BELIEVE men and women should conduct themselves according to the role of their gender in the traditional Christian sense that God intended. Homosexuality is an abomination before God and should be punished by death (Lev. 18:22, 20:13; Rom. 1:24–28, 32; I Cor. 6:9).

(http://www.kingidentity.com/doctrine)

The Christian Separatist Church Society

The Christian Separatist Church Society (CSCS), a splinter Christian Identity group, focus on the Identity belief of white supremacy. They refer to the Bible as the Separatist Scriptures. According to their Web site (http://www.christian-separtist.org/other/welcome.html), church members proclaim that they are Christian Supremacists. They believe the true Christian faith is superior to all other religions and that God gave the gift of race. They believe that God did not intend for people to mix the races. They clearly state, "[W]e do not believe in wholesale genocidal murder for any peoples, and we do not believe that even a Marxist Communist state or its people have the right to take from or promote the taking from persons the inalienable rights granted to them by Almighty God." Yet, as one examines documents within the Web pages, an angrier, more hateful message emerges. For example, the following quotation is from an article entitled "Wake Up, Christian," in which members explain their points-of-view as not personal but rather a matter of absolute truth:

> The mongrel antichrists, regardless of what they may call themselves, are at war with the Living and True God, Jesus Christ. The Jewish antichrists like to attack Christian Separatists for no other reason than the fact that we believe Jesus Christ to be God in the flesh, and we believe that the New Testament is the Final Revelation of Almighty God.
>
> Jews manifest themselves as liars by trying to pretend that they are the only antichrists that we have spoken up against. We are against all enemies of God— homosexuals, gypsies, white people who hate God, Identity groups that hate God and are judaized, and white Judeo churches that hate God and are judaized or heathenized. Therefore, every time a humanist, a materialist, an antichrist plutocrat, communist, or whatever an antichrist wants to call himself, attacks Christianity and the essential beliefs of Christianity, then he manifests himself to be an antichrist ...
>
> It is true that we Christian Separatists detest the enemies of God. Yet, the filthy, Talmudic Jew likes to describe anybody who disagrees with his or insane points-of-view as haters. The truth is that the Christian Separatists are not haters. We are lovers of the Lord Jesus Christ. We Christian Separatists teach

that the Word of God must be obeyed and believed objectively, without impos-
ing one's personal feelings or operating in feelings. In other words, our views of
Christ-hating, Talmudic Jews or humanists or homosexuals are not our personal
points-of-view, or at least, they were not our personal points-of-view before we
became indwelled by the Living Holy Spirit of Truth. We Christian Separatists
simply repeat the just judgments of a just and true Living God.

(www.christianseparatist.org/aw/aw980926.html)

Like similarly situated religious organizations, the CSCS lists articles or briefs
that further articulate their belief system on their Web site. For example, the CSCS
offers readers a series of articles titled "Antichrist Watch." They use the word "anti-
christ" to distinguish those who they believe have not been "anointed" by Jesus.
Even like-minded individuals from other Identity-linked organizations are labeled
antichrists and are given the title "Rabbi," which one can only interpret, on the
basis of their belief system, to be hateful in tone (Harrell, n.d.)

Westboro Baptist Church

Established in 1955 by Pastor Fred Phelps, the Westboro Baptist Church exists as
an Old School (or Primitive) Baptist Church. Church members engage in regular
sidewalk demonstrations to oppose homosexuality, claiming that homosexuals are
"soul-damning, nation-destroying filth." Their hateful message is prominently
displayed on the Internet (http://www.godhatesfags.com). They proudly carry
large signs containing biblical words and sentiments, including messages such as
"God Hates Fags," "Fags Hate God," "Aids Cures Fags," "Thank God for Aids,"
"Fags Burn in Hell," "God Is Not Mocked," "Fags Are Nature Freaks," "God Gave
Fags Up," "No Special Laws for Fags," and "Fags Doom Nations." They preach
the following:

> "GOD HATES FAGS"—though elliptical—is a profound theological state-
> ment, which the world needs to hear more than it needs oxygen, water and
> bread. The three words, fully expounded, show:
>
> 1. the absolute sovereignty of "GOD" in all matters whatsoever (e.g.,
>   Jeremiah 32:17, Isaiah 45:7, Amos 3:6, Proverbs 16:4, Matthew 19:26,
>   Romans 9:11–24, Romans 11:33–36, etc.).
> 2. the doctrine of reprobation or God's "HATE" involving eternal retri-
>   bution or the everlasting punishment of most of mankind in Hell for-
>   ever (e.g., Leviticus 20:13,23, Psalm 5:5, Psalm 11:5, Malachi 1:1–3,
>   Romans 9:11–13, Matthew 7:13,23, John 12:39–40, 1 Peter 2:8, Jude
>   4, Revelation 13:8, 20:15, 21:27, etc.), and

3. the certainty that all impenitent sodomites (under the elegant metaphor of "FAGS" as the contraction of faggots, fueling the fires of God's wrath) will inevitably go to Hell (e.g., Romans 1:18–32, 1 Corinthians 6:9–11, 1 Timothy 1:8–11, Jude 7, etc.).

4. The only lawful sexual connection is the marriage bed. All other sex activity is whoremongery and adultery, which will damn the soul forever in Hell. Heb. 13:4. Decadent, depraved, degenerate and debauched America, having bought the lie that It's OK to be gay, has thereby changed the truth of God into a lie, and now worships and serves the creature more than the Creator, who is blessed forever. Amen! Rom. 1:25. But the Word of God abides. Better to be a eunuch if the will of God be so, and make sure of Heaven. Mat. 19:12. Better to be blind or lame, than to be cast into Hell, into the fire that never shall be quenched. Mk. 9:43–48. Abstain, you fools.

(www.godhatesfags.com/main/aboutwbc)

These examples provide only a brief glimpse into the belief systems of three religious organizations that proudly share their beliefs on the Internet. It should be noted that all three examples represent Christian-based belief systems and thus are not representative of the religious justification for hate utilized by other religious traditions. These quotations do seem to suggest, however, that adherents are bound by the absolute truth claims of their religious beliefs and the belief that their religion is supreme.

Measuring Hate Crime

Measuring the prevalence of hate crime is a daunting task because of the often ambiguous and complex nature of crime and the inherent difficulty of separating out bias-related motivations from other motivations. In contrast, the examples provided at the opening of this chapter were easily identified by officials as hate crimes because the motivations and affiliations of the defendants were clearly verified by the defendants themselves or witnesses and others known to the defendants. Also, the specific details and circumstances of each of these crimes fit within the legal definition of hate crime. Although these crimes provided officials a clear-cut example of hate crime in action, they are not necessarily representative of the types of hate crime that are often reported, since such crimes involve a number of different elements, of which bias or hate may be only a small part.

In fact, recent research has found the ambiguity in many seemingly bias-related crimes to be a great source of confusion and frustration for law enforcement officials and ultimately to affect the accuracy of national hate crime statistics (Nolan, McDevitt, Cronin, & Farrell, 2004). Of course, other factors, such as a police officer's own preconceived ideas about the victims and their perceived group membership as well as departmental factors that either encourage or discourage the documentation of hate crime, are also legitimate concerns in the gathering of accurate hate crime statistics (Balboni & McDevitt, 2001). Nolan & Akiyama (2002) found that police agencies that reported hate crimes were different from those that did not in that they had higher levels of support for hate crime reporting from their local government and departmental officials, had implemented an internal mechanism to prevent misidentification, and had provided better training. In addition, police agencies that reported hate crimes had demonstrated a stronger desire to support their communities and to improve the overall relationship between the police and the community. They also had reported higher levels of concern about the seriousness of hate and their role in dealing with it.

The accuracy of hate crime statistics has even been challenged by lawmakers concerned about hate crime legislation. For example, in July 2001, the U.S. Senate Republican Policy Committee published a report in which they challenged the accuracy of hate crime statistics. The committee conducted a review of the seventeen hate crime murders documented by the FBI in 1999. After investigating the details of each of these murders, the committee concluded that only nine of the seventeen were verifiable hate crime murders. In fact, they found that one case from Bullhead City, Arizona, that had been reported as a hate crime murder was actually an aggravated assault (Oliphant, 2001).

Despite these controversies, the U.S. attorney general has been obligated by law to collect and report data about hate crime since the passage of the Hate Crimes Statistics Act (HCSA) in 1990. The act (P.L. 101-275) was an attempt to regulate the consistency of reporting of hate crime by individual states by requiring the U.S. attorney general to collect statistical data on hate or bias crime "to provide for the acquisition and publication of data about crimes that manifest prejudice based on race, religion, homosexuality or heterosexuality, or ethnicity." Since 1990, amendments have been made through two other pieces of legislation. Section 320926 of the Violent Crime Control and Law Enforcement Act of 1994 (P.L. 103-322) added crimes against persons with disabilities. Section 7 of the Church Arson Prevention Act of 1996 (P.L. 104-155) reauthorized the HCSA and removed the sunset clause that had been embedded in the original legislation. Despite the difficulties in measurement, Congress has continued its commitment to understanding and tracking the prevalence of hate crime in the United States more fully.

Before the passage of the HCSA, there were no prevalence data from which to evaluate the frequency or characteristics of hate crime on a national level, although not-for-profit organizations such as the Anti-Defamation League, the Southern Poverty Law Center, and the National Gay/Lesbian Task Force Policy Institute (all described below) had long documented instances of violence or vandalism against particular victims (Levin & McDevitt, 2002). The HCSA was intended to institutionalize the collection of data related to hate crime, and the attorney general delegated the responsibility to the FBI through the Uniform Crime Reporting (UCR) system, the method by which police agencies report the crimes that are known to them (discussed in Chapter 8).

Given the mandate of the HCSA of 1990, one might assume that a template had been created within the UCR system through which to gauge trends in hate crime across the nation. Yet the documentation of hate crime has proven to be difficult indeed. As mentioned earlier, the reporting of hate crime incidents requires some knowledge of the motivation of offender(s), not just the recording of various criminal acts. This adds another dimension to the responsibilities of law enforcement personnel who investigate such crimes and report on them via the UCR system.

Nolan and Akiyama (2002) note that the number of law enforcement agencies participating in the program to measure hate crimes has increased substantially since its creation in 1990; however, the volume of hate crimes reported has remained very stable. They note that in 1992 there were a total of 6,181 law enforcement agencies participating in the program, covering approximately 51 percent of the population. In 1992, a total of 7,466 hate crime incidents were reported. These reports were gathered by a very small number of law enforcement agencies, since approximately 82 percent of the participating agencies noted zero hate crimes during the reporting period. In 1999, when 12,122 law enforcement agencies noted their participation in the program, virtually the same number of hate crimes were reported: a total of 7,876. Out of more than 12,000 participating law enforcement agencies, 85 percent recorded that zero hate crimes had occurred in their jurisdiction during the reporting period. This trend appears to have continued. In data compiled by the Anti-Defamation League's (2006a) Washington Office from FBI reports, in 2000 a total of 11,690 police agencies reported a total of 8,063 crimes, and in 2004 a total of 12,711 agencies reported a total of 7,649 crimes. The FBI reports that in 2005, a total of 12,417 police agencies reported a total of 7,163 incidents of hate crime involving a total of 8,300 offenses and 8,804 victims (FBI, 2006).

The Southern Poverty Law Center (2001), in an article entitled "Discounting Hate," charges that the UCR system is capturing only a small proportion of the hate crime that actually occurs, arguing that the real figure is likely to be closer to 50,000 crimes per year. In a survey of officials from fifty states, the center asked about specific incidents of hate crime that had been reported in the media but were not documented in the UCR system. The center found a wide range of explanations for the discrepancies, including the issues already described here; however, the problem of "false zeroes" was most disconcerting. False zeroes are created when police agencies do not file a hate crime statistical report and the administrator submits a zero instead of showing that the agency did not file a report. Such a practice creates an instant error in data collection, and, according to the center, the FBI concedes that false-zero reporting is widespread. It certainly does seem unlikely that 85 percent of some 12,000 police agencies would have zero hate crime incidents in any given year. Other issues recognized included police agencies dismissing various acts as the work of juveniles, problems with the interpretation and definition of hate crime legislation in various states, and bureaucratic errors.

Other concerns are connected to the limitations of the UCR system itself. The NIBRS is a revised version of the UCR system that is intended to increase the utility of crime reporting. The NIBRS is a new data collection tool that enables the police to document the situational context of crime, rather than simple frequency counts. Although adoption has been slow, a growing number of law enforcement agencies are taking up the new crime reporting method.

The ability to record the situational context of crime (Maxfield, 1999) may become indispensable to discerning hate crime. For example, Bureau of Justice Statistics statistician Kevin J. Strom (2001) prepared a report using data from the NIBRS for the period 1997–1999. In 1977 a total of 1,878 police agencies from ten states submitted data via the NIBRS, and in 1999 there were 3,396 agencies from seventeen states. These agencies reported about 3,000 bias-related crimes during this period, of which 61 percent were motivated by racial bias, 14 percent by religious bias, 13 percent by sexual orientation bias, 11 percent by ethnicity or national origin bias, and 1 percent by disability bias. Among the racially motivated hate crimes, 60 percent targeted African Americans and about 30 percent targeted whites. Among crimes motivated by religious bias, the majority were anti-Jewish crimes or crimes against unnamed religious groups. Among crimes against sexual orientation, virtually all were targeted toward male and female homosexuals. Crimes committed as a result of an ethnic or national origin bias affected Hispanics most frequently. About 60 percent of the hate crimes were violent in nature; this is in contrast to the 5.4 million other crime incidents reported, of which only one in five involved violence. The majority of suspects in these crimes were white males. In addition, Strom (2001) notes that there are two general barriers to hate crime reporting; one involves factors related to victims reporting such incidents and the other involves factors associated with police recording of such incidents as bias-related crimes.

Strom (2001) also notes that in 2000 the National Crime Victimization Survey was amended to include questions to uncover hate crime victimizations that go unreported to the police. The questions ask victims about the basis for their belief that the crime they experienced was motivated by bias. Preliminary data reveal that like many other crime victims, victims of bias-related crimes do not report them to the police. Thus, it is probably fair to assume that victim nonreporting, coupled with the difficulties police have in categorizing hate crime, results in very low rates of reported hate crime. At this time, there is every reason to believe that actual hate crime occurs with much greater frequency than official reports reveal.

Combating Hate Crime

Public Policy Responses

Responding to hate crime has been marked by controversy since the conceptual delineation of hate crime as a distinct form of criminal behavior emerged in the 1970s. As with other social problems, remedies for fighting such criminal behavior came to rest with the development of new criminal statutes. Legislation proliferated that was centered on the basic premise that crimes motivated by hate are morally reprehensible and thus are deserving of their own distinct criminal statutes or enhanced sanctions. Lawmakers responded by crafting policies that either created a new category of crime, amended existing law, or increased the sanctions against offenders who commit certain crimes because of hate or bias. Since the 1970s, the majority of states in the United States have adopted at least one statute that relates to hate crime, although these statutes have taken different forms.

The Anti-Defamation League (2006b) monitors the statutory provisions regarding hate crime in the states. The organization notes that all states, with the exception of Wyoming, have adopted at least one hate crime statute. While forty-six states have statutory provisions that provide a criminal penalty for bias-motivated violence or intimidation, not all states specifically cover all potential victim groups. For instance, in Idaho, criminal penalties for bias-related violence do not apply to biases regarding sexual orientation, gender, or disability. With the exception of Wyoming, the states without an enhanced criminal penalty for hate crime have a statute relating to institutional vandalism. Most states have historically had legislation to address specific problems affecting religious institutions such as vandalism or the disturbance of religious worship (Brooks, 1994). Also, many states have adopted provisions that permit civil action (ADL, 2006b).

Controversy related to hate crime legislation has centered on the ambiguity of hate crime laws and the appropriateness of designing statutes with enhanced penalties for offenses based on the motivation of the offender. The enhanced penalty statutes rank bias-related wrongdoing higher than would be customary for similar crimes. So, for example, an offender who committed assault consistent with a hate crime statute might find himself with a stiffer sentence than a perpetrator who assaulted someone for another reason. Some argue (Adams, 2005) that such penalty enhancements are legally flawed and unnecessary because criminal law already provides mechanisms by which hate-related violence can be prosecuted. Also, because some state statutes defined groups of victims and perpetrators, they created circumstances in which certain people were protected by the law while others were not (Jenness, 2002–2003) and the types of perpetrators who can be prosecuted were defined. This "slippery slope" has made hate crime policy, implementation, and analysis all the more difficult (McPhail, 2000).

There is evidence, however, that the controversy surrounding hate crime legislation has begun to settle. Over time, the courts have augmented the definition of hate crime as a distinct form of criminal behavior. For example, Phillips and Grattet (2000) examined thirty-eight appellate court opinions relating to the constitutionality of hate crime cases from 1984 to 1999. They found that over time, judicial discourse transformed the legal ambiguity of hate crime legislation into a more standardized set of legal arguments from which challenges to hate crime legislation can be brought forth. Their analysis showed that a stable pattern of interpretation has emerged. This has, in essence, helped to establish legal meaning and the legitimacy of hate crime as a special category of crime. Phillips and Grattet also note that appeals in hate crime convictions have declined since their height in the early 1990s, and cases involving hate motivations have seen higher conviction rates in more recent years. Both indicators are additional signs that the legal meaning of hate crime has become more concrete and determinate. The U.S. Supreme Court decision in *Wisconsin v. Mitchell* (1993) also seems to have helped resolve some of the legal disputes. In this case, the Court considered whether a state's enhanced penalty for a crime committed against a victim because of bias was a violation of the First Amendment. The Court ruled that the First Amendment does not preclude a state from enhancing criminal penalties in response to bias motivations.

Congress has enacted several pieces of legislation that relate to hate crimes, although such statutes are limited to violent crimes motivated by the victim's race, religion, or national origin. Efforts to expand the list of potential targets of hate crime have been unsuccessful. The FBI investigates civil rights violations related to bias-motivated crime on the basis of five federal statutes: 18 U.S.C. 241 (Conspiracy Against Rights), 18 U.S.C. 245 (Interference with Federally Protected Activities), 18 U.S.C. 247 (Damage to Religious Property; Obstruction in Free Exercise of Religious Beliefs), 42 U.S.C. 3631 (Criminal Interference with Right to Fair Housing), and 18 U.S.C. 844(h) (Using Explosives or Fire in the Commission of a Felony). It is important to note that the HCSA of 1990 (mentioned earlier) and its subsequent amendments allow for the collection of statistical data related to hate crimes committed against persons or property motivated by bias on the grounds of race, religion, ethnicity, national origin, disability, and sexual orientation; however, because other federal statutes do not include similar language, the FBI does not have jurisdiction over hate crimes motivated by bias against sexual orientation, and their investigation of hate crimes motivated by a disability bias is generally reserved for incidents related to housing rights.

Law Enforcement Initiatives

In addition to enforcing state or federal hate crime laws, law enforcement officials have been collaborating to combat hate crime with new initiatives. For example, in 1996, the president established the National Church Arson Task Force (NCATF), a multijurisdictional task force responsible for investigating arsons, bombings, or attempted bombings, at or near houses of worship. After the creation of the NCATF, the U.S. attorney general established local Church Arson Task Forces within each U.S. attorney district. According to the FBI, a total of 790 investigations have been conducted since 1999 under this initiative. A total of 343 individuals have been arrested in cases involving 259 church arsons. Of those arrested, 68 were charged with federal violations, and the remainder were charged with violations of state laws (FBI, 2005). Many more arsons have gone unsolved.

In a similar vein, in 1997, the attorney general convened a Hate Crimes Working Group (HCWG) to examine the problem of hate crime in the United States. The working group recommended a national hate crimes initiative. As a result, a Hate Crimes Working Group was established in each U.S. attorney district. Each district was to convene a working group comprising federal, state, and local law enforcement officials as well as representatives from the local communities within the district. This created a network and planning structure in which the various regions of the country could work collaboratively.

Advocacy/Watchdog Groups

Law enforcement officials cannot and should not be considered the only line of defense against hate crime. Advocacy groups play a critical role in combating hateful action. Advocacy can take on a variety of different perspectives. At the level of the individual, advocacy organizations can help victims of hate crime by ensuring they are treated fairly by officials in the criminal justice system and have access to services and information. For instance, the Southern Poverty Law Center assists victims of hate crime by bringing legal action against individuals and groups who espouse hate. Advocacy organizations also combat hate crime on a broader scale. They educate professionals and laypeople about the impact of hate and advocate for appropriate legislative reform. In some instances, they serve as "watchdog" organizations, observing or surveying the activities of various groups who publicly espouse hate doctrines. Three different organizations that have had a significant influence in terms of creating social change and partnering with law enforcement to combat hate crime are noted here.

Southern Poverty Law Center

In 1971, civil rights attorneys Morris Dees and Joe Levin founded the Southern Poverty Law Center (SPLC) in Montgomery, Alabama. As an outgrowth of their commitment to the ideals of racial equality, the center's roots are grounded in the early pro bono civil rights lawsuits Dees and Levin took on during the 1960s, which helped to implement the Civil Rights Act of 1964 and the Voting Rights Act of 1965, and resulted in the desegregation of recreational facilities, restructuring of legislative districts, and integration of the Alabama State Troopers. Eventually, Dees and Levin sought national support for their work and established the SPLC as a small civil rights law firm dedicated to fighting discrimination and to making the rights afforded to citizens in the U.S. Constitution a living reality.

As part of their fight against discrimination, the SPLC began investigating hate groups after a group of more than a hundred Klansmen attacked participants in a civil rights demonstration in Decatur, Alabama, in 1979. Members of the Invisible Empire Klan descended on the peaceful marchers, shooting two in the head and face and assaulting others with clubs and sticks. The FBI responded to the incident, but their investigation did not turn up enough evidence to make any arrests. The SPLC responded by filing a civil suit against the Ku Klux Klan in 1980. In the case, *Brown v. Invisible Empire, Knights of the Ku Klux Klan* (CV-80-1449), the SPLC achieved a settlement that required the Klansmen to rescind their membership in the Klan, to participate in a two-hour course on race relations as well as community service, and to refrain from white supremacist activities. Eventually, enough evidence was gathered to convict nine of the Klansmen of criminal charges.

The case led the center to create a system to monitor the hate activity of various Ku Klux Klan organizations across the county. Originally called the Klanwatch, the project eventually expanded to involve the monitoring of different hate groups and was renamed the Intelligence Project. Today, the SPLC monitors hate and extremist activity across the nation through the Intelligence Project and provides updates to law enforcement, the media, and the public through a quarterly *Intelligence Report* (accessible at http://www.splcenter.org).

Since the inception of the Intelligence Project, the SPLC has worked to bring criminal hate activities to the criminal and civil courts for resolution. This work has not been uncontroversial, although it is sometimes difficult to ascertain exactly where such controversy comes from. For example, in June 2005, Joe McCutchen of Fort Smith, Arkansas, denounced his labeling by the SPLC as a white supremacist/extremist. McCutchen, an activist fighting against illegal immigration in Arkansas, was linked by the SPLC in 2001 to the Council of Concerned Citizens, which the SPLC describes as a white supremacist group (Kellams, 2005).

Ken Silverstein (2000), in an editorial in *Harper's Magazine* entitled "The Church of Morris Dees," sharply criticized both the center and one of its founders, Morris Dees. Silverstein's concern focuses on the center's continued fundraising activities, despite the fact that the SPLC has already accumulated a robust financial portfolio. His article, which includes comments made by past staff members or associates, charges that the center's resources are not adequately distributed to fight discrimination in areas of critical need; instead, they are used for the surveillance of private citizens who belong to hate groups and for suing the leaders of these groups for crimes their members commit. He claims that although such strategies may be well intentioned, they should give civil libertarians cause for concern.

Despite such criticisms, the media continues to consult the SPLC on matters involving hate crimes. Also, the direct link to the SPLC Web site from the FBI's Web page on hate crime suggests the FBI considers at least some of SPLC's watchdog activities credible.

Anti-Defamation League

Another prominent advocacy group dedicated to fighting hate crime is the Anti-Defamation League (ADL). The league was founded in 1913 by Sigmund Livingston, a Chicago attorney, with the intention of eradicating negative images of Jewish people in the print media and on stage and screen. The ADL has worked toward legislative reform and has combated anti-Semitism on a number of different fronts.

In more recent times, the league has broadened its scope to include all other vulnerable populations. It is committed to fighting "unjust and unfair discrimination against and ridicule of any sect or body of citizens." Its goal, to "expose and combat the purveyors of hatred in our midst, responding to whatever new challenges may arise," has remained constant throughout the years (ADL, 2001). It gathers, analyzes, and disseminates intelligence information on extremist and hate activity for law enforcement officials, enhancing the ability of law enforcement to combat serious threats; it also provides assistance, support, and resources on security to the Jewish community (http://www.adl.org).

Lesbian, Gay, Bisexual, and Transgender (LGBT) Advocacy

Hate crime is often targeted against members of the LGBT community. Many lesbian, gay, bisexual, and transgender people routinely experience disrespect, harassment, and violence. The rhetoric of religious leaders and antigay politicians creates a supporting climate for such pervasive victimization. For example, Reverend Fred Phelps, pastor of the Westboro Baptist Church in Topeka, Kansas (discussed above), routinely sends his parishioners to demonstrate at the funerals of homosexuals as part of the Church's antigay activism. In October 2004, he sent a group to the Crossroads Church of God during the funeral service for Scotty Joe Weaver, an eighteen-year-old gay man who had been brutally murdered in Alabama. Although robbery appeared to be the main motive in this case, prosecutors noted that the nature and severity of the attack against Scotty suggested hate played a substantial role. Reverend Phelps's parishioners appeared outside the church holding signs with slogans such as "God hates fags" and "God hates America" (the latter intended to suggest that God unleashed his anger at America for its tolerance of homosexuality through natural disasters and terrorist attacks; AP, 2004; Meenan, 2004). Apparently the harassment of the LGBT community knows no bounds. Funeral protests by members of the Westboro Baptist Church have prompted some lawmakers to propose legislation to ban protests of any kind during funerals (O'Connor, 2006).

The fight against harassment of, and violence toward, the LGBT community has involved several advocacy organizations. For example, the National Gay and Lesbian Task Force, Inc. is a national advocacy group working to promote the rights of gay and lesbians. Founded in 1973, the task force played a pivotal role in ending the classification of homosexuality as a mental illness, lifting the prohibition on gays and lesbians being employed by the federal government, and bringing the problem of HIV/AIDS to national attention. As a political activist organization seeking equality for the LGBT community, the task force has also taken a leading role in combating violence against the community. For instance, the Policy Institute provides research and policy analysis to support the equality goals of the organization. Its mission is to "create a world that respects and makes visible the diversity of human expression and identity where all people may fully participate in society" (http://www.thetaskforce.org). The Policy Institute conducts research to document the demographics of the LGBT community and analyzes the ways in which various policies will affect its members. The organization seeks to become a powerful voice in educating the public to recognize the parallels between sexism, racism, or classism and homophobia, transphobia, or biphobia. This necessarily involves exposing homophobic attacks against members of the LGBT community.

National Coalition of Anti-Violence Programs

The NCAVP is a network of more than twenty anti-violence programs that monitor and respond to incidents of bias and violence against and within the LGBT community. Such incidents include domestic violence, HIV-related violence, rape, and sexual assault. The NCAVP also monitors "pick-up" crimes, where the victim is "picked up" by someone and then robbed, assaulted, or murdered. The coalition is responsible for orchestrating a national response to such violence. As part of its charge, the coalition publishes an annual report documenting bias-related incidents targeting LGBT individuals. The 2004 report (Patton, 2005) indicates that 1,792 anti-LGBT incidents, involving a total 2,131 victims and 2,637 offenders, occurred in 2004, as reported by only eleven NCAVP organizational members. Patton (2005) notes several disturbing trends in the data, one of which is the increased use of weapons and the increase in the number of incidents perpetrated by a member of an organized hate group.

Part IV
The Abuse
of Religious Authority

Clergy Misconduct: An Overview

In 1991, a Tennessee teenager named Michael mistakenly grabbed a microcassette tape from the filing cabinet in the choir room of his Central Baptist Church in Hixson, Tennessee. As a member of the church youth choir, Michael had been taking drum lessons at the church and thought the tape was one on which he had recorded some of his performances. Little did he know that his discovery of the tape would ultimately lead to a sexual abuse investigation involving one of his church leaders, Brother Don McCary. The tape held conversations between the youth minister McCary and a young boy at the church. Sickened by what she heard on the tape, Michael's mother Jane promptly shared it with her husband, and they presented the tape to chief of police Eugene McCutcheon, who was a member of the same church. The chief assigned two detectives to investigate.

The investigators found much incriminating evidence in McCary's church office, including photographs of his victims, semen-soaked clothing, a briefcase full of pornographic material, condoms, motel keys with notations indicating which youth he had stayed with in which motel, and additional tapes of conversations between McCary and his victims. The investigation led to the exposure of the sexual abuse of several young boys. The boys reported that McCary had showered them with gifts, taken them on trips, and made them engage in various sexual acts over a long period. They told investigators that the sexual abuse occurred both at the church and at McCary's residence. The investigation concluded with the arrest and conviction of McCary in 1992. He was convicted of thirteen sex offenses against four male victims aged twelve to fifteen and was sentenced to a term of seventy-two years in state prison (*State v. McCary*, 1996).

McCary appealed, and the Tennessee Supreme Court reversed his convictions and remanded the case for a new trial, finding that the trial court had improperly admitted evidence in the original trial. As McCary approached retrial, the Court granted his motion for a severance of trials and his request to act as his own attorney in two of the trials. In August 1997 he was convicted in two separate trials on two counts of aggravated sexual battery, one count of sexual battery, and four counts of statutory rape and was sentenced to thirty-four years. Later that year, in the two remaining cases, McCary pled guilty to three counts of rape and two counts of assault. The Court imposed a sentence of thirty-eight years, which was to be served concurrently with his previous thirty-four-year sentence.

In 1998, McCary filed a petition for post-conviction relief on the cases in which he had pled guilty, but the Court denied his application (*State v. McCary*, 2003). He also appealed his convictions in the two new trials that had concluded in 1997. Although he used a number of legal arguments, one of the most interesting challenges he raised involved the appropriateness of some of the religious references made by the special prosecutor during closing arguments in the case of one of the victims—comments such as:

> You know, the good thing that comes out of this case is that when you first hear it, your faith is just shaken. You wonder, How can God allow this to happen in His church, it happen at all, but in His church with a pastor. How can everybody in that church miss it? How can this poor young boy be put in that position so that perhaps a year of his life he thinks about killing himself? But my faith is stronger because of this … For some reason, my faith walks through this case and … watches as the evidence developed. (*State of Tennessee v. Donald C. McCary*, 2003).

The Court of Criminal Appeals of Tennessee at Knoxville agreed with McCary and found these comments to be inflammatory and improper. Judge Gary R. Wade delivered the opinion of the court: "At no time did he submit that the defendant should be convicted of aggravated sexual battery for touching J.B. Instead, he argued exclusively that the defendant deserved conviction because of his hypocrisy and his immorality." Given that the jury had not been instructed to disregard such statements and that the state had been forewarned about making such comments in the previous trial, the court reversed the convictions from this trial. The convictions in the other trial were affirmed.

The special prosecutor may have taken some liberties in his closing arguments, but such comments are easy to understand given that Don McCary was a man of the cloth. The details of the case tell a torrid story of abuse and betrayal. Not only did McCary engage in criminal activities that victimized some of the boys in his church, but he also abused the power and authority vested in him by his parishioners.

At the time of writing, McCary is still serving time in a Tennessee prison; however, the story does not end here. Don McCary is one of three brothers, all ministers at various times, who have been convicted of crimes related to the sexual abuse of children. Don's twin brother, Ron McCary, pled guilty to the aggravated rape of a six-year-old boy in 1991 and was sentenced to twenty-five years. According to court records, he had forced the boy to perform oral sex on him while he was babysitting him. Before this charge, Ron had had other scrapes with the law. He had been suspected of child molestation in 1987 while working at the Brainerd United Methodist Church. Yet, according to news reports, the investigation appeared to be obstructed by the chief of police (the same police chief who ordered the investigation of Don McCary), and Ron was never charged. Ron engaged in other crimes for which he was ultimately arrested. In 1989 he was arrested for buying marijuana from an undercover police officer. Shortly after that arrest he was arrested for shoplifting, public drunkenness, and contributing to the delinquency of a minor in a situation in which he and a fifteen-year-old stole two 12-packs of beer from a store (Sohn, 1992).

Yet the story does not end here either. Don and Ron's older brother, Richard, also has a criminal history involving the sexual abuse of minors. Richard pled guilty to three charges of child molestation in San Jose, California, in 1980. In 1982 he was arrested for child molestation in Georgia and sentenced to five years on probation and fined $1,000. He was also sentenced to three years in prison for sexually abusing his eight-year-old stepson in California and was released from prison after two years in 1985. He blamed at least some of his problems on a cult group he claimed to be part of called the People of the Name, a group he linked to Jim Jones and the Peoples Temple (Sohn, 1992).

The criminal cases involving the McCary brothers illustrate the reality that clergy are not immune from engaging in criminal behavior. When they do participate in criminal activity, their crimes are all the more noteworthy because of the special bond community members have with their faith leaders. These crimes are religion related by virtue of the fact that religious leaders and their lay workers abuse their religious authority when they participate in criminal behaviors. Don McCary used his position as a minister to attract, groom, and sexually abuse young boys. Parents trusted him to work with and care for the boys in an appropriate, professional manner. As this chapter illustrates, the abuse of religious authority has consequences beyond the criminal offenses committed by the offenders. Crimes perpetrated by clergy or trusted church workers victimize not only individuals but the entire church community.

This chapter explores religion-related crime when clergy, high-level church officials, or lay leaders engage in criminal activity to further their own individual or institutional purposes. Unlike the other types of religion-related crime described in this text, religion itself has little to do with the commission of the crimes of interest here. Instead, religion may provide the social context in which such crimes can flourish. Here we explore the issue of clergy abusing their religious authority to commit crime or to cover it up. This chapter also considers religious institutions that either actively participate in crime or, through neglect, place their institution and parishioners at risk of criminal victimization. The next chapter provides a more detailed exploration of several types of abuse of religious authority, particularly those that violate criminal laws.

Conceptualizing the Problem

When religious leaders take advantage of their social position within a faith-based community to commit crime, they violate a critical bond of trust. Clergy, regardless of their particular faith, are generally held in very high regard by their followers and citizens at large. Men and women of the cloth are revered and are often expected to uphold higher moral standards than the average citizen. As with doctors, police officers, and military personnel, we expect that clergy and those employed by them will demonstrate integrity and operate within strict ethical and legal boundaries. Not only are clergy expected to demonstrate such propriety; they are often looked upon by their followers to set the standard for appropriate behavior within the context of a particular religious creed. Believers look to their church leaders to provide advice and support regarding some of life's most challenging problems, and, thus, church leaders are expected to be the moral compass that guides and directs followers to live more holy existences.

Within this context, most religious traditions consider their faith leaders to be "holy" or "divine." Most followers would have difficulty imagining that the supreme leaders of their faith communities could do any harm. Among Christian denominations, this concept is referred to as "priestly numinosity," loosely meaning that faith leaders are assumed to be divine or numinous (Lebacqz & Barton, 1991). Bowker (2000) defines the numinous as "the non-rational elements in what is experienced in religion as the 'Holy'" (p. 419). In Jewish traditions, the rabbi is considered the *mara d'atra* (master of the place), the last word on religious decisions and standards within the community (Fried, 2002, p. 7). In other words, clergy are considered to be the direct representatives of God (Wells, 2003) and, therefore, have a sacred power that few others in society have. Followers tend to have blind faith in their clergy and those whom they have entrusted to work within the religious organization.

Certainly, clergy should, at a minimum, be able to follow the guidelines established by law, especially when such secular laws are not in conflict with religious doctrines. Thus the abuse by clergy of their high social standing is a betrayal of the highest proportion. Anson Shupe (1998) describes this phenomenon as "clergy malfeasance" and defines it as "the exploitation and abuse of [a] religious group's believers by trusted elites and leaders of that religion" (p. 1).

There are many other occasions when trusted elites exploit and abuse the authority vested in them by committing crimes; thus, it makes sense that we begin our discussion with an examination of how the abuse of religious authority might be consistent with other types of crime committed by trusted elites. Social scientists have studied deviance by trusted elites, although much of that attention has been focused on those in high-level corporate positions who commit crime purely for financial gain. Referred to as "white-collar crime," these crimes are generally committed by individuals of high social rank and respectability within the context of their legal occupational duties. Although no standard definition of white-collar crime is accepted by all social scientists, the National White Collar Crime Center (http://www.nw3c.org) drafted the following definition of white-collar crime after convening a panel of experts in 1996:

> Illegal or unethical acts that violate fiduciary responsibility of public trust committed by an individual or organization, usually during the course of legitimate occupational activity, by persons of high or respectable social status for personal or organizational gain. (Helmkamp, Ball, & Townsend, 1996, p. 331)

Friedrichs (2004) makes an interesting distinction in his definition of white-collar crime by referring to offenders as "trusted criminals." Although he acknowledges that "trust" itself is relative and can also be a component of other types of crimes, individuals who commit white-collar crime are able to do so because of the inherent trust involved in their legitimate or proclaimed occupational status. Although we might consider religious leaders as having a larger commitment to their work than employment, the reality is that for many, religious leadership is a service for which they are paid. So, just like individuals in the medical, legal, and academic professions who engage in criminal or unethical behavior, religious leaders who commit crime provide an example of white-collar crime.

This notion of "occupational crime," or what Green (1990) defines as "any act punishable by law that is committed through opportunity created in the course of an occupation which is legal" (p. 12), certainly fits the crimes describes here. One could argue that members of the clergy who commit criminal acts are really not so different from other white-collar criminals. Yet, since religious leaders "typically take sacred vows to uphold religious doctrine that uniformly denounces theft, violence, and exploitation," Friedrichs (2004) argues that for many, "the notion of religious crime may be the most disturbing of all forms of crimes by professionals" (p. 103).

The abuse of religious authority also may be viewed as a form of "corporate crime," a term that generally refers to crimes involving corporate violence, corporate abuses of power, fraud, or economic exploitation (Friedrichs, 2004). Shupe (1998) points out that it makes sense to consider the crimes committed by clergy as similar to elite deviance because of the corporate status of many churches and denominations. Many churches are legal entities in that they own property and assets, like other corporate bodies.

Although the vast majority of crime committed by clergy is intended to meet more personal needs, not to enhance the financial status of the religious institution, in some circumstances religious institutions have not acted differently than corporations in attempting to cover up crime to protect their bottom lines. We might argue the semantics, but there may not be that much difference between a corporation engaging in criminal activity to secure its financial future and a religious institution sweeping the crimes committed by its leaders under the carpet to protect the institution or the cleric from legal intervention and bad publicity. Both are seeking to protect the future of the institution, albeit their methods may be vastly different. Religious institutions that adopt an institutional protection agenda use scripture and doctrines to distort the truth (Fortune & Longwood, 2004), and the pain and suffering of victims are minimized or virtually unacknowledged.

Rosoff, Pontell, and Tillman (2002), in their coverage of white-collar crime, consider examples of religious fraud and corruption. Their focus on the misappropriation of funds by various televangelists and the practice of phony faith healing underscores the appropriateness of viewing such crimes as white-collar crimes.

One important distinction should be made between crimes that represent the abuse of religious authority and other types of white-collar crime. That distinction involves the relationship between the perpetrator and the victim. Although all white-collar crimes have victims, many of whom suffer very grave losses, the relationship between the religious leader and his or her victim is likely to be more personal. Victimization by clergy can therefore be an emotionally painful experience for victims, their families, and the congregation as a whole. The betrayal of trust often extends beyond the fiduciary responsibility of the religious leader to involve personal relationships and commitments. This shatters the images most of us have about religious leaders. Could it be that even the most sacred among us can fall prey to the evils of crime? It certainly appears that way.

Jeffrey Windy, a Roman Catholic priest from the Diocese of Peoria, pled guilty to conspiring with five other men to manufacture and distribute GHB (gamma hydroxybutyric acid), commonly known as the "date rape drug." Reports indicate twenty-five gallons of a precursor chemical used in the making of GHB were sold to St. Patrick's parish in Sheffield, Illinois, where Reverend Windy worked (Leitsinger, 2002). Father Windy and the other men were using the drug to help them achieve their weightlifting goals. Windy was sentenced to seventy months in prison. The diocese relieved him of his duties upon his arrest in 2002 (Diocese of Peoria, 2002).

As with other people found in possession of controlled substances, drug addiction was the likely motive in this crime; however, whatever the exact reasons, Father Windy abused the power, authority, and freedom vested in him as a Catholic priest. Shupe (1998) aptly notes that religious organizations are structured around inequities in the distribution of power between leaders and followers. Religious groups should be understood in terms of this power hierarchy, since inevitably it is the authority of the leader that creates the opportunity to commit crime. As Finkelhor, Gelles, Hotaling, and Straus (1983) have argued in regard to families, the risk of abuse is highest in situations in which the differential in power is greatest. That power differential may create a context or an opportunity in which crime can flourish. For example, one must have unrestricted access to the financial resources of a religious organization to steal from the church coffers. Similarly, one must have unfettered contact with children to abuse them. Since clerics are usually the most trusted members of religious organizations, they tend to have free rein. As you may recall, we discussed similar themes in previous chapters in our exploration of destructive religious organizations.

Conceptualizing these issues has been a difficult task for scholars. It is important to acknowledge that the abuse of religious authority can take many forms, not all of which violate criminal statutes. Unethical or unprofessional behavior, when it causes harm to parishioners, church workers, or other clergy, should also be considered an abuse of religious authority. For example, Reverend Pamela Cooper-White (1991) argues that it is a violation of ethical boundaries when pastors engage in sexual or romantic relationships with their parishioners. She notes that "there can be no authentic consent in a relationship involving unequal power" (p. 196). Another concern is sexual harassment, which is prohibited by state and federal civil law. Sexual harassment involves unwanted sexual advances (even subtle ones) in the workplace or educational institutions in which there is an imbalance in power between the parties (Underwood, 2003). Clergy, lay leaders, and church workers must acknowledge the inherent power in the roles that they assume within religious organizations and that sexual exploration of any kind is therefore likely to cross critical boundaries.

To fully conceptualize the abuse of religious authority we must also consider larger-scale cases in which religion has been used to harm populations for purposes of conquest and imperialism (Kimball, 2002; Shupe & Iadicola, 2000). In addition, when religious leaders use religion as a call to action in defense or support of some political agenda (as described in previous chapters), this may be an abuse of religious authority. It is probably fair to assume that throughout history the abuse of religious authority has, in some form, played a significant role in the relationship between religion, crime, and violence. In fact, it is probably fair to say that to some extent, all of the religion-related crime explored in this text could be viewed as an abuse of religious authority.

The aim of this text, in its survey of religion-related crime in the United States, is to create a framework in which the dynamics of various forms of religion-related crime can be distinguished. Thus, unlike the other chapters in this text, the topics covered in this chapter relate directly to crimes committed by clergy or other powerful lay leaders for their own personal gain. This will help us distinguish this phenomenon from others described in this text.

Crimes of the Cloth: Measuring the Problem

As mentioned throughout this text, few criminologists have taken on the issue of religion-related crime; crimes that involve an abuse of religious authority are no exception. Most attention has been centered on the sexual exploitation of children by clergy. In fact, a plethora of scholarly and popular literature has surfaced since the sexual abuse scandal plaguing the Catholic Church was first unveiled (e.g., Bartunek, Keenan, & Hinsdale, 2005; Burkett and Brunie, 1993; Dokecki, 2004; Fortune & Longwood, 2004; Jenkins, 1996; Rossetti, 1996). The literature has focused on several themes, including defining and theorizing the problem, the institutional response of religious organizations, and treatment for abuse victims and clergy offenders.

A growing body of literature under the more general rubric of clergy malfeasance has added greatly to our understanding of this phenomenon (Shupe, 1995, 1998; Shupe, Stacey, & Darnell, 2000). Also, white-collar crime experts (Friedrich,

2004; Rosoff, Pontell, & Tillman, 2002) have begun to conceptualize clergy malfeasance as a subset of white-collar or occupational crime. It is within this paradigm that we are likely to come to a deeper understanding of the broader social context of criminal activity by clergy.

Despite this scholarly attention, much of our understanding continues to be influenced by journalistic reports of the arrest, prosecution, and conviction of faith leaders. Religious leaders from all faiths have been charged with a wide range of criminal offenses, including violent and nonviolent crimes; fraud, embezzlement, and sexual abuse appear to be among the most common. In some cases, the criminal activity has shown no bounds.

- In November 2006 a preacher from Hickman Community Church in LaGrange, California, Howard Douglas Porter, was arrested at the Mexican border as he was making his way back from a trip to Mexico, where he was starting a new mission. Reports indicate that he had befriended an eighty-five-year-old man who had millions of dollars in stocks and real estate in a trust fund. Porter eventually had himself named as the trustee of the fund, with the church named as the beneficiary. Porter was charged with murder, attempted murder, and embezzlement for deliberately crashing his truck to kill the man in a scheme to gain access to the trust fund. The victim's family urged police to investigate the case because this was the second time Porter had been in a serious automobile crash with the victim. In 2002, Porter's car veered off the road and struck a tree and the elderly man became disabled (Munoz, 2006a, 2006b).
- In May 2006, Reverend Gerald Robinson, a Roman Catholic priest from Ohio, was convicted of murdering Sister Margaret Ann Pahl in a chapel twenty-six years earlier (Ewinger, 2006).
- Rabbi Fred Neulander from Cherry Hill, New Jersey, was convicted in 2002 of contracting with a hit man to kill his wife so that he could continue his affair with another woman (Mulvihill, 2006).
- David Cartee, a former pastor from Rivers of Life Fellowship in Steelville, Minnesota, was sentenced to a seven-year prison term when he pled guilty to felony charges involving the theft of $10,000 from his church in December 2001. He was also implicated on arson charges after his church was destroyed by fire; however, the arson charges were dismissed for lack of evidence (O'Neil, 2001).

Since one can easily find a plethora of similar examples in the news media, it is unlikely that these cases are indicative of a few bad apples. Yet one should also be cautious of the extent of media coverage of these crimes, because the news media are known to use such stories for their own financial gain (Surette, 1998). These types of crime stories are very compelling, and thus reporters take no risk in choosing to publish them over other stories from their community. In fact, some may argue that given the fiduciary responsibility of clergy, journalists have an obligation to cover these cases when they arise to alert the public to potential danger.

The reality is that we currently have no accurate way of officially measuring, or even estimating, the extent to which faith leaders are involved in criminal activity. As discussed in previous chapters, the Uniform Crime Reporting (UCR) system offers limited ability to analyze crime data to track the occupational or religious status of perpetrators or victims. Even the National Crime Victimization Survey is limited in this regard. Although there is no reason to believe that clergy participate disproportionately in criminal activity, it is likely that as a whole, clergy participate in crime more frequently than most of us would ever have considered. On the basis of a cursory review of anecdotal evidence available through journalistic reports, it is feasible that members of the clergy are prosecuted for crimes at least as frequently as other elite professionals.

Yet, given the social role of clergy, it is likely that individual victims would be even more reluctant to report crimes by clergy to law enforcement officials. Thus, it is feasible that much of the crime committed by clergy is dealt with outside the formal criminal justice system. Some victims have remained silent, while others have reported the offenses directly to other religious leaders on the assumption that the offending clergy member would be dealt with in an appropriate manner. For example, the sexual abuse scandal involving the Catholic Church seems to indicate that when victims or their parents came forward to report an offense, reports were made directly to the church or diocese in the expectation that the Church would handle things suitably. Sadly, this was not always the case. Thus, cases in which clergy are arrested and prosecuted likely represent only a small proportion of the crimes committed by clergy.

Scholars have begun to track the prevalence of clergy misconduct using survey research, although much of the research is focused on sexual misconduct. Although the results of such surveys are revealing and warrant our attention, we must recognize that not all of the offenses reported are violations of criminal law. Yet it is fair to say that at a minimum, a pattern of unethical misconduct has emerged that suggests some clergy have routinely abused their religious authority for their own personal gain.

For example, Seat, Trent, and Kim (1993) surveyed senior pastors of Southern Baptist churches in several states. Out of a total of 277 senior pastors who participated in the study, 14.1 percent self-reported that they had engaged in inappropriate sexual contact for a minister, and more than 70 percent indicated that they had knowledge of another pastor engaging in sexual misconduct with a congregant. In comparing the survey results with those of similar studies involving sexual misconduct by professionals such as psychologists, nurses, social workers, and psychiatrists, Seat, Trent, and Kim (1993) report that the prevalence of sexual misconduct by clergy was higher, with the exception of psychiatrists.

Mental health practitioners were surveyed by Bottoms, Shaver, Goodman, and Qin (1995) to capture the extent of religion-related child abuse in their caseloads. Survey respondents reported a total of 1,652 cases of ritualistic or religion-related child abuse of adult survivors or child victims. A total of 177 cases were determined to have involved an offender who had religious authority. The perpetrators were most often priests or ministers; however, some cases involved nuns, youth ministers, and at least one tribal medicine man and one archbishop. Interestingly, some of the mental health professionals who participated in the study noted that they did not consider sexual abuse by a religious leader different from abuse by any other perpetrator. Bottoms and associates (1995) argue that victimization by faith leaders is less likely to be reported and more likely to "promote painful confusion in young victims that make its long-term psychological consequences difficult to bear" (p. 94).

In a national survey of 578 Catholic nuns, Chibnall, Wolf, and Duckro (1998) found that sexual trauma among nuns was not uncommon. In fact, they found that the lifetime prevalence of sexual trauma for these nuns was nearly 40 percent, with nearly 30 percent reporting sexual trauma during their religious life. A total of 599 incidents of child abuse, sexual exploitation, work sexual harassment, or intracommunity sexual harassment were reported. More than 18 percent of the sisters had been sexually abused as children (which is lower than the figure for the general population of adult women); in these cases, about 10 percent of their abusers were members of the clergy (both men and women). In religious life, the nuns reported that other sisters accounted for nearly 45 percent of the 383 incidents of exploitation and work or intracommunity harassment. The authors estimate that about 34,000 of the 85,000 sisters with active orders at the time of the survey had been victims of some form of sexual trauma (Chibnall, Wolf, & Duckro, 1998), and some of that trauma was inflicted by other women.

Stacey, Darnell, and Shupe (2000) conducted a preliminary analysis of the prevalence of sexual abuse by faith leaders by reviewing numerous national and local publications. Their review yielded a study sample of 337 cases in which victims had reported that clergy had sexually abused them. The cases represented a total of

1,620-plus victims of 409-plus clergy offenders. Also, they found ample evidence of cases from around world, suggesting that the issue is not restricted to the United States, as others have suggested (Jenkins, 1996). In addition, in a survey of 1,067 residents of the Dallas–Fort Worth metropolitan area, they found that 7.4 percent of the respondents had personal knowledge of clergy abuse from either their own experience or the experience of their friends, family, or co-workers.

The most glaring indication of the prevalence of sexual abuse by clergy has recently been documented by researchers at John Jay College of Criminal Justice on behalf of the United States Conference of Catholic Bishops. In response to the scandals involving the sexual abuse of minors by Catholic priests, the Conference of Catholic Bishops established the Charter for the Protection of Children and Young People in 2002. A National Review Board was created to study the exact nature and scope of sexual abuse of minors by Catholic clergy. The study, titled *The Nature and Scope of the Problem of Sexual Abuse of Minors by Catholic Priests and Deacons in the United States,* is an unprecedented examination of allegations of sexual abuse of minors by priests during the period 1950 to 2002. The study also estimated the financial impact those cases have had on the Church.

This exhaustive study revealed that during the fifty-two-year period examined, a total of 4,392 priests were cited in allegations made by 10,667 victims. Of this total, law enforcement officials were contacted about 1,021 of the priests, which led to criminal charges being filed in 384 of the cases. For those cases where information was available, 252 priests were convicted of charges and at least 100 served time in prison for their offenses. Interestingly, of the 195 dioceses and eparchies that participated in the study, only seven did not have any sexual abuse allegations against any of the priests serving in their ministries, suggesting that the problem is widespread rather than clustered in any one jurisdiction. Researchers estimate that the priests and deacons involved in sexual abuse allegations represent about 4 percent of the total population of priests and deacons serving during this period (John Jay College of Criminal Justice, 2004).

What do these surveys suggest? A number of important preliminary conclusions can be drawn from these studies. First, it is clear that some clergy actively engage in inappropriate sexual behavior that at a minimum is unbecoming and inconsistent with their pastoral care duties, and often is downright criminal. Second, these studies also suggest that the problem is not restricted to any one region of the country or any particular denomination. Also, since evidence of sexual abuse is available in other parts of the world, it is not only a U.S. phenomenon. Third, and consistent with sexual abuse cases involving other types of offenders, the reporting of such offenses to law enforcement officials is low. This suggests that the cases reported to police officials are likely to represent only the tip of the iceberg. Finally, although these studies cannot definitively provide a prevalence rate, the results do suggest that sexual abuse perpetrated by clergy may be more consistent with the abuse perpetrated by others than originally thought—a disturbing point if one expects clergy to abide by a different code of conduct and set of moral standards from the average Joe.

This preliminary research, because of its focus on sexual misconduct, reveals little about clergy participation in other types of criminal or unethical behavior. Although some scholars have attempted to look beyond sexual abuse for other examples of clergy misconduct (Shupe, 1995, 1998; Shupe, Stacey, & Darnell, 2000), scholarly research regarding the prevalence of these other forms of violent or property crime is virtually nil. The next chapter attempts to shed some light on three different types of abuses of religious authority: economic crimes, personal crimes, and organizational crimes.

Crimes of the Cloth: Economic, Personal, and Organizational Crime

One Sunday morning in early January 2007, a vigil, sponsored by the Survivors Network of Those Abused by Priests (SNAP), was held in Albany, New York, on the steps of the Holy Cross Church. Those in attendance were joined by sexual abuse survivors and advocates in fifty-four other cities across the nation in marking the fifth anniversary of the first *Boston Globe* news story that implicated the Catholic Church in a sexual abuse scandal—one the Church is still reeling from today. The news article spoke of priests sexually abusing children and of the Church going to great lengths to cover up this abuse. The article sparked 850 articles about hundreds of priests. Carrying signs, photos, and candles, survivors stood outside the Catholic church to focus attention on the plight of victims and their families, to request that bishops disclose the names of offending clergy, and to call for the Church to stop trying to prevent cases from going to civil trials (Higgins, 2007).

Although the sexual abuse scandal within the Catholic Church can be traced back many years (Jenkins, 1996), the breaking story within the Boston diocese in early 2002 prompted a national dialogue about the criminal abuse of religious authority. As discussed in the previous chapter, conceptualizing and categorizing crimes by clergy is a difficult task. It is especially difficult because much of the attention, perhaps rightly so, has centered on the sexual abuse of minors, and thus few have addressed the wider range of clergy misconduct. Shupe (1998) addresses this imbalance in his description of clergy malfeasance by categorizing three different forms of deviance by religious elites: sexual, economic, and authoritative. This typology makes good intuitive sense, since the vast majority of crimes committed by clergy neatly fit into one of these three categories.

Shupe and Iadicola (2000) enhance this typology by further distinguishing between individual and organizational crime. Their open systems model looks to explain the clergy malfeasance through the examination of the interrelationship among the individual member of the clergy, the religious institution, and the broader social environment in which the religious organization functions. Indeed, understanding the criminal deeds of clergy requires us to appreciate the social, economic, and political contexts in which those clergy operate. In other words, clergy are successful in their criminal deeds not because they operate in a vacuum but because of a complex set of situational relationships between the clergy member, the religious organization, and the outside world.

As Shupe and Iadicola (2000) point out, relationships between religious organizations, the state, the media, and the local criminal justice system influence how clergy misconduct is discovered, defined, and dealt with. For example, a police department may have no difficulty pursuing a criminal investigation into the reported activities of the leader of a fringe religious group, especially if that religious group has had a tumultuous relationship with the local community. Yet the same police department might ignore or respond reluctantly to criminal complaints made against a pastor who is well known within law enforcement circles. Jenkins (1996) remarks on the ease with which the Roman Catholic Church was historically able to collaborate with local media to ensure reports of sexual misconduct remained private. Burkett and Brunie (1993) discuss how the structure of the Catholic Church enables bishops to deal with sexual abuse cases in secrecy.

In a similar vein, it is also important to recognize the distinct role that belief systems play in how perpetrators, their colleagues, and victims interpret and frame the criminal behaviors of clergy. Belief systems can influence how victims and religious institutions respond to criminal behaviors once they have occurred. How a religious group views the notions of sin, penance, atonement, retribution, forgiveness, and so on is likely to affect their response to a member of their flock who has broken the law.

In addition, victims may be reluctant to report certain criminal actions to the authorities owing to their obligation to forgive. In the case of sexual abuse, young victims often feel great shame at being involved in sexual acts that are forbidden by religious regulation. Even though they are not responsible for the sexual abuse, victims tend to blame themselves for engaging in such acts and being powerless to stop them (Horst, 1998). Martin Moran's (2005) poignant memoir, *The Tricky Part*, chronicles his experience of being sexually abused by a church camp counselor. The abuse began when he was twelve years old and lasted for the better part of three years. Like other victims of child sexual abuse, he blamed himself for what had happened to him. His strong Catholic upbringing, with its prescriptions on sexual morality, coupled with his emerging adolescent thought processes, played a significant role in how he conceptualized the abuse. As a result, he experienced intense shame and a self-degradation that followed him well into adulthood and ultimately led him to attempt suicide.

Thus, when clergy or church workers commit criminal acts, they do so within the confines of a particular set of religious beliefs and with the influence of the structure and the social boundaries of their religious organization. These factors, combined with individual physical, psychological, or economic concerns, can create circumstances in which the crimes committed by clergy can be ignored or tolerated within the religious organization. It is in this sense that religious institutions have become co-conspirators. Suffice it to say that this is a complex but dynamic set of interrelationships.

Yet it should also be acknowledged that despite these distinctive characteristics, clergy who abuse their religious authority by violating the law often do so in very ordinary ways. This chapter reviews the complex features of some clergy-committed crime, while also attending to some of the more commonplace criminal activities that make certain clergy virtually indistinguishable from other types of criminals. Toward this end, this chapter provides examples of abuses of religious authority in three general categories: economic crimes, crimes against persons, and organizational abuses of authority. Also, it underscores the experiences of victims, for whom the abuse of religious authority can have particularly devastating consequences.

Economic Crimes

Economic crimes are those in which the perpetrator engages in criminal activity for financial gain. Economic crimes involve a wide range of activity, most notably fraud, embezzlement, and larceny. The following examples highlight the nature and scope of crimes committed by clergy of different faiths for economic gain.

Religious Worker Visa Fraud

The Religious Worker Visa Program, administered by the U.S. Citizenship and Immigration Services (USCIS), allows churches, synagogues, or mosques in the United States to sponsor visas for foreign nationals with religious training and experience so that they can come to the United States to work in a religious capacity.

U.S. Immigration and Customs Enforcement (ICE) agents have taken a special interest in religious worker visa fraud since an August 2005 report issued by the Office of Fraud Detection and National Security (FDNS) detailing rampant fraud in the religious visa worker program. The Benefit Fraud Assessment study concluded that fraud was involved in 72 of the 220 religious worker petitions reviewed (USCIS, 2006). This represents a fraud rate of 33 percent, an obvious concern for immigration and law enforcement officials, especially in a post–September 11 world.

Although citizens have participated in a variety of fraudulent schemes to obtain religious worker visas for foreign nationals, of particular concern are those cases where the motives are financial, since the sums of money involved can be large. Fraud investigations by ICE agents have resulted in numerous arrests; in December 2006 thirty-three individuals of different nationalities and religions from eight states and the District of Columbia were arrested in connection with religious visa fraud (Hart, 2006).

For instance, Pastor Dong Wan Park from Tacoma Hope Korean Church, in Tacoma, Washington, was convicted of conspiracy, visa fraud, and obstruction of justice for his role in a religious worker visa fraud scheme. Court reports indicate that he charged up to $30,000 to Korean nationals for providing fraudulent application paperwork, including fake transcripts from a Korean seminary and a certificate of ordination from a Korean Bishop, so that they could obtain religious worker visas in the United States. He had advertised in Korean-language newspapers that immigration visas were available through his church. Park sponsored the nationals to serve as associate pastors at his church; however, there was no evidence any of them had ever been employed by the church. Officials reported that Pastor Park also tried to get the petitioners to change their stories to mislead investigators and to hide any evidence that they had paid him to provide the documents. Although Park claimed the money was to be donated to the church, prosecutors showed evidence that he withdrew money at tribal casinos (AP, 2006). After his conviction, Park fled to South Korea for asylum; however, he was deported and sent back to the United States to face punishment (*Seattle Post-Intelligencer*, 2006).

Religious Fraud

Religious fraud is a general term, used here to describe circumstances in which a religious leader raises money for a supposedly religious purpose and then misappropriates the funding to serve his or her personal needs. This may involve a wide range of fraudulent "religious commerce" activities (Rosoff, Pontell, & Tillman, 2002, p. 207), such as collecting donations for fraudulent faith healing, appealing to large-scale television audiences for donations to support the work of the ministry, or requesting that followers invest in various financial opportunities. Several examples help illustrate how clergy have been involved in crimes that have yielded them large financial rewards and in some instances have bilked followers out of millions of dollars.

Perhaps the most notorious example is from Florida. Gerald and Betty Payne and several associates, founders of Greater Ministries International (GMI) in Tampa, Florida, were sentenced in 2001 in a U.S. District Court for multiple charges of conspiracy, mail fraud, and money laundering. The Paynes were carrying out a classic Ponzi scheme. Ponzi schemes are named after the infamous white-collar criminal, Charles Ponzi, who ran such a scheme in 1919–1920 to bilk 20,000 investors of $10 million (Rosoff, Pontell, & Tillman, 2002). Ponzi schemes are generally operated by a central person or company who pays high returns to investors out the money paid into the venture by new investors.

The Paynes recruited their investors from various Christian groups, promising that God would double their money. Investors were attracted to the scheme via biblical passages and were told that state and federal securities laws did not apply to them because the investments were really "gifts" to the Church and the repayments to investors were really "blessings," thus not subject to taxes (Pennsylvania Securities Commission, 1999).

In another case, Reverend Kevin Thompson of the Bay Area Family Church, Holy Spirit Association for Unification of World Christianity, in San Leandro, California, was sentenced on federal charges in January 2007 for a poaching scheme involving baby leopard sharks. He was sentenced to one year and one day in prison and ordered to pay $100,000 in restitution for violating the Lacey Act, which makes it a federal offense to knowingly sell or purchase fish, wildlife, or plants captured or uprooted in violation of any underlying law. In California, the law places a limit of thirty-six inches on any commercial harvest of leopard sharks (USDOJ, 2007).

Fishing plays an important role in Pastor Thompson's church (also called Ocean Church), which is affiliated with the Unification Church, headed by Reverend Sun Myung Moon. Thomson realized he could make a fortune distributing leopard sharks on the black market, since the sharks are prized among certain fish collectors. Federal investigators uncovered an elaborate ring of illegal leopard shark trafficking that centered on Thompson. The investigation led officials to consider whether the infamous Reverend Sun Myung Moon was also involved in the illegal operation, especially given that some of his church members control True World Foods, a company that supplies seafood for sushi (Gammon, 2006, 2007).

Ocean Church has a presence on the Internet (http://www.oceanchurch.org.) where they proclaim "the ocean is a classroom and a cathedral."

Cases such as these demonstrate how easy it is for (so-called) religious leaders to engage in economically beneficial criminal activities under the guise of religion. Such crimes usually pass under the radar of most law enforcement officials and thus are generally not brought to attention of authorities unless someone suspects wrongdoing and reports their suspicions to the authorities. As you might imagine, it is difficult to ascertain the validity of the religious calling of those who engage in religious fraud. Since people of strong faith willingly donate millions of dollars each year to religious causes and ministries, and some do so blindly because of their faith, there is reason for concern.

In fact, in the 1990s a Christian ministry called Wall Watchers, founded by Howard "Rusty" Leonard and his wife Carolyn, was established in part to bring about accountability in Christian ministries. As the ministry evolved it broadened its scope to evaluate the financial transparency of ministries and make those data available to the public. In 2000, Wall Watchers introduced Ministry Watch (http://www.ministrywatch.com), which now serves as an online database of financial profiles and rankings of more than 400 of the largest Christian church and parachurch ministries in the United States. Ministry Watch provides the donating public with critical information to inform their giving decisions. Religious ministries are graded on their financial efficiency and their transparency in providing their financial and organizational records; if it is warranted, they can be flagged with a donor alert. A profile is provided of each ministry in the database, which includes a narrative description of the religious organization and a summary of what supporters and critics have to say about it.

Embezzlement

Embezzlement is the taking of money or property that is entrusted to one's care but is actually owned by someone else. In the case of clergy, embezzlement usually involves the theft of church assets or cash by a clergy member who has some legitimate role in overseeing the funds. A recent case from Palm Beach, Florida, may go down in history as one of the most notorious examples of embezzlement and collusion ever uncovered by police officials. This case illustrates that clergy, given their social position, can literally get away with millions of dollars before their indiscretions are revealed.

In this case, Monsignor John Skehan, a Roman Catholic priest from St. Vincent Ferrer Church in Delray Beach, Florida, and his successor, Reverend

Francis Guinan, were arrested in September 2006 after an extensive investigation by the Florida Department of Law Enforcement. Both are charged with the misappropriation of $8.6 million of church funds over forty years. News reports are unclear as to when these two priests met, but it appears they have been in collusion with each other—and with others—for many years. In 1984 they formed SHAG Inc., a mortgage loan scheme, with another archdiocese of Venice priest, Michael Hickey. Their partnership also led them to invest in race horses in Ireland in the 1990s. Father Guinan took over the parish at St. Vincent after Monsignor Skehan retired in 2003. Investigators have traced their spending on all kinds of lavish vacations, real estate properties, gambling, an extensive coin collection, as well as women and their children. They both had girlfriends who were former bookkeepers of the church and no doubt indispensable in keeping their spending habits secret (LaForgia, 2006; O'Connor & Slater, 2006; Slater, 2006; Thompson, 2006; Wides-Munoz, 2006). At the time of writing, the case continues to unfold, but prosecutors have released hundreds of documents related to the investigation, some of which the media have made available online (Franceschina & Diaz, 2007).

Forgery

The crime of forgery involves activities such as creating a false document, altering a genuine existing document, or signing someone else's name to a document without permission. Commonly forged documents include contracts, identification cards, and legal documents. Forgery usually involves the intent to defraud someone or to steal something and thus often accompanies fraud and embezzlement. For example, Reverend Randy Radic, the pastor from First Congregational Church in Ripon, California, was arrested for forgery and embezzlement after he forged documents in 2002 to embezzle church property: the deed to the home he had lived in as pastor of the church. The house was owned by the church, and as pastor he was able to live there rent free. Once in possession of the deed he was able to take out home equity loans on the property. He secured a total of five loans, totaling $370,000. When he could no longer make the payments on the loans, he declared bankruptcy and sold the church and parsonage for $525,000 (AP, 2005).

Originally charged with ten felonies with enhancements, he pled guilty in January 2006 to one count of grand theft by embezzlement and was sentenced to sixteen months in prison and ordered to pay restitution. In a dramatic twist, he approached prosecutors for an additional deal to reduce his prison sentence to time served in return for testifying in the murder trial of Roy Gerald Smith, who was accused of killing a forty-six-year-old woman in Ripon. His testimony would have been based on statements that Smith had made to him while they both were incarcerated. Prosecutors agreed to the deal (Miller, 2007), but Smith, a registered sex offender, pled guilty and Radic did not need to testify. Despite this turn of events, prosecutors plan to uphold their end of the bargain, since Radic upheld his (Smith, 2007).

Tax Evasion/Tax Fraud

In instances of tax evasion and tax fraud, clergy have misrepresented their tax status, refused to pay taxes, or filed fraudulent tax returns. In some cases clergy have done so with their own personal financial gain in mind. Yet some clergy do so as part of a larger church movement to resist the regulations of the federal government. In these instances, clergy have refused to apply for tax-exempt status or to incorporate on the premise that the government has no authority to regulate churches in any way, shape, or form. They argue that for a church to go through the process of applying for tax-exempt status (as most churches readily do) is the equivalent of acknowledging that the government has a right to control the church. Two examples illustrate this point.

In 2006, federal officials arrested evangelist Kent Hovind on fifty-eight federal charges related to his willful failure to pay federal taxes and evading tax-reporting requirements. His wife, Jo Hovind, was also arrested and named as a co-defendant on forty-four of the charges. Hovind, also known as Dr. Dino, is a creationist who owned and operated a Creation Science Ministry from his home in Pensacola, Florida, which housed a dinosaur theme park. According to the park's Web site (http://www.dinosauradventureland.com), Dinosaur Adventure Land is a place where dinosaurs and the bible meet. A central tenet of the Creation Science Ministries is that dinosaurs and humans shared time on earth together and that dinosaurs may still roam the earth. Internal Revenue Service officials charged Hovind for failure to withhold quarterly taxes for his employees, whom he classified as missionaries and paid in cash (Kauffman, 2006a, 2006b). In January 2007 Hovind was sentenced to ten years in prison and ordered to pay restitution to the IRS (Stewart, 2007). He is currently in a federal prison facility in Pensacola.

Another example hails from Indianapolis. The Indianapolis Baptist Temple (IBT) and pastors Greg J. Dixon and his son Greg A. Dixon lost a long-standing dispute with the IRS and had their church property seized by federal officials in 2001. The church had not paid taxes in seventeen years and had refused to register as a charity under section 501(c)3 of the Internal Revenue Code. They went through a three-year legal battle with the federal government that resulted in the court issuing a seizure order (SPLC, 2001). In anticipation of the seizure, the Dixons rallied support from like-minded church members and other antigovernment extremists, resulting in a ninety-two-day standoff (ADL, 2001). All ended peacefully when the church was repossessed by federal officials, although Pastor Dixon had to be strapped to a gurney and rolled out of the church (King, 2006).

The Hovinds and the Dixons represent a coalition of approximately 100 churches nationwide that promote a "theology of Christian resistance to earthly government" (SPLC, 2001, n.p.). Their coalition, the Unregistered Baptist Fellowship (UBF; http://www.unregisteredbaptistfellowship.com) explains their views as follows:

> We believe that civil government occupies a sphere of sovereignty which is separate and distinct from that of the New Testament Church, and just as the church may not take up the sword of the magistrate, so civil government is prohibited from taking up the spiritual keys of the church or usurping any authority over it. The authority of civil government ends at the threshold of the church, since it can have no jurisdiction in the realm of church government or any assembly of the Lord Jesus Christ.

The Southern Poverty Law Center (2001) argues that the UBF has attracted a number of different extremists to its cause, some of whom actively promote a pro-hate agenda against homosexuals, abortion providers, African Americans, Jewish people, and/or the government. Despite the arrest and conviction of Kent Hovind and the loss of church property by the IBT, the UBF appears to be moving its agenda forward, and thus it is likely that more pastors will face criminal charges in the future.

These examples of tax fraud are illustrative of religion-related crime that could be easily defined in a number of different ways, since the clergy involved are intentionally breaking the law on the basis of some theological principle and they do so in hopes of spurring on policy reform. Thus, this form of tax evasion could also readily be considered a theologically-based or reactive/defensive religion-related crime. It is included as an example of an abuse of religious authority because clergy are making the decision to break the law in their official capacity as church leaders, and such decisions ultimately had consequences for their followers.

Personal Crimes/Sexual Abuse of Minors

Personal crimes are those that involve direct physical contact with individual victims, such as rape, sexual abuse and other sex crimes, robbery, physical assault, and murder. Members of the clergy have been arrested and convicted of all different types of personal crimes, some of which have been described elsewhere in this text. Yet of all the different abuses of religious authority recognized here, none has gained as much media attention as the sexual abuse of children by trusted clergy. This attention is for good reason, since the physical and emotional well-being of children has been at stake. Also, the integrity of certain religious institutions has been called into question when it has been determined some high-level religious officials have actively covered up such crimes or have at minimum denied the seriousness of their impact on victims and their families. Therefore, child sexual abuse by clergy, and the surrounding scandal, provides perhaps the best illustration of the complex dynamics at work when a member of the clergy engages in wrongdoing within the confines of a strong, yet insular, religious tradition.

A case from the diocese of Superior in Wisconsin illustrates these points. On February 5, 2002, Dan O'Connell, owner of O'Connell Family Funeral Home in Hudson, Wisconsin, and one of his employees, James Ellison, were shot and killed at the funeral home. After a four-year investigation, police concluded that Father Ryan Erickson, a parish priest at St. Patrick's Church, where Dan was a member, was responsible for the deaths of Dan and James. The motive for the killings was likely linked to the fact that Dan had discovered information that the priest had been sexually abusing children and/or giving them alcohol. The investigation also revealed that Father Erickson had a long history of abuse, alcohol problems, and other erratic behaviors, yet the Church continued to have him serve his priestly duties. During the investigation, Father Erickson committed suicide. A special hearing was held after the suicide in which a judge determined that there was probable cause to rule that the priest had committed the murders (*Janesville Gazette*, 2006).

Charges of child sexual abuse have been made against clergy from different faiths; however, much of the attention in the past two decades has centered on Roman Catholic priests and the way the Church has chosen to respond to reports of sexual violation by the priests in their employ. The issue surfaced in the 1980s and reached fever pitch in 2002 with the resignation of Cardinal Bernard Law of the Boston archdiocese. At the time of his resignation, the Boston archdiocese was wrestling with almost 500 legal claims and lawsuits filed by individuals alleging abuse by more than 100 priests within the archdiocese (Pfeiffer, 2002).

Perhaps the most notorious priests convicted of child sexual abuse, who were under the supervisory control of Cardinal Law, were Reverend Paul R. Shanley and Reverend John Geoghan. It appeared that Cardinal Law and other high-ranking religious officials had a blatant disregard for the predatory sexual behavior of priests such as Shanley and Geoghan. Once the abuse was discovered, public pressure ultimately prompted the cardinal to resign his post.

Shanley was originally charged with ten counts of child rape and six counts of indecent assault and battery in the molestation of six boys while he was the pastor of St. Jean's parish in Newton, Massachusetts, although he has been accused of molesting about twenty-five people (Belluck, 2002). During Shanley's court hearings, the Boston archdiocese was required to release more than 800 pages of documentation establishing the Church's knowledge of Reverend Shanley's abusive behavior during his career as a priest. For example, Bishop Thomas V. Daily promoted Shanley to lead a parish even though he had knowledge that Shanley had been giving speeches outside of the Boston area supporting sexual relationships between men and boys (Belluck, 2002). Shanley was even known to have attended a meeting in 1978 of the North American Man–Boy Love Association (NAMBLA) (Robinson & Farragher, 2002). Even after the Boston archdiocese had paid monetary settlements to several of Shanley's victims, Cardinal Law did not oppose Shanley's request to run a guesthouse in New York City that often housed students (Robinson & Farragher, 2002). Over the course of four decades, Cardinal Law and other officials chose to deal with Shanley's criminal indiscretions by moving him from parish to parish.

A similar pattern emerged with Reverend John Geoghan, who was sentenced to a prison term of nine to ten years in Massachusetts for abusing a young boy in a public swimming pool, although records indicated he had molested many other children as well. The sentencing judge, Middlesex Superior Court judge Sandra Hamlin, sentenced Geoghan to the maximum term and stated that he was "a threat to any young boy 'who may have the misfortune to be in contact with him'" (Farragher, 2003, n.p.). In August 2003 the defrocked priest was murdered in his cell at the Souza-Baranowski Correctional Center by fellow inmate Joseph L. Druce.

Organizational Abuse of Religious Authority

As the Shanley and Geoghan cases suggest, the Catholic Church failed to deal with these priests in an appropriate manner. In fact, Cardinal Law was subpoenaed to testify in May 2002 regarding his lack of response to repeated and credible complaints of criminal behavior in a lawsuit brought by eighty-six plaintiffs accusing him and others in the Boston archdiocese of negligent behaviors. Documents that detail the extent to which the archdiocese failed to handle the predatory abusive behavior of Shanley and Geoghan (as well as documents on cases from other communities) are available on a Web site dedicated to documenting patterns of sexual abuse (http://www.bishopaccountability.org). Not only are the actions of the individual offending priests a concern, but so is the broader response of the religious institution to complaints of such misconduct.

It appears, at least in these case examples, that the Church's actions ultimately perpetuated the criminal actions of priests within its control. The term "organizational abuse of authority" applies to situations in which religious organizations respond to criminal acts by the clergy in its employ in such a way as to benefit and protect the institution rather than the victims. The Catholic Church is by no means the only religious institution that has abused its authority in this manner; however, the sheer frequency with which cases have surfaced in recent years within the Catholic Church has resulted in a firestorm of public attention and provides an excellent example of the role of the religious institution in the criminal misdeeds of its clergy. You might be asking yourself why an organization would take such a risk when young children are involved. Although there is no definitive answer to that question, a number of factors are likely to have played a role, as discussed in Chapter 10.

Historically, religious institutions have chosen to police their own, and in the cases of Catholic priests such as Shanley and Geoghan, this was clearly a strategy that only placed more children in danger. The Church's actions seem to suggest that it was not eager to yield any power or authority to laypeople in the civil government since, like many other religious organizations, it has always viewed itself as above or at least separate from the government of the United States (Kurst-Swanger & Ryniker, 2003). Certainly, the ingrained notion of the separation of church and state plays a role in perpetuating this situation.

It is also important to note that other professional groups, such as police, lawyers, doctors, and government officials, have struggled with how to appropriately discipline members of their own ranks who have engaged in some form of misconduct. Just as members of a police department, a law firm, or a medical practice would be hard pressed to report a colleague or subordinate to law enforcement officials, it would be difficult for religious leaders to do the same. This is especially true within the context of a belief system shared by religious leaders and followers that is focused on forgiveness and views clergy as not merely employees but as people with a special, holy relationship with God. Although other professional groups have struggled with disciplinary actions when their members engage in criminal behavior, these groups have not routinely had to deal with their members sexually abusing children while performing their professional duties, nor do these other professions have a history of continuing to place children at risk of abuse. Certainly, the Catholic Church has struggled to involve the authorities, despite the fact that the safety of children has been involved.

Most state legislatures have not considered members of the clergy to be mandated reporters of child abuse and neglect. Since most child protection systems are intended to respond specifically to cases of child abuse and neglect involving parents or guardians, cases in which a member of the clergy is the perpetrator are likely to be considered a law enforcement issue rather than a specific child protective service issue, unless the member of the clergy is specifically in a caretaking role. It may follow that many religious leaders are uneducated about what constitutes child sexual abuse and the extent of injury to the cognitive, physical, and emotional development of children when abuse occurs. Terry and Leland Smith (2006) report that "education about the problem of sexual abuse is the most recognized pathway to the safety of all" (p. 53).

Theresa Krebs (1998) points out that the structures within the Catholic Church itself serve to facilitate pedophilia among clergy. She cites the Church's international nature, its organizational hierarchy, and its form of governance as central factors in the patterned denial of abuse. These organizational realities have maintained the secrecy of abusive behaviors and insulated the offenders from community retribution. Also, the aging population of priests and the lack of younger individuals willing to commit to the priesthood may have been a factor in keeping offending priests active within the Church.

Regardless of the factors involved, some people have vehemently argued that the Church should be held liable for its actions. For example, Arthur Austin, an alleged victim of sexual abuse by Reverend Paul Shanley, stated, "If the Catholic Church in America does not fit the description of organized crime, then Americans seriously need to examine their concept of justice" (Robinson & Farragher, 2002, p. A1). As a result, the Church has since had to face litigation for its role in perpetuating the sexual abuse of children.

Numerous scholars have examined the issue of sexual abuse within the Catholic Church and the Church's organizational and administrative responses from a number of perspectives (Bartunek, Keenan, & Hinsdale, 2006; Dokecki, 2004; Fortune, 2004; Fortune & Longwood, 2004; Jenkins, 1996); however, perhaps the most courageous research conducted to date has been commissioned by the Catholic Church itself. As mentioned in Chapter 11, in June 2002 the U.S. Conference of Catholic Bishops approved the Charter for the Protection of Children and Young People. This charter established a National Review Board, made up of laypeople, who were charged with the task of ensuring that a comprehensive study was conducted into the true nature and scope of the sexual abuse of minors by clergy. The National Review Board commissioned scholars from the John Jay School of Criminal Justice of the City University of New York to conduct the study. The study was intended to reveal the number and nature of allegations of sexual abuse against individuals under the age of eighteen by Catholic priests between the years 1950 and 2002 and to document the financial impact those crimes have had on the Church. The full report is available to the public on the Web site of the U.S. Conference of Catholic Bishops (http://www.usccb.org/nrb/johnjaystudy).

The researchers gathered data for the study from several sources. A profile of each diocese was drawn up that detailed various characteristics such as size, total number of abuse allegations, and the expenditures involved in responding to such allegations. A survey was conducted of church records relating to individual priests against whom allegations had been made as well as information regarding the alleged victims and the nature of the abuse allegations. Researchers contracted with Ernst and Young, an accounting firm, to protect the confidentiality of the information by stripping data of all identifiers so as to maintain the confidentiality of the victims and priests who became subjects in the study. The study was conducted from March 2003 through February 2004, and information was gathered from 195 dioceses and 140 religious communities.

The results of the study are very revealing. A total of 4,392 priests had at least one allegation of abuse made against them during the period of the study. Although estimating how this number relates to the overall number of priests in active service during this period is difficult, the researchers estimated that this number represented about 4 percent of all active priests. A total of 149 priests (or 3.5 percent of the total) had more than ten allegations of abuse, involving a total of 2,960 abuse victims. Therefore, these 149 priests were responsible for 26 percent of the total number of allegations.

A total of 10,667 individuals made allegations of child sexual abuse by priests. More than 50 percent of the victims (50.9) were between the ages of eleven and fourteen, 27.3 percent were aged fifteen to seventeen, and 16 percent were between eight and ten years old. Almost 6 percent of the victims were under the age of seven. Therefore, nearly 73 percent of the victims were fourteen years old or younger. Eighty-one percent of the victims were male. The sexual abuse allegations took many different forms, including touching over the victim's clothing, touching under the victim's clothing, cleric performing oral sex, victim disrobing, and penile penetration. Just 141 reported incidents included only verbal abuse and/or the use of pornography.

At the time of the study, law enforcement officials were contacted regarding a total of 1,021 priests, which represents about 24 percent of the total number of priests who had allegations made against them. The available information indicates that 252 priests were convicted in criminal court, and about 100 of them were given prison terms (this represents about 2 percent of the total number of priests against whom allegations were made). The study also confirmed that the Church bore a huge financial cost as a result of these abuses. A total of $572 million was paid by dioceses and religious communities to compensate victims, treat victims, treat offending priests, and settle attorneys' fees. This figure does not include the $85 million settlement in the archdiocese of Boston related to the cases described above (USCCB, 2004; Terry & Leland Smith, 2006).

This study determined that the problem of sexual abuse is in fact widespread, touching nearly all of the dioceses and religious communities in the sample at some time during the study period. Although many dioceses struggled with the development of sexual abuse policies before this research (Kurst-Swanger & Ryniker, 2003), the Church has responded to these issues with vigor. The U.S. Conference of Catholic Bishops crafted the Charter for the Protection of Children and Young People (USCCB, 2005), in which they state that "it is within this context of the essential soundness of the priesthood and of the deep faith of our brothers and sisters in the Church that we know we can meet and resolve this crisis for now and the future" (p. 6).

As part of its commitment to resolving the sexual abuse issue, the Church issued what are referred to as "essential norms" for diocesan and eparchial policies in terms of how to deal with allegations of sexual abuse of minors by priests or deacons. Under these essential norms, dioceses and eparchies are required to have written policies related to the sexual abuse of minors consistent with canon law and must file their policy with the U.S. Conference of Catholic Bishops. The norms also require that each diocese or eparchy assign a person to coordinate pastoral care for those persons affected by sexual abuse by clerics (USCCB, 2006). As part of this requirement, the Office of Child and Youth Protection has established programs and services to heal those affected by sexual abuse. Victim assistance coordinators have been assigned in each of the dioceses around the country. Coordinators are able to assist victims in making formal complaints to their diocese or eparchy and can set up personal meetings with the leaders of the church and provide ongoing support.

In fact, it appears as though the Office of Child and Youth Protection has a central role in implementing the goals and objectives of the charter. This new office was established in 2002 as part of the U.S. Conference of Catholic Bishops' formal organizational response to the sexual abuse issue. The office has three main responsibilities: assisting each diocese and eparchy in implementing programs to ensure the safety of children as they engage in church activities, developing an audit mechanism by which compliance with the responsibilities set forth in the charter could be assessed and preparing an annual compliance report that is to be available to the public. The current executive director of the center is Teresa M. Kettelkamp, a retired colonel from the Illinois State Police (USCCB, 2007a).

Central to the work of the Office of Child and Youth Protection are the annual audits established to provide a mechanism by which the Church could continually track sexual abuse allegations and compliance with various mandates. The Center for Applied Research in the Apostolate of Georgetown University presented the report on the 2006 audit results. The audit revealed that 635 new credible allegations of child sexual abuse were made against clerics in 2006 by a total of 632 individuals against a total of 394 priests or deacons. It is important to note that of the 635 new allegations, "14 of the allegations (or 2 percent) involved children under the age of 18 in 2006, while the remaining allegations were made by adults who are alleging abuse as minors in previous years" (USCCB, 2007b, p. 8). This is to be expected, since many child victims of sexual assault do not disclose abuse until they are adults. For example, Ponton and Goldstein (2004) found that on average the male victims of clergy abuse in their study waited more than eighteen years to disclose their victimization. This reality of child sexual abuse means that regardless what changes the Church makes for the future, allegations are likely to continue to emerge as those abused years ago come of age to report.

The audit also revealed that in 2006 the Church paid out a total of $332.9 million in costs associated with sexual abuse allegations. Although this figure represents a decline in costs over previous years, audits reveal that for the years 2004–2006, the costs to the Church have totaled more than $918 million (USCCB, 2007b).

Article 12 of the charter requires local dioceses and eparchies to engage in safe environment training and education for all members of the Church community. The Church established a Safe Environment Work Group to address concerns related to the implementation of safety training and to engage scholars in prevention education and sexual abuse in the dialogue about appropriate training for children and young people.

All in all, it appears as though the Catholic Church has taken very positive steps in its organizational response to the problem of the sexual abuse of minors by members of the cloth. The Church has established policies, feedback mechanisms, workgroups, and training and created a process by which victims can receive assistance from church representatives. Although for many victims the Church's response may be considered a day late and a dollar short, it is probably fair to say that much of this reform came about only as a direct result of public pressure from media exposure and litigation. It would also be fair to say that a problem as embedded and complex as this is also resistant to quick fixes; sustainable change will require a cultural shift within the ranks of the Church. Thus the Church will need to be vigilant in continually evaluating itself to make effective long-term change. In the meantime, litigation continues. For instance, in July 2007 the archdiocese of Los Angeles settled a lawsuit involving more than 500 victims for about $660 million. Settlements in the United States to date have cost the Roman Catholic Church in the United States about $1.5 billion, with the financial burden directly on the dioceses (Goodstein, 2007).

Although new allegations continue to surface, at least a more transparent process appears to be in place to deal more appropriately with the problem. Rest assured, there are plenty of scholars, journalists, and survivor advocacy groups continuing to monitor progress and to call Church officials to task if old organizational practices are maintained. For instance, a Massachusetts-based nonprofit organization hosts a Web site dedicated to doing just that (http://www.BishopAccountability.org). The site is intended to record and expose the responses of bishops in various dioceses to the criminal behavior of their priests. The Web site also serves as a repository of available public records regarding the sexual abuse crisis and includes a database of priests who have been publicly accused of abuse in each diocese across the United States.

Now that systems of intervention have been begun, it is important that the Church continue to focus on prevention and to create an ongoing dialogue on issues of abuse and violence in any form. Perhaps other religious institutions will learn from its mistakes and follow its lead toward the "promise to protect, pledge to heal."

Victims of Clergy Abuse

As mentioned previously, experiencing abuse by a trusted member of the clergy can be a devastating experience for victims. This is especially true for young people, whose sexual identities and sense of self are yet to emerge fully. At its very core, sexual abuse in any form is a very personal violation. Victims are affected in numerous ways, depending on the extent and frequency of abuse. For many abused by clerics, the violation is also a spiritual one.

Horst (1998) eloquently describes the debilitating role that shame plays in the recovery from sexual abuse violations by victims of clergy sexual abuse. Such shame can leave demoralizing wounds that emotionally cripple, ultimately spilling over into all aspect of victims' lives. "Victims feel that they must have been really bad, since this holy, God-like person singled them out for the abuse" (Horst, 1998, p. 24). Complicating the experience for some victims is their participation in the abusive acts and their powerlessness to stop them, especially if the offending cleric showered them with gifts or forbidden "treats" such as alcohol or pornography. Young people also believe they are somehow to blame for the sexual violations if they experienced any arousal or sexual gratification from the acts. Coming to understand that arousal is a normal biological response in sexual encounters, even in situations of abuse, is an important element of healing. Moran (2005) confirms this in his memoirs, recounting in vivid detail the thoughts and feelings that he experienced while his body was being violated by an adult church camp counselor.

Also at stake is faith. Horst (1998) states that those abused in a religious setting essentially "miss experiencing the unconditional love of God" (p. 26). McLaughlin (1994) found that those abused by clergy decreased their church attendance and participation. The rituals of religious worship are tainted by abuse, especially since clergy are considered representatives of God (Wells, 2003).

There is no doubt that some victims of abuse experience intense feelings of hurt and shame that have a profound impact on their lives as they grow and develop into adulthood. Researchers have also identified that many victims experience anger, a loss of spirituality, sexual difficulties, depression, sleeplessness, and/or substance abuse as adults (Fater & Mullaney, 2000; Ponton & Goldstein, 2004). These findings are consistent with the findings of other researchers for adult survivors of child sexual abuse when the offender is a family member. Children who are sexually violated are likely to experience some impact to their cognitive, physical, and emotional development, depending on factors such as the level of violation and the frequency (Kurst-Swanger & Petcosky, 2003).

Victims of sexual abuse by clergy, as well as victims of other types of crime committed by clergy, do not have to recover alone. A variety of services and support networks are available across the nation and on the Internet. Services are available to help minimize the impact of crime on victims and their families and include information and referral, assistance with civil and criminal legal procedures and processes, counseling, support groups, crisis intervention, shelter, advocacy, and financial assistance through state crime victim compensation programs. Services for crime victims have been established in different federal, state, or local venues, including law enforcement agencies, prosecutors' offices, hospitals, courts, and nonprofit community-based organizations.

Like survivors of other types of crimes, survivors of clergy abuse have come together to support each other. A number of organizations have formed to provide support and advocacy. The Survivors Network of Those Abused by Priests (http://www.snapnetwork.org/) is one such organization. It has a network of local chapters and provides survivors with support via Internet-based support groups and discussion boards. The organization also provides information to survivors and their families and serves as a watchdog advocacy organization. The organization keeps an eye on how various dioceses around the country are handling allegations. Although the Church has taken a bold step in establishing victim assistance services within the Church for those sexually abused by priests, it is important that independent support networks such as SNAP exist to provide unbiased support for survivors.

Another lay support and advocacy organization that emerged as a result of the child sexual abuse crisis is the Voice of the Faithful (VOTF; http://www.votf. org/index.html). VOTF's mission is to support survivors of abuse, to support priests who are working to heal survivors and effect change, and to shape structural change with the Church.

The Healing Alliance (http://www.healingall.org), originally named Victims of Clergy Abuse LinkUP, was established to raise awareness of clergy abuse and to support the recovery of victims of clergy abuse in Chicago in the early 1990s; however, it found that survivors of other kinds of trauma were also in need of support. It provides information and resources to survivors about the nature of trauma and healing.

Crusade Against Clergy Abuse is an advocacy Web site hosted by the families of murder victims Dan O'Connell and James Ellison (murdered by Father Ryan Erickson) to inform and to encourage others to get involved in advocating for reform within the Catholic Church (http://www.crusadeagainstclergyabuse. com/index.html). They seek to reform the Church to protect children, support survivors, and make Church officials accountable for their actions or neglect. Their five-point plan for reform seeks to make bishops and cardinals accountable for their decisions, requires the Church to disclose to the public the names of clergy who have been proven to be abusive, requires the Church to acknowledge its mistakes publicly, requires religious elites to reach out to survivors in tangible ways to provide support and healing and links to law enforcement officials, and encourages religious leaders to support legislation to eliminate criminal and civil statutes of limitations on child sexual abuse litigation.

In addition, for those abused by nuns, an organization named Abuse by Nuns (http://www.abusebynuns.com) provides survivors with support, information, advocacy, and a venue to share their thoughts and feelings through an Internet discussion board.

As these examples illustrate, today there is ample support for those abused by clergy, and many organizations are actively working to ensure change occurs in the organizational practices of religious institutions when clergy misuse their power and authority. For many victims, recovery requires a type of spiritual healing or renewal that may challenge or redefine their faith. It is important that religious institutions play a role in that healing process.

Part V
Conclusion

12

Final Thoughts and Future Directions

I wrote this book to explore the nexus between religion and crime. I hope your journey through this text ends with the recognition that religion-related crime is worthy of future research and inquiry. I have suggested a three-pronged typology intended to frame an ongoing dialogue about the role of religion in the commission of crime and to demonstrate the scope of the problems that arise when legal and religious principles conflict. The book has explored examples of religion-related crime within this typology. The examples provided were meant to be selective rather than exhaustive, and were chosen because of their salience for scholars and professional practitioners from a variety of disciplines, including legal, medical, social work, psychology, criminal justice, sociology, and religious studies. With its focus on recent criminal activity, this book was intended to shed some light on the debates between religious and secular communities, the legal issues raised by such debates, and some of the dilemmas posed to public policy making and implementation.

Although each chapter reviews a different category of religion-related crime, a number of important common themes emerge. First, given our history and the fact that the United States is one of the most religiously diverse countries in the world, it is likely that debates will continue to rage about where to draw the line between religious freedom and the law. It is important to safeguard religious freedom; however, it is clear that legal boundaries must exist. It is important that the law be used to protect others from injurious religious practices, especially those citizens who are most vulnerable. It is clear that the Constitution was crafted with the knowledge that religion was especially important in the lives of U.S. citizens and thus worthy of recognition and special protection. Yet this special protection does not license religious individuals or institutions to be above the law. Thus, the law must serve the dual role of protecting religious freedom while protecting people from it—a daunting task indeed.

Second, this text illustrates that religion-related crime can occur and flourish in a number of settings for a number of reasons. Theology is not always a central feature of crime commission, but it is inextricably in the mix of factors associated with religion-related crime. Thus, it is important that legal, medical, and behavioral health professionals understand the complex nature of religious belief systems and how they can affect the behavior and decision making of otherwise law-abiding citizens.

Third, in addition to understanding individual behavior, we must consider the dynamic interactions of group and institutional behaviors. Groups and their leaders tend to engage in self-protective behaviors when challenged by internal or external pressures, especially if those pressures represent a real or perceived threat to the belief system of the leader or group. Some groups might dissolve and dwindle as result of external pressure; for others their resolve will only strengthen. This appears to be true of all kinds of groups where membership is based on some common bond or goal. Groups experience both internal and external pressures, either of which can result in abusive and criminal behavior. We should not ever underestimate the level of destruction that is possible when people think their goals or beliefs are being challenged, especially if other mental health and social concerns exist.

Fourth, we must recognize that clergy and other people of strong faith are not beyond behaving criminally. As a society, we might hold religious people in high regard and as such be in social denial as to their ability to be involved in harmful social actions. This text demonstrates that even the most pious of individuals can be guilty of heinous criminal atrocities. They must be held accountable for their actions. We must recognize that clergy are human, regardless of whatever social roles they play.

Fifth, despite the lack of formal mechanisms to measure religion-related crimes, it does appear as though they occur with enough frequency to warrant the concern of criminal justice practitioners and human service professionals. With history as our teacher, it is prudent that law enforcement officials approach religion-related crime with caution. It is important to understand the depth, complexity, and contours of religiosity and the characteristics of different religious environments. In the future, conflicts between religious people or groups and the government are likely to erupt, and a number of kinds of crime may result.

Finally, this volume explores criminal or neglectful behavior within a religious framework in an effort to help us better understand and predict deviance. Further investigation may reveal that religiosity and faith communities provide unique social environments in which to study the contours of deviance. Within the field of criminology it is time we move beyond viewing religion and religious communities as only positive agents of social control. This book illustrates that religion and crime coalesce in more ways than have ever fully been acknowledged.

Although this text is intended to serve as an initial exploration of the various types of religion-related crime and to highlight the related body of literature that currently exists, a few words about what might be accomplished in the future are in order. First, it is important that the social, political, and legal issues related to religion-related crime be openly discussed both in faith circles and among secular practitioners. It is critical that these communities address how such issues affect all their constituents. A dialogue between the leadership of various religious communities and local law enforcement and human service providers can promote problem solving and boundary setting before incidents occur, providing a mechanism from which both religious and secular institutions could benefit. It might be possible to find creative ways in which religious organizations can stay true to their belief system within the confines of the law. Such discussions have begun in some areas, and perhaps this text will help illustrate the need for continued dialogue.

The burden may lie with law enforcement officials, who should make it a point to get to know the religious communities in their jurisdiction. Building common understanding can only help to improve communication in the future if problems erupt. Reaching out to religious communities, especially those on the fringe, should be deliberate and part and parcel of an ongoing community-based policing model. Positive interactions between religious communities and the police in times of peace can only help to open lines of communication in times of turmoil. Along the same lines, the police and other secular practitioners (such as health officials) can certainly bridge communication gaps by educating religious communities about the purpose and intent of the law. Of course, this is all easier said than done, especially if one is trying to interact with religious groups that purposefully isolate themselves from the comings and goings of the community.

Law enforcement officials and other secular practitioners should also educate themselves about the distinct belief systems, customs, rituals, and customs of the religious groups in their communities. Even if a religious group has abhorrent practices, demonstrating a respect for the religious tradition as whole can help to improve communication. At a minimum, understanding specific religious traditions can assist law enforcement officials in tailoring their responses to meet the challenges posed by those grounded in religious zeal. It is important that both religious leaders and secular practitioners engage in an open dialogue whenever possible to prevent an escalation of fear and anxiety.

At the same time, it is critical that religious organizations reexamine their own responses to the crimes that are committed within their church communities. This would include a review of the policies, customs, and practices followed when clergy or church workers violate the law. Organizations will continue to be held accountable if they ignore any criminal activity that is reported to them; thus religious organizations should work to prevent criminal activity within their own ranks. They must find new procedures and policies to deal with clergy and other church workers who exhibit problem behaviors. Working closely with social workers, psychologists, psychiatrists, and other mental health professionals when problem behaviors are first identified may help prevent more severe acts of deviance in the future. As in many other types of organizations and corporations, this can be accomplished within the religious environment itself if a group chooses to make such professional services available within the formal structure of the organization.

Religious groups also have a responsibility to educate themselves on issues such as domestic violence, child sexual abuse, neglect, and sexual harassment so that they come to understand the ramifications of these crimes. They should also become knowledgeable about the secular services available in their communities to assist their parishioners in these matters. A variety of crime victim assistance services and protective agencies are available to assist victims and their families, and religious leaders should feel comfortable referring parishioners to them. In the same vein, secular services should reevaluate their ability to provide services to a religiously diverse population.

First and foremost, religious organizations should educate themselves so that they can better protect the safety of their parishioners. Also, religious leaders have a responsibility to educate their followers as to the legality of any particular religious practice or custom. Followers should be well aware of what their participation in a specific religious activity or religiously motivated action might mean for their future interaction with the law. In the end, the solution to much religion-related crime may lie within religious institutions themselves.

Public policy must also be refined to better address religion-related crime. As this text notes, legal boundaries are often vague and unclear. For instance, current state statutes regarding immunization exemptions are often difficult to unravel, making it hard for both religious followers and health professionals to determine appropriate boundaries. Although such legal boundaries are often intended to be blurred, so as to better address individual cases, such vagueness can make it difficult to set standards that can benefit both religious freedom and the community at large. For now, civil and criminal remedies will likely be needed to continue to test the limits of religious freedom case by case.

As we examine the complex, multidimensional phenomenon of religion-related crime more closely, we must also acknowledge the role that the Internet may play in the future in uniting like-minded individuals who see violence as a way to prove or demonstrate their faith. Although it is likely that only a handful of individuals are promoting such a high degree of violence, their ability to recruit and mobilize others through the Internet is a reality. As long as some believe that criminal activity is a necessary part of their ministry or that their religious beliefs serve as a call to action, then it is likely the threat of future violence will only continue to grow. In a post–September 11 society, it is important that law enforcement officials and others continue to monitor groups whose messages are inherently violent in intent. The potential for future acts of domestic terrorism is very real and should be not underestimated. The continued monitoring of Internet "chatter" is a wise investment to protect innocent citizens from the wrath of those who justify their actions within a religious context.

It is obvious that religion-related crime is of particular interest to practitioners who must interact with a diverse population of people and circumstances, but it is equally important that social scientists from all fields continue to study the characteristics of different forms of religion-related crime. It is important that research unravel the complex cognitive, emotional, and physical domains of religion and religiosity and how they translate into deviant behavior. Of particular concern is the relationship between religion, mental health, and criminal behavior. We may find that mental health concerns play a critical mediating role in translating religious fervor into criminal action. Also, we may have much to gain by continuing to study group behavior and how religious views, practices, and customs impact the behavior of groups, especially those believed to be at risk of erupting into violence.

Finally, as a specific call to criminologists, I hope this text spurs continued attention to the various dynamics it explores. I believe there is great value in gaining a better understanding of how religion, religiosity, and conversion figure as a mechanism of criminological theory. From my research, I would argue that religion's relationship to crime is multidimensional, as it tends simultaneously to have psychological, familial, social, cultural, and institutional components. Thus, criminologists are challenged to examine the issues across micro, meso, and macro levels of analysis, keeping in mind the historical evolution of particular religious groups. In this vein, much may be gained by the academic collaboration of those who study religion with those who study crime and criminal justice. Since this text raises more questions that it answers, there are many conceptual and empirical avenues left to explore.

References

Chapter 1 Religion-Related Crime: An Introduction

Applegate, B.K., Cullen, F.T., & Fisher, B.S. (2000). Forgiveness and fundamentalism: Reconsidering the relationship between correctional attitudes and religion. *Criminology, 38*(3), 719–753.

Baier, C.J., & Wright, B.R.E. (2001). If you love me, keep my commandments: A meta-analysis of the effect of religion on crime. *Journal of Research in Crime and Delinquency, 38*(1), 3–21.

Bainbridge, W.S. (1989). The religious ecology of deviance. *American Sociological Review, 54*, 288–295.

Bainbridge, W.S. (1992). Crime, delinquency and religion. In J.F. Schumker (Ed.), *Religion and mental health* (pp. 199–210). New York: Oxford University Press.

Barkun, M. (1997). *Religion and the racist right: The origins of the Christian Identity Movement.* Chapel Hill: University of North Carolina Press.

Bennett, W.J., Dilulio, J.J., & Walters, J.P. (1996). *Body count: Moral poverty and how to win America's war against crime and drugs.* New York: Simon & Schuster.

Bowker, J. (2000). *Oxford concise dictionary of world religions.* Oxford: Oxford University Press.

Butler, J., Wacker, G., & Balmer, R. (2003). *Religion in American life: A short story.* New York: Oxford University Press.

Camp, S.D., Klein-Saffran, J., Kwon, O.K., Daggett, D.M., & Jospeh, V. (2006). An exploration into participation in a faith-based prison program. *Criminology and Public Policy, 5*(3), 529–550.

Chu, D.C. (2007). Religiosity and desistance from drug use. *Criminal Justice and Behavior, 34*(5), 661–679.

Clear, T.R., & Sumtner, M.T. (2002). Prisoners, prison, and religion: Religion and adjustment to prison. *Journal of Offender Rehabilitation, 35*(3–4), 127–160.

Cruz v. Beto. 405 U.S. 319 (1972).

Dammer, H.R. (2002). The reasons for religious involvement in the correctional environment. *Journal of Offender Rehabilitation, 35*(3–4), 35–58.

Dettmer v. Landon. 617 F.Supp. 592, 594 (D.C. Va. 1985).

Dettmer v. Landon. 799 F.2d 929 (4th Cir. 1986).

Earley, M.L. (2005). The role of nonprofits in the rehabilitation of prisoners. *Criminal Justice Ethics, 24*(1), 2–59.

Galanter, M. (1999). *Cults: Faith, healing, and coercion.* New York: Oxford University Press.

Gallop-Goodman, G. (2001). The answer to our prayers. *American Demographics, 23*(3), 20–21.

Grimsrud, T., & Zehr, H. (2002). Rethinking God, justice and treatment of offenders. *Journal of Offender Rehabilitation, 35*(3–4), 259–285.

Hadley, M.I. (2001). *The spiritual roots of restorative justice.* Albany: State University of New York Press.

Hanks, G.C. (1997). *Against the death penalty: Christian and secular arguments against capital punishment.* Scottsdale, PA: Herald.

Harvey, O.J. (1986). Belief systems and attitudes toward the death penalty and other punishments. *Journal of Personality, 54*(4), 659–676.

Hirschi, T., & Stark, R. (1969). Hellfire and delinquency. *Social Problems, 17,* 202–213.

Hoffman, B. (2006). *Inside terrorism.* New York: Columbia University Press.

Holbrook, C.A. (1987). Crime and sin in Puritan Massachusetts. In J.M. Day & W.S. Laufer (Eds.), *Crime, values and religion* (pp. 1–22). Norwood, NJ: Ablex.

Hostetter, E.C. (2005). Religious studies and crime. In S.Guarino-Ghezzi & A. Javier Trevino (Eds.), *Understanding crime: A multidisciplinary approach* (pp. 213–235). Cincinnati, OH: Anderson.

Jenkins, P. (1996). *Pedophiles and priests: Anatomy of a contemporary crisis.* New York: Oxford University Press.

Jenkins, P. (2000). *Mystics and messiahs: Cults and new religions in American history.* New York: Oxford University Press.

Jensen, K.D., & Gibbons, S.G. (2002). Shame and religion as factors in the rehabilitation of serious offenders. *Journal of Offender Rehabilitation, 35*(3–4), 209–224.

Johnson, B.R. (1987). Religious commitment within the corrections environment: An empirical assessment. In J.M. Day & W.S. Laufer (Eds.), *Crime, values and religion* (pp. 193–209). Norwood, NJ: Ablex.

Johnson, B.R. (2004). Religious programs and recidivism among former inmates in prison fellowship programs: A long-term follow-up study. *Justice Quarterly, 21*(2), 329–354.

Johnson, B.R., Larson, D.B., & Pitts, T.G. (1999). Religious programming, institutional adjustment, and recidivism among former inmates in prison fellowship programs. *Justice Quarterly, 14,* 145–166.

Kaminer, W. (1997). Unholy alliance. *American Prospect, 35*(November–December), 54–55.

Kimball, C. (2002). *When religion becomes evil: Five warning signs.* New York: HarperCollins.

Krakauer, J. (2004). *Under the banner of heaven: A story of violent faith.* New York: Anchor.

Kurst-Swanger, K., & Ryniker, M. (2003). Religion-related crime: Documentation of murder, fraud, and sexual abuse. In A.R. Roberts (Ed.), *Critical issues in crime and justice* (pp. 62–76). Thousand Oaks, CA: Sage.

Mackey, V. (1987). Punishment in the Scripture and tradition of Judaism, Christianity, and Islam. In J.M. Day & W.S. Laufer (Eds.), *Crime, values and religion* (pp. 23–110). Norwood, NJ: Ablex.

Marshall, C.D. (2001). *Beyond retribution: A New Testament vision for justice, crime and punishment.* Grand Rapids, MI: Eerdmans.

National Abortion Federation (NAF). (2007). NAF violence and disruption statistics: Incidents of violence and disruption against abortion providers in the U.S. and Canada. Retrieved August 10, 2007, from http://www.prochoice.org/about_abortion/violence/violence_statistics.html

O'Connor, T.P., & Perreyclear, M. (2002). Prison religion in action and its influence on offender rehabilitation. *Journal of Offender Rehabilitation, 35*(3–4), 11–34.

Reich, W. (1998). *Origins of terrorism: Psychologies, ideologies, theologies, states of mind.* Washington, DC: Woodrow Wilson Center Press.

Sherkat, D.E., & Ellison, C.G. (1999). Recent developments and current controversies in the sociology of religion. *Annual Review of Sociology, 75*(4), 363–394.

Shupe, A., Stacey, W.A., & Darnell, S.E. (2000). *Bad pastors: Clergy misconduct in modern America.* New York: New York University Press.

Skotnicki, A. (2000). *Religion and the development of the American penal system.* Lanham, MD: University Press of America.

Stark, R. (1987). Religion and deviance: A new look. In J.M. Day & W.S. Laufer (Eds.), *Crime, values and religion* (pp. 111–120). Norwood, NJ: Ablex.

White, J.R. (2005). *Terrorism and homeland security: An introduction.* Belmont, CA: Wadsworth.

Zehr, H. (2005). Commentary. In S. Guarino-Ghezzi & A. Javier Trevino (Eds.), *Understanding crime: A multidisciplinary approach* (pp. 237–240). Cincinnati, OH: Anderson.

Chapter 2 What Is Religion?

Anthony, D., & Robbins, T. (2003). Conversion and "brainwashing" in new religious movements. In J.R. Lewis (Ed.), *Oxford handbook of new religious movements* (pp. 243–297). New York: Oxford University Press.

Argyle, M. (2002). State of the art: Religion. *Psychologist, 15*(1), 22–26.

Bird, F., & Reiner, B. (1982). Participation rates in new religious movements and para-religious movements. *Journal for the Scientific Study of Religion, 21*(1), 1–14.

Bowker, J. (2000). *Oxford concise dictionary of world religions*. Oxford: Oxford University Press.

Clayton, R.R. (1968). Religiosity in 5-D: A Southern test. *Social Forces, 47*(1), 80–83.

Clayton, R.R. (1971). 5-D or 1? *Journal for the Scientific Study of Religion, 10*(March), 37–40.

Cornwall, M. (1989). The determinants of religious behavior: A theoretical model and empirical test. *Social Forces, 68*(2), 572–592.

Cornwall, M., Albrecht, S.L., Cunningham, P.H., & Pitcher, B.L. (1986). The dimensions of religiosity: A conceptual model with an empirical test. *Review of Religious Research, 27*(3), 226–244.

Dawson, L.L. (1998). *Cults in context: Readings in the study of new religious movements*. New Brunswick, NJ: Transaction.

Dynes, R.R. (1955). Church-sect typology and socio-economic status. *American Sociological Review, 20*(5), 555–560.

Eck, D.L. (2001). *A new religious America: How a "Christian country" has become the world's most religiously diverse nation*. San Francisco: HarperSanFrancisco.

Faulkner, J.E., & de Jong, G.F. (1966). Religiosity in 5-D: An empirical analysis. *Social Forces, 45*(2), 246–254.

Flinn, F.K. (1987). Criminalizing conversion: The legislative assault on new religions et al. In J.M. Day & W.S. Laufer (Eds.), *Crime, values, and religion* (pp. 153–191). Norwood, NJ: Ablex.

Galanter, M. (1999). *Cults: Faith, healing, and coercion*. New York: Oxford University Press.

Glock, C.Y. (1962). On the study of religious commitment. *Religious Education: Research Supplement, 42*(July–August), 98–110.

Glock, C.Y. (1964). The role of deprivation in the origin and evolution of religious groups. In R. Lee & M. Marty (Eds.), *Religion and social conflict* (pp. 24–36). New York: Oxford University Press.

Himmelfarb, H.S. (1975). Measuring religious involvement. *Social Forces, 53*(4), 606–618.

Johnstone, R.L. (1983). *Religion in society: A sociology of religion*. Englewood Cliffs, NJ: Prentice-Hall.

Kent, S.A., & Hall, D. (2000). Brainwashing and re-indoctrination programs in the Children of God/The Family. *Cultic Studies Journal, 17*, 56–78.

Kimball, C. (2002). *When religion becomes evil*. San Francisco: HarperSanFrancisco.

King, M.B., & Hunt, R.A. (1969). Measuring the religious variable: Amended findings. *Journal for the Scientific Study of Religion, 8*(June), 321–323.

King, M.B., & Hunt, R.A. (1972). Measuring the religious variable: Replication. *Journal for the Scientific Study of Religion, 11*(September), 240–251.

Levine, S.V. (1984). *Radical departures: Desperate detours to growing up*. New York: Harcourt Brace & Co.

Lofland, J., & Skonovd, N. (1981). Conversion motifs. *Journal for the Scientific Study of Religion, 20*(4), 373–385.

Lofland, J., & Stark, R. (1965). On becoming a world-saver: A theory of conversion to a deviant perspective. *American Sociological Review, 30*, 863–874.

Loveland, M.T. (2003). Religious switching: Preference development, maintenance, and change. *Journal for the Scientific Study of Religion, 42*(1), 147–157.

Martin, D.A. (1962). The denomination. *British Journal of Sociology, 13*(1), 1–14.

Partridge, C. (2004). *New religions: A guide. New religious movements, sects and alternative spiritualities.* New York: Oxford University Press.

Rambo, L. (1993). *Understanding religious conversion.* New Haven, CT: Yale University Press.

Richardson, J.T. (1994). The ethics of "brainwashing" claims about new religious movements. *Australian Religious Studies Review, 7*, 48–56.

Richardson, J.T., & Ginsberg, G. (1998). A critique of "brainwashing" evidence in light of Daubert: Science and unpopular religions. In H. Reece (Ed.), *Law and science: Current legal issues*, Vol. 1 (pp. 265–288). New York: Oxford University Press.

Roof, W.C. (1989). Multiple religious switching: A research note. *Journal for the Scientific Study of Religion, 28*(4), 530–535.

Rossano, M.J. (2006). The religious mind and the evolution of religion. *Review of General Psychology, 10*(4), 346–364.

Snow, D.A., & Machalek, R. (1984). The sociology of conversion. *Annual Review of Sociology, 10*, 167–190.

Sommerville, C.J. (2000). Interpreting seventeenth-century English religion as movements. *Church History, 69*(4), 749–769

Stark, R., & Glock, C.Y. (1968). *Patterns of religious commitment. American piety: The nature of religious commitment*, Vol. 1. Berkeley: University of California Press.

Swatos, W.H. (1998). Chuch-sect theory. In W.H. Swatos (Ed.), *Encyclopedia of religion and society.* Walnut Creek, CA: AltaMira. Retrieved July 22, 2007, from http://hirr. hartsem.edu/ency/cstheory.htm

U.S. v. Fishman. 743 F.Supp. 713 (N.D. Cal. 1990).

Wellman, J.K., & Tokuno, K. (2004). Is religious violence inevitable? *Journal for the Scientific Study of Religion, 43*(3), 291–296.

Zellner, W., & Petrowsky, M. (1998). Freedom Park. In W.W. Zellner & M. Petrowsky (Eds.), *Sects, cults, and spiritual communities: A sociological analysis* (pp. 157–176). Westport, CT: Praeger.

Chapter 3   Religion, Crime, and the First Amendment

Abadinsky, H. (2001). *Drugs: An introduction.* Belmont, CA: Wadsworth.

American Academy of Pediatrics (AAP). (1999). Religious Liberty Protection Act: Possible danger to children. September 9. Retrieved May 27, 2005, from http://www.aap. org/advocacy/washing/rlpa9_99.htm

American Civil Liberties Union (ACLU). (1999). Effect of the Religious Liberty Protection Act on state and local civil rights laws. January 25. Retrieved May 27, 2005, from http://www.aclu.org/ReligiousLiberty/ReligiousLiberty.cfm?ID=8997&c=29

Angrosino, M. (2002). Civil religion redux. *Anthropological Quarterly, 75*(2), 239–268.

Braunfeld et al. v. Brown. 366 U.S. 599 (1961).

Brent, J.C. (1999). An agent and two principles: U.S. Court of Appeals responses to *Employment Division, Department of Human Resources v. Smith* and the Religious Freedom Restoration Act. *American Politics Quarterly, 27*(2), 236–266.

Brent, J.C. (2003). A principle-agent analysis of U.S. Courts of Appeals responses to *Boerne v. Flores. American Politics Research, 31*(5), 557–570.

Butler, J., Wacker, G., & Balmer, R. (2003). *Religion in American life: A short history.* New York: Oxford University Press.

Cantwell v. Connecticut. 310 U.S. 296, 303, 304 (1940).

Carmella, A.C. (1993). State constitutional protection of religious exercise: An emerging post-*Smith* jurisprudence. *Brigham Young University Law Review,* 275–325.

Church of the Lukumi Babalu Aye, Inc. and Ernesto Pichardo v. City of Hialeah. 508 U.S. 520 (1993).

City of Boerne v. Flores, Archbishop of San Antonio, et al. 521 U.S. 507 (1997).

Cleveland et al. v. U.S. 329 U.S. 14 (1946).

Davis v. Beason. 133 U.S. 333 (1890).

Employment Division, Department of Human Resources of Oregon v. Smith et al. 485 U.S. 660, 670 (1988) (*Smith I*).

Employment Division, Department of Human Resources of Oregon v. Smith et al. 494 U.S. 872 (1990) (*Smith II*).

Esbeck, C. (1994). Table of United States Supreme Court decisions relating to religious liberty, 1789–1994. *Journal of Law and Religion, 10*, 5573–5588.

Everson v. Board of Education. 330 U.S. 1, 15 (1947).

Fisher, L. (2002). *Religious liberty in America: Political safeguards.* Lawrence: University Press of Kentucky.

Gaustad, E.S. (2003). *Proclaim liberty throughout all the land: A history of church and state in America.* New York: Oxford University Press.

Geller, J.R. (2003). The Religious Land Use and Institutionalized Persons Act of 2000: An unconstitutional exercise of Congress's power under section five of the Fourteenth Amendment. *New York University Journal of Legislation and Public Policy, 6*, 561–587.

Gordon, S.B. (2002). *The Mormon question: Polygamy and constitutional conflict in nineteenth- century America.* Chapel Hill: University of North Carolina Press.

Ignagni, J.A. (1993). U.S. Supreme Court decision-making and the free exercise clause. *Review of Politics, 55*, 511–529.

Irons, P. (1997). *May it please the court: The First Amendment.* New York: New Press.

Marsh v. State of Alabama. 326 U.S. 501 (1946).

Prince v. Commonwealth of Massachusetts. 321 U.S. 158 (1944).

Reynolds v. U.S. 98 U.S. 145 (1879).

Sherbert v. Verner. 374 U.S. 398 (1963).

Tucker v. State of Texas. 326 U.S. 517 (1946).

Two Guys from Harrison-Allentown, Inc. v. McGinley. 366 U.S. 582 (1961).

United States v. Ballard. 322 U.S. 78 (1944).

Way, F., & Burt, B.J. (1983). Religious marginality and the free exercise clause. *American Political Science Review, 77*(3), 652–665.

Wisconsin v. Yoder. 406 U.S. 205 (1972).

Witte, J. (2000). *Religion and the American constitutional experiment: Essential rights and liberties.* Boulder, CO: Westview.

Chapter 4   Crimes against Children

American Academy of Pediatrics (AAP) Committee on Bioethics. (1988). Religious exemptions from child abuse statutes. *Pediatrics, 81*(1), 169–171.

American Academy of Pediatrics (AAP) Committee on Bioethics. (1997). Religious objections to medical care. *Pediatrics, 99*(2), 279–281.

Asser, S.M., & Swan, R. (1998). Child fatalities from religion-motivated medical neglect. *Pediatrics, 101*(4), 625–629.

Attleboro sect couple facing jail over duty of care issue. (2002, March 31). *Cultic Studies Review, 1*(1). Retrieved January 24, 2006, from http://www.culticstudiesreview.org/csr_news/csr_newsgirl/Attleboro sect_2002_01_31.htm

Aviles, J.M., Whelan, E., Hernke, D.A., Williams, B.A., Kenny, K.E., O'Fallon, W., & Kopecky, S.L. (2001). Intercessory prayer and cardiovascular disease progression in a coronary care unit population: A randomized controlled trial. *Mayo Clinic Proceedings, 76,* 1192–1198.

Bader, C.D. (2003). Supernatural support groups: Who are the UFO abductees and ritual-abuse survivors? *Journal for the Scientific Study of Religion, 42*(4), 669–678.

Bartkowski, J. (1996). Beyond biblical literalism and inerrancy: Conservative Protestants and the hermeneutic interpretation of scripture. *Sociology of Religion, 57*(3), 259–273.

Baumrind, D. (1996). A blanket injunction against disciplinary use of spanking is not warranted by the data. *Pediatrics, 98*(4), 828–831.

Belitz, J., & Schacht, A. (1992). Satanism as a response to abuse: The dynamics and treatment of satanic involvement in male youths. *Adolescence, 27*(108), 855–872.

Bottoms, B.L., Shaver, P.R., Goodman, G.S., & Qin, J. (1995). In the name of God: A profile of religion-related child abuse. *Journal of Social Issues, 51,* 85–111.

Bowker, J. (2000). *Oxford concise dictionary of world religions.* New York: Oxford University Press.

Bozeman, J.M., & Palmer, S.J. (1997). The Northeast Kingdom Community Church of Island Pond, Vermont: Raising up a people for Yahshua's return. *Journal of Contemporary Religion, 12*(2), 181–190.

Children's Healthcare Is a Legal Duty (CHILD). (2006). Data on injuries to children because of religion-based medical neglect. Retrieved January 20, 2006, from http://www.childrenhealthcare.org/legal.htm

Coleman, J. (1994). Presenting features in adult victims of Satanist ritual abuse. *Child Abuse Review, 3*, 83–92.

Commonwealth v. Barnhart. 497 A.2d 616 (Pa. Super. 1985).

Commonwealth v. Cottam. 616 A.2d 988 (Pa. Super. 1992).

Cyan, J.R. (1997). The banning of corporal punishment: In child care, school and other educative settings in the U.S. *Childhood Education, 63*, 146–153.

Day, R.D., Peterson, G.W., & McCraken, C. (1998). Predicting spanking of younger and older children by mothers and fathers. *Journal of Marriage and the Family, 60*, 79–94.

Ellement, J. (2004, February 11). Woman admits role in child's death. *Boston Globe.* Retrieved January 24, 2006, from http://www.boston.com/news/local/massachusetts/articles/2004/02/11/woman_admits_role…

Ellison, C.G., Bartkowski, J., & Segal, M.L. (1996). Do conservative Protestants spank more often? Further evidence from the National Survey of Families and Households. *Social Science Quarterly, 77*, 663–673.

End All Corporal Punishment of Children (EACPC). (2007). Global summary of the legal status of corporal punishment of children. Retrieved August 11, 2007, from http://www.endcorporalpunishment.org

Feikin, D.R., Lezotte, D.C., Hamman, R.F., Salmon, D.A., Chen, R.T., & Hoffman, R.E. (2000). Individual and community risks of measles and pertussis associated with personal exemptions to immunization. *Journal of the American Medical Association, 284*, 3145–3150.

Finkelhor, D., Meyer Williams, L., & Burns, N. (1988). *Nursery crimes: Sexual abuse in day care.* Newbury Park, CA: Sage.

First Church of Christ, Scientist. (2006). About Christian Science. Retrieved January 20, 2006, from http://www.tfccs.com

Fraser, G.A. (1990). Satanic ritual abuse: A cause of multiple personality disorder. *Journal of Child and Youth Care,* Special Issue, 55–66

Friedman-Ross, L., & Aspinwall, T.J. (1997). Religious exemptions to the immunization statutes: Balancing public health and religious freedom. *Journal of Law, Medicine and Ethics, 25*, 202–209.

Gelles, R.J. (1997). *Intimate violence in families.* Thousand Oakes, CA: Sage.

Gershoff, E.T. (2002). Corporal punishment by parents and associated child behaviors and experiences: A meta-analytic and theoretical review. *Psychological Bulletin, 128*(4), 539–579.

Gershoff, E.T., Miller, P.C., & Holden, C.W. (1999). Parenting influences from the pulpit: Religious affiliation as a determinant of parental corporal punishment. *Journal of Family Psychology, 13*(3), 307–320.

Gibb, T. (2001, June 1). Prayerful parents in prison for death. *Post Gazette News.* Retrieved January 24, 2006, from http://www.post-gazette.com/regionstate/20010601faith5.asp

Giles-Sims, J., Staus, M.A., & Sugarman, D.B. (1995). Child, maternal, and family characteristics associated with spanking. *Family Relations, 44*(2), 170–177.

Greven, P. (1991). *Spare the child: The religious roots of punishment and the psychological impact of physical abuse.* New York: Knopf.

Heller, J. (1998, October 1). It's freedom vs. responsibility: Religious beliefs go up against parental obligations when it comes to a child in need of medical help. *St. Petersburg Times.*

Hinman, A.R., Orenstein, W.A., Williamson, D.R., & Darrington, D. (2002). Childhood immunization: Laws that work. *Journal of Law, Medicine and Ethics, 30*(3), 122–132.

Hunt v. Hunt. 162 Vt. 423 (1994).

Hutchins, S., Markowitz, L., Atkinson, W., Swint, E., & Hadler, S. (1996). Measles outbreaks in the United States, 1987–1990. *Pediatric Infectious Disease Journal, 15*(1), 31–38.

Jackson, S., Thompson, R., Christiansen, E.H., Colman, R.A., Wyatt, J., Buckendahl, C.W., Wilcox, B.L., & Peterson, R. (1999). Predicting abuse-prone parental attitudes and discipline practices in a nationally representative sample. *Child Abuse and Neglect, 23*(1), 15–29.

Jehovah's Witnesses in the State of Washington et v. King County Hospital Unit no. 1 et al. 390 U.S. 598 (1968).

Kaunitz, A.M., Spence, C., Danielson, T.S., Rochat, R.W., & Grimes, D.A. (1984). Perinatal and maternal mortality in a religious group avoiding obstetric care. *American Journal Obstetrics and Gynecology, 150,* 826–831.

Kurst-Swanger, K., & Petcosky, J. (2003). *Violence in the home: Multidisciplinary perspectives.* New York: Oxford University Press.

Lanning, K. (1991). Ritual abuse: A law enforcement view or perspective. *Child Abuse and Neglect, 15,* 171–173.

Lanning, K. (1992). *Investigator's guide to allegations of "ritual" child abuse.* Quantico, VA: Behavioral Science Unit, National Center for the Analysis of Violent Crime, Federal Bureau of Investigation, FBI Academy.

Larzelere, R.E. (1996). A review of the outcomes of parental use of no abusive or customary physical punishment. *Pediatrics, 98*(4), 824–828.

Lewis, D.O., Yeager, C.A., Swica, Y., Pincus, J.H., & Lewis, M. (1997). Objective documentation of child abuse and dissociation in 12 murderers with dissociative identity disorder. *American Journal of Psychiatry, 154*(12), 1703–1710.

Lewis, I.M. (2003). Trance, possession, shamanism and sex. *Anthropology of Consciousness, 14*(1), 20–39.

Lloyd, D.W. (1992). Ritual child abuse: Definitions and assumptions. *Journal of Child Sexual Abuse, 1*(3), 1–14.

Lovett, K. (2001, October 4). Upstate "soap" cult fined for child labor. *New York Post.*

Lundman v. First Church of Christ, Scientist. 95-534 (Dist.Ct., Hennepin, Co. Minn) (1996).

McKown v. Lundman. 91-8197 (Dist. Ct., Hennepin, Co., Minn) (1995).

Miller, T.W., Veltkamp, L.J., Kraus, R.F., Lane, T., & Heister, T. (1999). An adolescent vampire cult in rural America: Clinical issues and case study. *Child Psychiatry and Human Development, 29*(3), 209–219.

Monopoli, P.A. (1991). Striking a new balance between sincere religious belief and a child's right to medical treatment. *Pepperdine Law Review, 18*(2), 319–352.

National Clearinghouse on Child Abuse and Neglect Information (NCCANI). (2003). *Report laws: Religious exemptions, 2003 child abuse and neglect state statutes series ready reference.* Children's Bureau, Administration for Children and Families, U.S. Department of Health and Human Services. Retrieved January 23, 2006, from http://nccanch.acf.hhs.gov

National Law Journal. (1996, February 5). Reductions: Verdicts reduced after trial, Pg. C18 and faith healer held liable for death, p. A8.

Noblitt, J.R., & Perskin, P.S. (2000). *Cult and ritual abuse: Its history, anthropology, and recent discovery in contemporary America.* Westport, CT: Praeger.

Novotny, T., Jennings, C.E., Doran, M., March, C.R., Hopkins, R.S., Wassilak, S.G., & Markowitz, L.E. (1988). Measles outbreaks in religious groups exempt from immunization laws. *Public Health Reports, 103*(1), 49–54.

Nunnally, D. (2004, July 10). Minister convicted of felony child abuse: Exorcism that killed boy may bring 5 years in prison. *Milwaukee Journal Sentinel.*

O'Laoire, S. (1997). An experimental study of the effects of distant, intercessory prayer on self-esteem, anxiety and depression. *Alternative Therapies in Health and Medicine, 3*(6), 38–53.

Pagelow, M.D. (1984). *Family violence.* New York: Praeger.

Plastine, L.M. (1993). "In God we trust": When parents refuse medical treatment for their children based upon their sincere religious beliefs. *Constitutional Law Journal, 3*(1), 123–160.

Pollard, D.A. (2002). Banning corporal punishment: A constitutional analysis. *American University Law Review, 52,* 447–492.

Prince v. Massachusetts. 321 U.S. 158 (1944).

Reynolds, D. (2004, August 20). Hemphill sentenced over boy's "exorcism" death. *Inclusion Daily Express.*

Rodier, D.N. (1999, November 1). State court rulings. *Pennsylvania Law Weekly,* p. 5.

Rota, J.S., Salmon, D.A., Rodewald, L.E., Chen, R.T., Hibbs, B.F., & Gangarosa, E.J. (2001). Processes for obtaining nonmedical exemptions to state immunization laws. *American Journal of Public Health, 91,* 645–653.

Salmon, D.A., Haber, M., Gangarosa, E.J., Phillips, L., Smith, N.J., & Chen, R.T. (1999). Health consequences of religious and philosophical exemptions from immunization laws: Individual and societal risk of measles. *Journal of the American Medical Association, 282,* 47–53.

Scott, S. (2001). *The politics and experience of ritual abuse beyond disbelief.* Buckingham, U.K.: Open University Press.

Sedlak, J.J., & Broadhurst, D.D. (1996). Executive summary of the third National Incidence Study of Child Abuse and Neglect. Retrieved January 18, 2006, from http://www.nccanch.acf.hhs.gov/pubs/statsinfo/nis3.cfm

Sicher, F., Targ, E., Moore, D., & Smith, H.S. (1998). A randomized double-blind study of the effect of distant healing in a population with advanced AIDS. Report of a small scale study. *Western Journal of Medicine, 169*(6), 356–363.

Simpson, W. (1989). Comparative longevity in a college cohort of Christian Scientists. *Journal of the American Medical Association, 262,* 1657–1658.

Simpson, W. (1991). Comparative mortality in two college groups. *Mortality and Morbidity Weekly Report, 40,* 579–582.

Straus, M.A. (1994). *Beating the devil out of them: Corporal punishment in American families.* New York: Lexington.

Straus, M.A., & Paschall, M.J. (1998, August). *Corporal punishment by mothers and child's cognitive development: A longitudinal study.* Durham: University of New Hampshire, Family Research Laboratory.

Swan, R. (2000). When faith fails children—religion-based neglect: Pervasive, deadly… and legal? *Humanist, 60*(6), 11–16.

U.S. Department of Health and Human Services (USDHHS). (2005). Long-term consequences of child abuse and neglect. Retrieved January 30, 2006, from http://www.nccanch.acf.hhs./pubs/factsheets/long_term_consequences.cfm

U.S. Department of Health and Human Services (USDHHS). (2006). Child maltreatment: 2004. Retrieved August 11, 2007, from http://www.acf.hhs.gov/programs/cb/pubs/cm04/index.htm

Walker, S.R., Tonigan, J.S., Miller, W.R., Corner, S., & Kahlick, L. (1997). Intercessory prayer in the treatment of alcohol abuse and dependence: A pilot investigation. *Alternative Therapies in Health and Medicine, 3*(6), 79–86.

Yeager, C.A., & Lewis, D.O. (1997). False memories of cult abuse. *American Journal of Psychiatry, 154*(3), 435.

Chapter 5   Crimes against Women

Adams, B. (2006, February 11). Physician finds rare disease in FLDS kids. *Salt Lake Tribune.*

Adams, B., & Manson, P. (2006, August 29). Polygamist sect leader Warren Jeffs arrested in Las Vegas. *Salt Lake Tribune.* First story, Local.

Ali, Y. (1993). *The meaning of the Holy Qur'an: New edition with revised translation and commentary.* Brentwood, MD: Amana.

Altman, I., & Ginat, J. (1996). *Polygamous families in contemporary society.* New York: Cambridge University Press.

Anderson, C.M. (2000). The persistence of polygyny as an adaptive response to poverty and oppression in Apartheid South Africa. *Cross-Cultural Research, 34*(2), 99–112.

Arrington, L.J., & Bitton, D. (1979). *The Mormon experience: A history of the Latter Day Saints.* New York: Knopf.

Associated Press (AP). (2005, August 1). *Psychologists have challenge in uncooperative patients.* State and Regional. Salt Lake City.

Associated Press (AP). (2006, February 9). Doctor: Birth defects increase in polygamy community. Retrieved April 6, 2006, from http://azcentral.com/health/news/articles/0209PolygamyBirthDefect09-ON.html

Associated Press (AP). (2007, June 30). Jeff's traffic stop ruled legal. St. George, Utah.

Atkins, C.L. (1999). Why I am interested in kidney disease. Retrieved April 10, 2006, from http://www.cc.utah.edu/~da6202.why.htm

Bartkowski, J. (1996). Beyond biblical literalism and inerrancy: Conservative Protestants and the hermeneutic interpretation of scripture. *Sociology of Religion, 57*(3), 259–273.

Bartkowski, J. (1997). Debating patriarchy: Discursive disputes over spousal authority among evangelical family commentators. *Journal for the Scientific Study of Religion, 36*(3), 393–410.

Battaglia, L.J. (2001). Conservative Protestant ideology and wife abuse: Reflections on the discrepancy between theory and data. *Journal of Religion and Abuse, 2*(4), 31–45.

Bowker, J. (2000). *Oxford concise dictionary of world religions.* New York: Oxford University Press.

Brinkerhoff, M.B., Grandin, E., & Lupri, E. (1992). Religious involvement and spousal violence: The Canadian case. *Journal for the Scientific Study of Religion, 31*(1), 15–31.

Brooke, J. (1998, August 23). Utah struggles with a revival of polygamy. *The New York Times.* Retrieved April 5, 2006, from http://www.ishipress.com/utah-pol.htm

Butler, J., Wacker, G., & Balmer, R. (2003). *Religion in American life: A short history.* New York: Oxford University Press.

Cardarelli, A.P. (Ed.). (1997). *Violence between intimate partners: Patterns, causes and effects.* Boston: Allyn & Bacon.

Church of Jesus Christ of Latter Day Saints v. U.S. 136 U.S. 1, 49 (1890).

Dada-Adegbola, H.O. (2004). Socio-cultural factors affecting the spread of HIV/AIDS in Africa: A case study. *African Journal of Medicine and Medical Sciences, 33*(2), 179–182.

Davies, D.J. (2004). The Church of Jesus Christ of Latter-Day Saints (Mormonism). In C. Partridge (Ed.), *New religions: A guide: New religious movements, sects and alternative spiritualities* (pp. 32–35). New York: Oxford University Press.

Davis v. Beason. 133 U.S. 333 (1890).

Department of Public Safety, Utah Highway Patrol (2006). History 1980–1989: Return to Marion. Retrieved April 4, 2006, from http://highwaypatrol.utah.gov/history/chapter4/448.html

Dobash, R., & Dobash, R. (1979). *Violence against wives.* New York: Free Press.

Dougherty, J. (2005, September 22). Under siege: Polygamists are barricading their homes in the midst of mounting legal assaults by authorities. *Phoenix New Times.*

Durose, M.R., Wolf Harlow, C., Langan, P.A., Motivans, M., Rantala, R.R., & Smith, E.L. (2005, June). *Family violence statistics: Including statistics on strangers and acquaintances.* Bureau of Justice Statistics, Office of Justice Programs, U.S. Department of Justice. NCJ 207846.

Eigenberg, H.M. (2001). *Women battering in the United States: Till death do us part.* Prospect Heights, IL: Waveland.

Elbedour, S., Onwuegbuzie, A.J., Caridine, C., & Abu-Saad, H. (2002). The effect of polygamous marital structure on behavioral, emotional, and academic adjustment in children: A comprehensive review of the literature. *Clinical Child and Family Psychology Review, 5*(4), 255–271.

Ellison, C.G., Bartkowski, J.P., & Anderson, K.L. (1999). Are there religious variations in domestic violence? *Journal of Family Issues, 20*(1), 87–113.

Gelles, R.J. (1997). *Intimate violence in families.* Thousand Oaks, CA: Sage.

Goddard, T., & Shurtleff, M. (2006). Safety Net directory: Agencies and organizations helping victims of domestic violence and child abuse in polygamous communities. Retrieved April 4, 2006, from http://www.azag.gov/victims_rights/safetyNetDirectory.pdf

Gordon, S.B. (2002). *The Mormon question: Polygamy and constitutional conflict in nineteenth-century America.* Chapel Hill: University of North Carolina Press.

Hassouneh-Phillips, D. (2001a). Marriage is half of faith and the rest is fear of Allah: Marriage and spousal abuse among American Muslims. *Violence against Women, 7*(8), 927–946.

Hassouneh-Phillips, D. (2001b). Polygamy and wife abuse: A qualitative study of Muslim women in America. *Health Care for Women International, 22,* 735–748.

Hollenhorst, J. (2006, February 9). Birth defect is plaguing children in FLDS towns. *Deseret Morning News.*

Holmes, K.E. (2005, July 28). Muslims in Philadelphia shun men who abuse their wives. *Herald News,* p. B06.

Horsburgh, B. (1995). Recent developments: Lifting the veil of secrecy: Domestic violence in the Jewish community. *Harvard Women's Law Journal, 18*(Spring), 171–213.

Hunt, S. (2005, July 27). Treatment, not trial for Mitchell; Judge rules Elizabeth Smart's alleged abductor mentally incompetent; Mitchell unfit to stand for trial, judge rules. *Salt Lake Tribune,* p. A1.

Interchurch Ministries of Nebraska (IMN). (2006). Domestic violence ministries: Faith communities' responses to domestic violence. Retrieved on February 26, 2006, from http://www.interchurchministries.org/Ministries/DV.htm

Kalmuss, D.S., & Strauss, M.A. (1982). Wife's marital dependency and wife abuse. *Journal of Marriage and the Family, 44*, 277–286.

Kossan, P. (2005, August 12). Colorado City school district faces bankruptcy. *Arizona Republic.* Retrieved on April 4, 2006, from http://www.azcentral.com/specials/special45/articles/0812coloradocity12.htm

Kossan, P. (2006, March 2). Residents refuse to pay land taxes in Colorado City. *Arizona Republic.* Retrieved April 4, 2006, from http://www.azcentral.com/specials/special45/articles/0302coloradocity02.html

Krakauer, J. (2004). *Under the banner of heaven: A story of violent faith.* New York: Anchor.

Kurst-Swanger, K., & Petcosky, J. (2003). *Violence in the home: Multidisciplinary Perspectives.* New York: Oxford University Press.

Mhalu, F.S., & Lyamuya, E. (1996). Human immunodeficiency virus infection and AIDS in East Africa: Challenges and possibilities for prevention and control. *East African Medical Journal, 73*(1), 13–22.

Miles, A. (2005). *Why Christian clergy must be involved in ending domestic violence.* Interfaith Council, NW. Circle of Caring: Leader Statements. Retrieved February 26, 2006, from http://www.interfaithw.org/miles.html

Nason-Clark, N. (1997). *The battered wife: How Christians confront family violence.* Louisville, KY: Westminster John Knox.

Nason-Clark, N. (2004). When terror strikes at home: The interface between religion and domestic violence. *Journal for the Scientific Study of Religion, 43*(3), 303–310.

Nebraska Domestic Violence Sexual Assault Coalition (NDVSAC). (2004, June 5). Statement against domestic violence. *The Voice.*

Newell, L.K., & Avery, V.T. (1984). *Mormon enigma: Emma Hale Smith: Prophet's wife, "elect lady," polygamy's foe, 1804–1879.* New York: Doubleday.

Nichols, J. (2003, October 5). Wives suing to bring end to abuse under polygamy. *Arizona Republic.* Retrieved April 4, 2006, from http://www.azcentral.com/specials/special45/articles/1015polygamywomen.html

Peek, C.W., Lowe, G.D., & Williams, L.S. (1991). Gender and God's word: Another look at religious fundamentalism and sexism. *Social Forces, 69*(4), 1205–1221.

Rabin, B., Markus, E., & Voghera, N. (1999). A comparative study of Jewish and Arab battered women presenting in an emergency room of a general hospital. *Social Work in Health Care, 29*(2), 69–84.

Reavy, P. (2007, February 27). Hearing on medicating Mitchell is postponed. *Deseret Morning News.*

Reynolds v. U.S. 98 U.S. 145 (1879).

Rosetta, L. (2005, February 14). Utah clergy to get domestic violence education. *Salt Lake Tribune,* p. B2.

Sargent, C., & Cordell, D. (2002). Polygamy, disrupted reproduction, and the state: Malian migrants in Paris, France. *Social Science and Medicine, 56*(9), 1961–1972.

Speckman, S. (2004, August 1). Aid sought for church's victims. *Deseret Morning News*. Retrieved April 5, 2006, from http://www.childbrides.org/boys_des_lost_boys. html

Taves, A. (1989). *Religion and domestic violence in early New England: The memoirs of Abigail Abbott Bailey*. Bloomington: Indiana University Press.

Thiessen, M. (2004, August 30). Grant to help domestic violence victims in polygamous communities. Associated Press. Retrieved April 6, 2006, from http://www.azcentral. com/families/articles/0830polygamy-dv-ON.html

Toppo, M., Tiwari, S.C., Dixit, G.C., & Nandeshwar. (2004). Study of STD pattern in Hamidia Hospital, Bhopal and its associated risk factors. *Indian Journal of Community Medicine, 29*(2), 65–66.

Van Wagoner, R.S. (1989). *Mormon polygamy: A history*. Salt Lake City, UT: Signature.

Walker, L. (1999). Fatal inheritance: Mormon eugenics. Retrieved April 6, 2006, from http://human-nature.com/science-as-culture/walker.html

Whipple, V. (1987). Counseling battered women from fundamentalist churches. *Journal of Marital and Family Therapy, 13*(3), 251–258.

Chapter 6   Illicit Drugs

Albaugh, B.J., & Anderson, P.O. (1974). Peyote in the treatment of alcoholism among American Indians. *American Journal of Psychiatry, 131*(11), 1247–1250.

Blackledge, R.D., & Taylor, C.M. (2003). *Psychotria viridis*: A botanical source of dimethyltryltryptamine (DMT). Drug Enforcement Administration, *Microgram Journal, 1*. Retrieved April 18, 2006, from http://www.usdoj.gov/dea/programs/forensicsci/microgram/journal_v1/mjournal_v1pg3.htm

Block, R.I., & Ghoneim, M.M. (1993). Effects of chronic marijuana use on human cognition. *Psychopharmacology, 110*(1–2), 219–228.

Bowker, J. (2000). *Oxford concise dictionary of world religions*. New York: Oxford University Press.

Brook, J.S., Cohen P., & Brook, D.W. (1998). Longitudinal study of co-occurring psychiatric disorders and substance use. *Journal of American Academy of Child and Adolescent Psychiatry, 37*, 322–330.

Busia, K., & Heckels, F. (2006). Jimson Weed: History, perceptions, traditional uses, and potential therapeutic benefits of the genus Datura. *HerbalGram: The Journal of the American Botanical Council, 69*, 40–50.

Centers for Disease Control and Prevention (CDC). (1984). Datura poisoning from hamburger—Canada. *Morbidity and Mortality Weekly Report, 33*(20), 282–283.

Centers for Disease Control and Prevention (CDC). (2003). Suspected moonflower intoxication—Ohio. *Morbidity and Mortality Weekly Report, 52*(33), 788–791.

City of Boerne v. Flores, Archbishop of San Antonio, et al. 521 U.S. 507 (1997).

Deloria, V., & Lytle, C.M. (1983). *American Indians, American justice.* Austin: University of Texas Press.

Doweiko, H.E. (2002). *Concepts of chemical dependency.* Pacific Grove, CA: Brooks/ Cole.

Drug Enforcement Administration (DEA) Office of Forensic Sciences, U.S. Department of Justice. (2004). Angel trumpet in Miami-Dade County, Florida. *Microgram Bulletin: Intelligence Alert, 37*(4), 70–71.

Drug Enforcement Administration (DEA), U.S. Department of Justice. (2005). Drugs of abuse. Report made available by the National Drug Intelligence Center. Retrieved May 2, 2006, from http://www.usdoj.gov/dea/pubs/abuse/doa-p.pdf

Drug Enforcement Administration (DEA), U.S. Department of Justice. (2006). Statistics and facts. Retrieved May 9, 2006, from http://www.dea.gov/statisticsp.html

Employment Division, Department of Human Resources v. Smith. 494 U.S. 872 (1990).

Fisher, L. (2002). *Religious liberty in America: Political safeguards.* Lawrence: University Press of Kansas.

Fuller, R.C. (2000). *Stairways to heaven: Drugs in American religious history.* Boulder, CO: Westview.

Garrity, J.F. (2000). Jesus, peyote, and the holy people: Alcohol abuse and the ethos of power in Navajo healing. *Medical Anthropology Quarterly, 14*(4), 521–542.

Gonzales, Alberto R., Attorney General et al. v. O Centro Espirita Beneficente Uniao Do Vegetal et al. 546 U.S. 418 (2006).

Gonzales, Attorney General et al. v. Raich et al. 125 S.Ct. 2195 (2005).

Green, B.E., & Ritter, C. (2000). Marijuana use and depression. *Journal of Health and Social Behavior, 41*(1), 40–49.

Halpern, J. (2004). American Indian religious freedom ... and a father's right to raise his child according to tradition. *Multidisciplinary Association for Psychedelic Studies Bulletin, 19*(2), 22–23.

Halpern, J., Sherwood, A.R., Hudson, J.I., Yurgelun-Todd, D., & Pope, H.G. (2005). Psychological and cognitive effects of long-term peyote use among Native Americans. *Biological Psychiatry, 58*(8), 624–631.

Herkenham, M., Lynn, A.B., Little, M.D., Johnson, M.R., Melvin, L.S., deCosta, B.R., & Rice, K.C. (1990). Cannabinoid receptor localization in the brain. *Proceedings of the National Academy of Sciences of the United States of America, 87*, 1932–1936.

Hudson, D.L. (2006, February 24). Tea and sympathy: High Court backs religion law. *American Bar Association Journal eReport.* Retrieved April 6, 2006, from http://www. abanet.org/journal/ereport/f24tea.html

Leary, T. (1964). The religious experience: Its production and interpretation. *Psychedelic Review, 1*, 324–346.

Lucas, A.M. (1995). Entheology. *Journal of Psychoactive Drugs, 27*(3), 293–295.

Lyman, M.D., & Potter, G.W. (2003). *Drugs in society: Causes, concepts and control.* Cincinnati, OH: Anderson.

MacRae, E. (1998). Santo Daime and Santo Maria: The licit ritual use of ayahuasca and the illicit use of cannabis in a Brazilian Amazonian religion. *International Journal of Drug Policy, 9*(5), 325–338.

Manson, P. (2006, February 23). Couple agree to end peyote use if feds drop drug charges. *Salt Lake City Tribune*, p. B5.

McBride v. Shawnee County, Kansas Court Services. 71 F.Supp.2d 1098 (Dkan. September 17, 1999).

Meier, K.J. (1994). *The politics of sin*. New York: M.E. Sharpe.

National Highway Traffic Safety Administration (NHTSA). (2000). Notes. Marijuana and alcohol combined severely impede driving performance. *Annals of Emergency Medicine, 35*, 398–400.

National Institute on Drug Abuse (NIDA). (2001, March). *Hallucinogens and dissociative drugs*. Research Report Series. National Institutes of Health, U.S. Department of Health and Human Services, publication 01-4209.

Native American Church v. Navajo Tribal Council. 272 F.2d 131 (10th Cir. 1959).

New Jersey Law Journal. (2006, March 6). *Gonzales, Attorney General, et al. v. O Centro Espirita Beneficente Uniao do Vegetal et al*. Constitutional law—Free exercise of religion.

Ofgang, K. (1997, January 29). "Religious Freedom" no defense to marijuana transportation—C.A. *Metropolitan News Enterprise*, p. 1.

Olsen v. Iowa, 808 F.2d 652, 653 (8th Cir. 1986).

Olsen v. Drug Enforcement Administration. 878 F.2d 1458 (D.C. Cir. 1989).

Parker, C. (2002). A constitutional examination of the federal exemptions for Native American religious use. *Brigham Young University Journal of Public Law, 16*, 89–112.

Partridge, C. (2004). *New religions: A guide. New religious movements, sects and alternative spiritualities*. New York: Oxford University Press.

Pascarosa, P., & Futterman, S. (1976). Enthnopsychedelic therapy for alcoholics: Observations in the peyote ritual of the Native American Church. *Journal of Psychedelic Drugs, 8*(3), 215–221.

Pascarosa, P., Futterman, S., & Halsweig, M. (1976). Observations of alcoholics in the peyote ritual: A pilot study. *Annals of the New York Academy of Science, 273*, 518–524.

Pasterchick, M.(2002). *Salvia divinorum*. News for DEA, Domestic Field Divisions, Newark Intelligence Bulletin, September. Retrieved April 18, 2006, from http://www.usdoj.gov/dea/pubs/states/newsrel/newark_intel_bulletin_salviap.html

People v. Peck. 52 Cal. App. 4th 351 (1996).

People v. Woody. 394 P.2d 813, 821 (1964).

Petrullo, V. (1934). *The diabolic root: A study of peyotism, the new Indian religion, among the Delawares*. Philadelphia: University of Pennsylvania Press.

Pope, H.G., & Yurgelun-Todd, D. (1996). The residual cognitive effects of heavy marijuana use in college students. *Journal of the American Medical Association, 275*(7), 251–527.

Reitmeyer, J., & Mathis, M. (2002, May 29). "Weedman" protests child-visitation ruling. *Burlington County Times*. Retrieved August 12, 2007, from http://hempevolution. org/media/burlington_county_times/bct020529.htm

Richards, W.A. (2005). Entheogens in the study of religious experiences: Current status. *Journal of Religion and Health, 44*(4), 377–389.

Roth, M.D., Arora, A., Barsky, S.H., Kleerup, E.C., Simmons, M., & Tashkin, D.P. (1998). Airway inflammation in young marijuana and tobacco smokers. *American Journal of Respiratory Critical Care Medicine, 157*(3), 929–937.

Ruck, C., Bigwood, J., Staples, D., Ott, J., & Wasson, R.G. (1979). Entheogens. *Journal of Psychedelic Drugs, 11*(1–2), 145–146.

Saliba, J. (2004). The Native American Church. In C. Partridge (Ed.), *New religions: A guide. New religious movements, sects and alternative spiritualities* (pp. 290–291). New York: Oxford University Press.

Saunders, N. (1995). Spiritual uses of MDMA in traditional religion. *Newsletter of the Multidisciplinary Association for Psychedelic Studies, 6*(6). Retrieved April 25, 2006, from http://www.maps.org/news-letters/v06n1/06133spi.html

Scanlan, D. (2005, October 20). UNF student arrest over toxic tea: A fellow student was hospitalized after drinking brew made with Angel Trumpet flowers. *Florida Times-Union (Jacksonville)*, p. B-5.

Scarcella, M.A. (2005, April 20). Woman in poison seed case gets 15 years. *Sarasota Herald-Tribune-Manatee Edition*, p. BM1.

Schaper, D., Siegel, R., & Block, M. (2006, March 20). Legal, herbal hallucinogenic draws teens, critics. *All Things Considered*. National Public Radio.

Shanon, B. (2002). Entheogens: Reflections on "psychoactive sacramentals." *Journal of Consciousness Studies, 9*(4), 85–94.

Sheffler, D.J., & Roth, B.L. (2003). Salvinorin A: The "magic mint" hallucinogen finds a molecular target in the kappa opioid receptor. *Trends in Pharmacology Science, 24*(3), 107–109.

Smith, H. (2003). *Cleansing the doors of perception: The religious significance of entheogenic plants and chemicals*. Boulder, CO: Sentient.

State v. Big Sheep. 242 P. 1067 (Mont. 1926).

Stewart, O.C. (1987). *Peyote religion: A history*. The Civilization of the American Indian Series, 181. Norman: University of Oklahoma Press.

Stewart, O.C. (1993). Peyote and the law. In C. Vecsey (Ed.), *Handbook of American Indian religious freedom* (pp. 44–62). New York: Crossroad.

Substance Abuse and Mental Health Services Administration (SAMHSA). (2005). *Results from the 2004 National Survey on Drug Use and Health: National findings*. NSDUH Series H-28, DHHS publication no. SMA 05-4062. Rockville, MD: Office of Applied Studies.

Tashkin, D.P. (1990). Pulmonary complications of smoked substance abuse. *Western Journal of Medicine, 152*(5), 525–530.

Town v. State ex rel. Reno, 377 So.2d 648 (Fla.1979), cert. denied, 449 U.S. 803, 101 S.Ct. 48, 66 L.Ed. 2d 7 (1980).

U.S. Food and Drug Administration (USFDA). (2003). List of firms receiving warning letters for marketing illegal street drug alternatives. Retrieved May 2, 2006, from http://www.fda.gov/bbs/topics/NEWS/ephedra/streetalternatives.html

U.S. v. Bauer, Treiber, Best, Meeks, Isarel, Wegner, Martinez, and Ramirez. 84 F.3d 1549, 1559. (1996).

U.S. v. Boyll. 774 F.Supp. 1333 (D.N.M. 1991).

U.S. v. Rush, 738 F.2d 497 (1st Cir.1984), cert. denied, 470 U.S. 1004 (1985).

Valdes, L.J. (1994). *Salvia divinorum* and the unique diterprene hallucinogen, salvinorin (divinorin) A. *Journal of Psychoactive Drugs, 26*(3), 277–283.

Witte, J. (2000). *Religion and the American constitutional experiment: Essential rights and liberties.* Boulder, CO: Westview.

Wu, T.C., Tashkin, D.P., Djahed, B., & Rose, J.E. (1988). Pulmonary hazards of smoking marijuana as compared with tobacco. *New England Journal of Medicine, 318*(6), 347–351.

Zinberg, N.E. (1984). *Drug, set, and setting: The basis for controlled intoxicant use.* New Haven, CT: Yale University Press.

Chapter 7   Destructive Religious Groups

Albanese, J. (2000). The causes of organized crime: Do criminals organize around opportunities for crime or do criminal opportunities create new offenders? *Journal of Contemporary Criminal Justice, 16*(4), 409–423.

Baker, T. (2001). Hostage negotiations: Paranoid and suicidal cults. *Journal of Police Crisis Negotiations, 1,* 99–111.

Balch, R.W. (1998).The evolution of a new age cult: From total overcomers anonymous to death at heaven's gate. In W.W. Zellner & M. Petrowsky (Eds.), *Sects, cults, and spiritual communities: A sociological analysis* (pp. 1–26). Westport, CT: Praeger.

Barker, E. (1995). The scientific study of religion? You must be joking. *Journal for the Scientific Study of Religion, 34,* 287–310.

Bohm, J., & Alison, L. (2001). An exploratory study in methods of distinguishing destructive cults. *Psychology, Crime and Law, 7,* 133–165.

Bowker, J. (2000). *Oxford concise dictionary of world religions.* New York: Oxford University Press.

Brown, D. (2003). *The Da Vinci Code.* New York: Doubleday.

Butler, J., Wacker, G., & Balmer, R. (2003). *Religion in American life: A short history.* New York: Oxford University Press.

Collins, C., & Frantz, D. (1994). Let us prey. *Modern Maturity, 37,* 22–32.

Dawson, L.L. (1998). *Cults in context: Readings in the study of new religious movements.* New Brunswick, NJ: Transaction.

Federal Bureau of Investigation (FBI). (1979). RYMUR (Jonestown). Investigation report concerning the assassination of U.S. Congressman Leo Ryan. U.S. Department of

Justice. Available online through the Freedom of Information Act. Retrieved May 23, 2006, from http://www.foia.fbi.gov/jonestown/rymsum1a.pdf

Federal Bureau of Investigation (FBI). (1999). Project Megiddo. Retrieved May 30, 2006, from http://www.cesnur.org/testi/FBI_updates.htm

Firestone, T.A. (1993). Mafia memoirs: What they tell us about organized crime. *Journal of Contemporary Criminal Justice, 9*(3), 197–220.

Galanter, M. (1999). *Cults: Faith, healing, and coercion.* New York: Oxford University Press.

Gaustad, E.S. (2003). *Proclaim liberty throughout all the land: A history of church and state in America.* New York: Oxford University Press.

Glock, C.Y. (1964). The role of deprivation in the origin and evolution of religious groups. In R. Lee & M. Marty (Eds.), *Religion and social conflict* (pp. 24–36). New York: Oxford University Press.

Hall, J. (1989). Jonestown and Bishop Hill. In R. Moore & F. McGehee III (Eds.), *New religious movements, mass suicide and the People Temple* (pp. 77–92). Lewiston, NY: Edwin Mellon.

Hill, M. (2002, October 7). MOVE 2002: Modern home, original beliefs. *Philadelphia Inquirer.*

Jenkins, P. (2000). *Mystics and messiahs: Cults and new religions in American history.* New York: Oxford University Press.

Kaplan, J. (1997). *Radical religion in America: Millenarian movements from the far right to the Children of Noah.* Syracuse, NY: Syracuse University Press.

Kelly, R.J., Chin, K., & Fagen, J. (1993). The structure, activity, and control of Chinese gangs: Law enforcement perspectives. *Journal of Contemporary Criminal Justice, 9*(3), 221–239.

Kimball, C. (2003). *When religion becomes evil: Five warning signs.* New York: HarperCollins.

Knox, G.W. (1999). Comparison of cults and gangs: Dimensions of coercive power and malevolent authority. *Journal of Gang Research, 6*(4), 1–39.

Krakauer, J. (2004). *Under the banner of heaven: A story of violent faith.* New York: Anchor.

Kurst-Swanger, K., & Petcosky, J. (2003). *Violence in the home: Multidisciplinary perspectives.* New York: Oxford University Press.

Kurst-Swanger, K., & Ryniker, M. (2003). Religion-related crime: Documentation of murder, fraud, and sexual abuse. In A.R. Roberts (Ed.), *Critical issues in crime and justice* (pp. 62–78). Thousand Oaks, CA: Sage.

Lalich, J. (1997). Dominance and submission: The psychosexual exploitation of women in cults. *Cultic Studies Journal, 14,* 4–21.

Levine, S.V. (1984). *Radical departures: Desperate detours to growing up.* New York: Harcourt Brace & Co.

Levine, S. (1999). Youth in terrorist groups, gangs, and cults: The allure, the animus, and the alienation. *Psychiatric Annals, 29*(6), 342–350.

Lewis, I.M. (1996). *Religion in context: Cults and charisma.* New York: Cambridge University Press.

Lofland, J., & Stark, R. (1965). On becoming a world-saver: A theory of conversion to a deviant perspective. *American Sociological Review, 30,* 863–874.

Mayer, J. (2001). Cults, violence and religious terrorism: An international perspective. *Studies in Conflict and Terrorism, 24*(5), 361–376.

Milgram, S. (1963). Behavioral study of obedience. *Journal of Abnormal and Social Psychology, 67,* 371–378.

Nishida, K. (2001). A social psychological analysis of Aum Shinrikyo's criminal behavior. *Japanese Journal of Social Psychology, 16*(3), 170–183.

Richardson, J.T. (1993). Definitions of cult: From sociological-technical to popular-negative. *Review of Religious Research, 34,* 348–356.

Richardson, J.T. (1994). The ethics of "brainwashing" claims about new religious movements. *Australian Religious Studies Review, 7,* 48–56.

Richardson, J.T. (2001). Minority religions and the context of violence: A conflict/interactionist perspective. *Terrorism and Political Violence, 13*(1), 103–133.

Ringe, S.H. (1992). The word of God may be hazardous to your health. *Theology Today, 49,* 367–376.

Robbins, T., & Anthony, D. (1995). Sects and violence: Factors enhancing the volatility of marginal religious movements. In S. Wright (Ed.), *Armageddon in Waco: Critical perspectives on the Branch Davidian conflict* (pp. 236–259). Chicago: University of Chicago Press.

Saliba, J.A. (2004). The Peoples Temple. In C. Partridge (Ed.), *New religions: A guide. New religious movements, sects and alternative spiritualities* (pp. 77–78). New York: Oxford University Press.

Schwartz, L.L., & Kaslow, F.W. (2001). The cult phenomenon: A turn of the century update. *American Journal of Family Therapy, 29,* 13–22.

Shelley, L.I., & Picarelli, J.T. (2002). Methods not motives: Implications of the convergence of international organized crime and terrorism. *Police Practice and Research, 3*(4), 305–318.

Southerland, M., & Potter, G. (1993). Applying organization theory to organized crime. *Journal of Contemporary Criminal Justice, 9*(3), 251–267.

Staub, E. (1985). The psychology of perpetrators and bystanders. *Political Psychology, 6*(1), 61–85.

Stewart, K., & Harding, S. (1999). Bad endings: American apocalypses. *Annual Review of Anthropology, 28,* 285–310.

Speckman, S. (2004, August 1). Aid sought for church's victims. *Deseret Morning News.* Retrieved April 5, 2006, from http://www.childbrides.org/boys_des_lost_boys.html

Whitsel, B.C. (2000). Catastrophic new age groups and public order. *Studies in Conflict and Terrorism, 23,* 21–36.

Wojcik, D. (2004). Apocalypticism and millenarianism. In C. Partridge (Ed.), *New religions: A guide. New religious movements, sects, and alternative spiritualities* (pp. 388–395). New York: Oxford University Press.

Wright, S.A., & Piper, E.S. (1986). Families and cults: Familial factors related to youth leaving or remaining in deviant religious groups. *Journal of Marriage and the Family, 48*, 15–25.

Zellner, W., & Petrowsky, M. (1998). Freedom Park. In W.W. Zellner & M. Petrowsky (Eds.), *Sects, cults, and spiritual communities: A sociological analysis* (pp. 157–177). Westport, CT: Praeger.

Chapter 8   Violence against Abortion Providers

Associated Press (AP). (2005, October 29). *Suspect arrested in anti-abortion activist attack.* State and Regional.

Associated Press (AP). (2007, May 24). *Sentencing set in arson at Davenport women's clinic.* State and Regional.

Baird v. Eisenstadt. 405 U.S. 438 (1972).

Baird-Windle, P., & Bader, E.J. (2001). *Targets of hatred: Anti-abortion terrorism.* New York: Palgrave.

Blanchard, D.A., & Prewitt, T.J. (1993). *Religious violence and abortion: The Gideon project.* Gainesville: University Press of Florida.

Bureau of Alcohol, Tobacco, Firearms and Explosives (BATF). (2006). Abortion clinic violence. Retrieved June 16, 2006, from http://www.atf.gov/explarson/abort_clinic. htm

Carlson, J.R. (1995). The future terrorists in America. *American Journal of Police, 14*(3–4), 71–91.

Centers for Disease Control (CDC) Coordinating Center for Infectious Diseases/Division of Bacterial and Mycotic Diseases. (2005, October 25). Anthrax. Retrieved June 20, 2006, from http://www.cdc.gov/ncidod/dbmd/diseaseinfo/anthrax_g.htm#Top

Feminist Daily News Wire. (2000, June 12). Bankruptcy bill in danger of protecting anti-abortion extremists. Retrieved July 1, 2006, from http://www.feminist.org/news/ newsbyte/uswirestory.asp?id=1300

Feminist Majority Foundation. (1996). Stalking law protects abortion provider. *Feminist Majority Newsletter, 8*(2). Retrieved July 5, 2006, from http://www.feminist.org/ research/report/82_twelve.html

Griswold v. Connecticut. 381 U.S. 479 (1965).

Guttmacher Institute. (2006, June 1). *State policies in brief: Protecting access to clinics.* Retrieved June 14, 2006, from http://www.guttmacher.org

Herbeck, D. (2004, June 19). Man accused of stalking police officer and 3 town officials. *Buffalo News,* Local, p. D3.

Kenney, D.J., & Reuland, M. (2002). Public order policing: A national survey of abortion-related conflict. *Journal of Criminal Justice, 30*(5), 355–368.

Life Research Institute. (1995). Abortion-related violence and alleged violence: An investigative report. Retrieved June 25, 2006, from http://geocities.com/kekogut/miscellaneous/Jan1995.pdf

Miller, N. (2001). Stalking laws and implementation practices: A national review for policymakers and practitioners. Institute for Law and Justice. Retrieved June 22, 2006, from http://www.ncvc.org/src/main.aspx?dbID=dash_Home

Mullen, P.E., Pathe, M., & Purcell, R. (2000). *Stalkers and their victims*. Cambridge, MA: Cambridge University Press.

National Abortion Federation (NAF). (2006). History of violence/butyric acid attacks. Retrieved May 22, 2006, from http://www.prochoice.org/about_abortion/violence/butyric_acid.asp

National Abortion Federation (NAF). (2007). NAF violence and disruption statistics: Incidents of violence and disruption against abortion providers in the U.S. and Canada. Retrieved August 10, 2007, from http://www.prochoice.org/about_abortion/violence/violence_statistics.html

NOW v. Scheidler. 510 U.S. 249 (1994).

Operation Rescue v. NOW. 126 S.Ct. 1264. (2006)

Planned Parenthood of the Columbia/Willamette Inc. v. American Coalition of Life Activists. No. 9935320 (9th Cir. March 28, 2001).

Purcell, R., Powell, M.B., & Mullen, P.E. (2005). Clients who stalk psychologists: Prevalence, methods, and motives. *Professional Psychology: Research and Practice, 36*(5), 537–543.

Reagan, L.J. (2000). Crossing the border for abortions: California activists, Mexican clinics, and the creation of a feminist health agency in the 1960's. *Feminist Studies, 26*(2), 323–348.

Roe et al. v. Wade, District Attorney of Dallas County. 410 U.S. 113.(1973).

Savage, C. (2005, April 19). Mass. Abortion clinic law allowed to stand. *Boston Globe*, National/Foreign, p. A2.

Scheidler v. NOW. 537 U.S. 393 (2003).

Scheidler v. NOW. 126 S.Ct. 1264 (2006).

Shannon, B. (2006, January 20). Health-clinic arson spurs insurance bill. *The Olympian*. Retrieved June 16, 2006, from http://www.theolympian.com

Shiffman, J. (2005, July 8). Man gets 19 years for mailing fake anthrax letters to abortion clinics. *Philadelphia Inquirer*.

Solinger, R. (2005). *Pregnancy and power: A short history of reproductive politics in America*. New York: New York University Press.

Taylor, K. (2006, May 22). Obituary Paul deParrie, staunch activist against abortion, dies at 56. *The Oregonian*, Local, p. D07.

U.S. Department of Justice (USDOJ). (2000). National Task Force on Violence Against Health Care Providers. Report on federal efforts to prevent and prosecute clinic violence 1998–2000. Retrieved May 22, 2006, from http://www.usdoj.gov/crt/crim/tfreppub.htm

U.S. Department of Justice (USDOJ). (2001, January). *National Task Force on Violence Against Health Care Providers.* Retrieved May 22, 2006, from http://www.usdoj.gov/crt/crim/faceweb.htm

U.S. Department of Justice (USDOJ). (2006, October 27). Robert Weiler pleads guilty in attempt to bomb an abortion clinic in Greenbelt: Also intended to shoot doctors who provided abortions. Retrieved on August 15, 2007, from http://www.usdoj.gov/usao/md/Public-Affairs/press_releases/press06/Weiler%20Guilty%20Plea.html

U.S. General Accounting Office (USGAO). (1998). *Abortion clinics: Information on the effectiveness of the Freedom of Access to Clinic Entrances Act.* Washington, DC: GAO/GGD-99-2.

Warren, L.J., MacKenzie, R., Mullen, P.E., & Ogloff, J.R. (2005). The problem behavior model: The development of a stalkers clinic and a threateners clinic. *Behavioral Sciences and the Law, 23,* 387–397.

Chapter 9   Hate Crimes

Adams, D.M. (2005). Punishing hate and achieving equality. *Criminal Justice Ethics,* Winter/Spring, 24(1),19–30.

Anti-Defamation League (ADL). (2001). History of the Anti-Defamation League: 1913–2000. Retrieved September 4, 2006, from http://www.adl.org/ADLHistory/intro.asp

Anti-Defamation League (ADL). (2006a). Comparison of FBI hate crime statistics 1991–2004. Retrieved September 8, 2006, from http://www.adl.org/combating_hate

Anti-Defamation League (ADL). (2006b). Anti-Defamation League state hate crime statutory provisions. Retrieved November 5, 2006, from http://www.adl.org

Associated Press (AP). (2004, October 18). Kansas anti-gay group pickets Alabama churches. *Bay Minette,* State and Regional.

Balboni, J.M., & McDevitt, J. (2001). Hate crime reporting: Understanding police officer perceptions, departmental protocol, and the role of the victim. Is there such a thing as a "love" crime? *Justice Research and Policy, 3*(1), 1–26.

Barkun, M. (1997). *Religion and the racist right: The origins of the Christian Identity Movement.* Chapel Hill: University of North Carolina Press.

Beirich, H., & Potok, M. (2004, Summer). Two faces of Volksfront: A growing and increasingly important neo-Nazi group claims it opposes any kind of political violence. Could it be true? *Southern Poverty Law Center Intelligence Report.* Retrieved September 15, 2006, from http://www.splcenter.org/intel/intelreport/article.jsp?aid=475&printable=1

Brooks, T.D. (1994). First Amendment–penalty enhancement for hate crimes: Content regulation, questionable state interests and non-traditional sentencing. *Journal of Criminal Law and Criminology, 84*(4), 703–742.

Federal Bureau of Investigation (FBI). (2004). Crime in the United States 2004: Hate crime. Retrieved September 13, 2006, from http://www.fbi.gov/ucr/cius_04/offenses reported/hate_crime/index.html

Federal Bureau of Investigation (FBI). (2005). Hate crimes. Retrieved November 5, 2006, from http://www.miami.fbi.gov/hate.htm

Federal Bureau of Investigation (FBI). (2006). Hate crime statistics 2005. Retrieved October 22, 2006, from http://www.fbi.gov/ucr/hc2005

Herrell, V.S. (n.d.). What do Christian Separatists believe, and why are we different? Retrieved November, 12, 2006, from http://www.christianseparatist.org/briefs/sb2.15.html

Jacobs, S.L. (2003–2004). The last uncomfortable "religious" question? Monotheistic exclusivism and textual superiority in Judaism, Christianity, and Islam as sources of hate and genocide. *Journal of Hate Studies, 3*, 133–143.

Jenness, V. (2002–2003). Engendering hate crime policy: Gender, the "dilemma of difference," and the creation of legal subjects. *Journal of Hate Studies, 2*, 73–97.

Kellams, L. (2005, June 30). Activist wants group to retract statements unfairly identified as extremist, he says. *Arkansas Democrat-Gazette (Little Rock)*.

Kimball, C. (2002). *When religion becomes evil: Five warning signs*. New York: HarperCollins.

Levin, J., & McDevitt, J. (2002). *Hate crimes revisited: America's war on those who are different*. Boulder, CO: Westview.

Maxfield, M.G. (1999). The National Incident-Based Reporting System: Research and policy implications. *Journal of Quantitative Criminology, 15*(2), 119–149.

Mayer, J. (2001). Cults, violence and religious terrorism: An international perspective. *Studies in conflict and terrorism, 24*(5), 361–376.

McPhail, B.A. (2000). Hating hate: Policy implications of hate crime legislation. *Social Science Review, 74*(4), 635–653.

Meenan, M. (2004, July 29–August 4). Young gay man brutally killed. *Gay City News 3*(331). Retrieved September 15, 2006, from http://www.gaycitynews.com/gcn_331/younggaymanbrutally.html

Nolan, J., & Akiyama, Y. (2002). Assessing the climate for hate crime reporting in law enforcement organizations: A force-field analysis. *The Justice Professional, 15*(2), 87–103.

Nolan, J.J., McDevitt, J., Cronin, S., & Farrell, A. (2004). Learning to see hate crimes: A framework for understanding and clarifying ambiguities in bias crime classification. *Crime Justice Studies, 17*(1), 91–105.

O'Connor, P. (2006, March 15). Rogers bill would ban protests at funeral. *The Hill*, p. 4.

Oliphant, L. (2001). How many were there? A closer look at the seventeen reported "hate-crimes" murders of 1999. U.S. Senate, Republican Policy Committee. July 12.

Retrieved October 3, 2006, from http://www.senate.gov/~rpc/releases/1999/cr071201.htm

Patton, C. (2005). Anti-lesbian, gay, bisexual, and transgender violence in 2004: A report of the National Coalition of Anti-Violence Programs. Retrieved October 14, 2006, from http://www.ncavp.org/publications/NationalPubs.aspx

Phillips, S., & Grattet, R. (2000). Judicial rhetoric, meaning-making, and the institutionalization of hate crime law. *Law and Society Review, 34*, 567–606.

Silverstein, K. (2000). The Church of Morris Dees. *Harper's, 301*(1806), 54–57.

Southern Poverty Law Center. (2001, Winter). Discounting hate: Ten years after federal officials began compiling national hate crime statistics, the numbers don't add up. *Intelligence Report*. Retrieved October, 6, 2006, from http://www.splcenter.org/intel/intelreport/article.jsp?pid=293

Strom, K.J. (2001, September). *Hate crimes reported in NIBRS, 1997–1999*. U.S. Department of Justice, Office of Justice Programs, Bureau of Justice Statistics Special Report, NCJ 186765.

Sun, K. (2006). The legal definition of hate crime and the hate offender's distorted cognitions. *Issues in Mental Health Nursing, 27*, 597–604.

Sykes, G., & Matza, D. (1957). Techniques of neutralization: A theory of delinquency. *American Sociological Review, 22*, 664–670.

Terrorist Research and Analytical Center (TRAC), Federal Bureau of Investigation. (1989). Christian Identity Movement: Right-wing terrorism matters. Freedom of Information/Privacy Acts Section. Retrieved November 11, 2006, from http://www.foia.fbi.gov/foiaindex/christianidentity.html

Turner, N. (2006). Responding to hate crimes: A police officer's guide to investigation and prevention. International Association of Chiefs of Police. Retrieved September 13, 2006, from http://www.theiacp.org/documents/index.cfm?fuseaction=document&document_id=141

U.S. Department of Justice (USDOJ). (2000, November 14). Indiana man sentenced to over 42 years for setting 26 churches ablaze. Retrieved September 16, 2006, from http://www.usdoj.gov/opa/pr/2000/ November/659cr.htm

Wisconsin v. Mitchell. 113 S.Ct. 2194 (1993).

Woolf, L.M., & Hulsizer, M.R. (2002–2003). Intra-and inter-religious hate and violence: A psychosocial model. *Journal of Hate Studies, 2*(5), 5–25.

Chapter 10   Clergy Misconduct: An Overview

Bartunek, J.M., Keenan, J.F., & Hinsdale, M. (2005). *Church ethics and its organizational context: Learning from the sex abuse scandal in the Catholic Church.* Lanham, MD: Rowman & Littlefield.

Bottoms, B.L., Shaver, P.R., Goodman, G.S., & Qin, J. (1995). In the name of God: A profile of religion-related child abuse. *Journal of Social Issues, 51*, 85–111.

Bowker, J. (2000). *Oxford concise dictionary of world religions*. New York: Oxford University Press.

Burkett, E., & Brunie, F. (1993). *A gospel of shame: Children, sexual abuse, and the Catholic Church*. New York: Penguin.

Chibnall, J.T., Wolf, A., & Duckro, P.N. (1998). A national survey of the sexual trauma experiences of Catholic nuns. *Review of Religious Research, 40*(2), 142–167.

Cooper-White, P. (1991, February 20). Soul stealing: Power relations in pastoral sexual abuse. *The Christian Century, 108*(6), 196–199. Retrieved January 7, 2007, from http://www.snapnetwork.org/psych_effects/soul_stealing_1.htm.

Diocese of Peoria. (2002). Top stories, week of November 17, *Catholic Post*. Retrieved December 26, 2006, from http://www.cdop.org/catholic_post/post_11_17_02/news.cfm

Dokecki, P.R. (2004). *The clergy sexual abuse crisis: Reform and renewal in the Catholic community*. Washington, DC: Georgetown University Press.

Ewinger, J. (2006, May 12). Priest convicted of killing nun in '80 Judge sentences Toledoan to 15 years to life; defense says verdict will be appealed. *Plain Dealer*, p. A1.

Finkelhor, D., Gelles, R.J., Hotaling, G.T., & Straus, M.A. (1983). *The dark side of families*. Beverly Hills, CA: Sage.

Fortune, M.M., & Longwood, W.M. (2004). *Sexual abuse in the Catholic Church: Trusting the clergy?* Binghamton, NY: Haworth Press.

Fried, S. (2002). *The new rabbi*. New York: Bantam.

Friedrichs, D.O. (2004). *Trusted criminals: White collar crime in contemporary society*. Belmont, CA: Wadsworth.

Green, G.S. (1990). *Occupational crime*. Chicago: Nelson-Hall.

Helmkamp, J., Ball, R., & Townsend, K. (1996). *Definitional dilemma: Can and should there be a universal definition of white collar crime?* Proceedings of the academic workshop. Training and Research Institute, National White Collar Crime Center, Morgantown, West Virginia. Retrieved January 2, 2007, from http://www.nw3c.org/research/site_files.cfm.?mode=p

Jenkins, P. (1996). *Pedophiles and priests: Anatomy of a contemporary crisis*. New York: Oxford University Press.

John Jay College of Criminal Justice. (2004). The nature and scope of the problem of sexual abuse of minor by priests and deacons in the United States. Washington, DC: United States Conference of Catholic Bishops. Retrieved December 20, 2006, from http://www.usccb.org/nrb/johnjaystudy/index.htm

Kimball, C. (2002). *When religion becomes evil: Five warning signs*. New York: HarperCollins.

Lebacqz, K., & Barton, R. (1991). *Sex in the parish*. Louisville, KY: Westminster John Knox.

Leitsinger, M. (2002, May 22). Priest, 5 others plead guilty in date-rape drug case. *Press and Sun Bulletin*.

Mulvihill, G. (2006, October 20). Rabbi convicted of having his wife killed wants third trial. The Associated Press. State & Local Wire. Mount Laurel, NJ.

Munoz, O. (2006a, November 30). Pastor arrested in alleged murder plot. Fresno, CA: Associated Press.

Munoz, O. (2006b, December 1). Preacher arrested in alleged murder plot. Fresno, CA: Associated Press.

O'Neil, T. (2001, December 21). Pastor will serve 7-year prison term for thefts. *St. Louis Post-Dispatch*, p. C11.

Rosoff, S.M., Pontell, H.N., & Tillman, R.H. (2002). *Profit without honor: White-collar crime and the looting of America*. Upper Saddle River, NJ: Prentice-Hall.

Rossetti, S.J. (1996). *A tragic grace: The Catholic Church and child sexual abuse*. Collegeville, MN: Liturgical Press.

Seat, J.T., Trent, J.T., & Kim, J.K. (1993). The prevalence and contributing factors of sexual misconduct among southern Baptist pastors in six southern states. *Journal of Pastoral Care, 47*(4), 363–370.

Shupe, A. (1995). *In the name of all that's holy: A theory of clergy malfeasance*. Westport, CT: Praeger.

Shupe, A. (1998). The dynamics of clergy malfeasance. In A. Shupe (Ed.), *Wolves within the fold: Religious leadership and abuses of power* (pp. 1–12). New Brunswick, NJ: Rutgers University Press.

Shupe, A., & Iadicola, P. (2000). Issues in conceptualizing clergy malfeasance. In A. Shupe, W.A. Stacey, & S.E. Darnell (Eds.), *Bad pastors: Clergy misconduct in modern America* (pp. 13–38). New York: New York University Press.

Shupe, A., Stacey, W.A., & Darnell, S.E. (2000). *Bad pastors: Clergy misconduct in modern America*. New York: New York University Press.

Sohn, P. (1992, January 4). A family's fall from grace: Three brothers follow path to charges of molestation. *Chattanooga Times*, p. A1.

Stacey, W.A., Darnell, S.E., & Shupe, A. (2000). How much clergy malfeasance is really out there? A victimization survey of prevalence and perceptions. In A. Shupe, W.A. Stacey, & S.E. Darnell (Eds.), *Bad pastors: Clergy misconduct in modern America* (pp. 187–213). New York, NY: New York University Press.

State of Tennessee v. Donald C. McCary. 119 S.W.3d 226 (2003); 2003 Tenn. Crim. Appl. LEXIS 17.

State v. McCary. 922 S.W.2d 511 (Tenn., 1996).

State v. McCary. 2003 Tenn. LEXIS 594 (Tenn., June 30, 2003).

Surette, R. (1998). *Media, crime, and criminal justice: Images and realities*. Belmont, CA: Wadsworth.

Underwood, A. (2003). Doing justice in cases of abuse of power: A legal perspective. *Journal of Religion and Abuse, 5*(1), 35–65.

Wells, K. (2003). A needs assessment regarding the nature and impact of clergy sexual abuse conducted by the Interfaith Sexual Trauma Institute. *Sexual Addiction and Compulsivity, 10*, 201–217.

Chapter 11   Crimes of the Cloth: Economic, Personal, and Organizational Crime

Anti-Defamation League (ADL). (2001). The consequences of right wing extremism on the Internet: Coordinating extremist events: "Patriot Confrontations". Retrieved January 22, 2007, from http://adl.org/internet/extremism_rw/cord_conf.asp

Associated Press (AP). (2005, November 5). Ripon minister accused of selling congregation's church, parsonage. State and Regional. Ripon, CA.

Associated Press (AP). (2006, June 6). Pastor convicted of conspiracy, visa fraud. State and Regional. Tacoma, WA.

Bartunek, J.M., Keenan, J.F., & Hinsdale, M.A. (Eds.). (2006). *Church ethics and its organizational context: Learning from the sex abuse scandal in the Catholic Church.* Lanham, MD: Rowman & Littlefield.

Belluck, P. (2002, October 29). Bishop knew Boston priest had praised man-boy sex. *The New York Times.* Retrieved April 4, 2007, from http://query.nytimes.com/gst/fullpage.html?sec=health&res=9807E0DD153FF93AA15753C1A9649C8B63&n=Top%2fReference%2fTimes%20Topics%2fPeople%2fS%2fShanley%2c%20Paul%20R%2e

Burkett, E., & Brunie, F. (1993). *A gospel of shame: Children, sexual abuse, and the Catholic Church.* New York: Penguin.

Dokecki, P.R. (2004). *The clergy sexual abuse crisis: Reform and renewal in the Catholic community.* Washington, DC: Georgetown University Press.

Farragher, T. (2003, November 30). In death, Geoghan triggers another crisis. *Boston Globe.* Retrieved April 7, 2007, from http://www.boston.com/news/local/Massachusetts/articles/2003/11/30/in_death_geoghan_tri

Fater, K., & Mullaney, J. (2000). The lived experiences of adult male survivors who allege childhood sexual abuse by clergy. *Issues in Mental Health Nursing, 21,* 281–295.

Fortune, M. (2004). Sexual abuse by priests: An institutional crisis in the Catholic Church. *Journal of Religion and Abuse, 6*(2), 17–22.

Fortune, M.M. & Longwood, M.W. (Eds.). (2004). *Sexual abuse in the Catholic Church: Trusting the clergy?* Binghamton, NY: Haworth Press.

Franceschina, P., & Diaz, M. (2007, March 8). Records detail secret lives of 2 priests accused of misappropriating $8.7 million. *South Florida Sun-Sentinel.* Retrieved March 19, 2007, from http://www.orlandosentinel.com/news/sfl-0308priests,0,5366854.story?coll=orl-news-headlines

Gammon, R. (2006, July 12). The Moonies and the sharks: How a Unification Church pastor went fishing for converts and snagged an indictment as America's most prolific poacher of baby leopard sharks. *East Bay Express.*

Gammon, R. (2007, January 31). The man v. Moon: As a local Moonie preacher is sentenced, evidence implicates the church's supreme leader in a shark-poaching scheme. *East Bay Express.*

Goodstein, L. (2007, July 15). Deal reported in abuse cases in Los Angeles. *The New York Times*, p. 1.

Hart, J. (2006). *ICE arrests 33 in religious worker visa scheme*. Retrieved February 6, 2007, from http://www.immigrateusa.us/index.php?option=com_content&task=view&id=555&Itemid=48

Higgins, D. (2007, January 8). Survivors of clergy sex abuse hold vigil: Albany joins in marking the fifth anniversary of the scandal's exposure. *Times Union*. Retrieved January 21, 2007 from http://timesunion.com/AspStories/storyprint.asp?StoryID=551568

Horst, E.A. (1998). *Recovering the lost self: Shame-healing for victims of clergy sexual abuse*. Interfaith Sexual Trauma Institute. Collegeville, MN: Liturgical Press.

Janesville Gazette. (2006, February 3). Priest believed to have killed two: Told of "wretched life." Retrieved June 11, 2007, from http://www.bishop-accountability.org/news2006/01_02/2006_02_03_AP_PriestBelieved

Jenkins, P. (1996). *Pedophiles and priests: Anatomy of a contemporary crisis*. New York: Oxford University Press.

Kauffman, C. (2006a, March 13). Creationist speaker "loose about the facts." *York Dispatch*, Local.

Kauffman, C. (2006b, July 20). 58 charges against anti-evolution speaker. *York Dispatch*, Local.

King, R. (2006, September 19). Baptist Temple bounces back after finding new home. *The Indianapolis Star*, State and Regional.

Krebs, T. (1998). Church structures that facilitate pedophilia among Roman Catholic clergy. In A. Shupe (Ed.), *Wolves within the fold: Religious leadership and abuses of power* (pp. 15–32). New Brunswick, NJ: Rutgers University Press.

Kurst-Swanger, K., & Petcosky, J. (2003). *Violence in the home: Multidisciplinary perspectives*. New York: Oxford University Press.

Kurst-Swanger, K., & Ryniker, M. (2003). Religion-related crime: Documentation of murder, fraud, and sexual abuse. In A.R. Roberts (Ed.), *Critical issues in crime and justice* (pp. 62–78). Thousand Oaks, CA: Sage.

LaForgia, M. (2006, October 24). 2nd Delray priest arrested, posts bond. *Palm Beach Post*, p. 1B.

McLaughlin, B.R. (1994). Devastated spirituality: The impact of clergy sexual abuse on the survivor's relationship with God and the Church. *Sexual Addiction and Compulsivity, 1*, 145–158.

Miller, I. (2007, February 16). Sentencing of ex-pastor again put off: Judge waiting to hear testimony Radic gives in separate murder trial. *Modesto Bee*, p. B1.

Moran, M. (2005). *The tricky part: A boy's story of sexual trespass, a man's journey to forgiveness*. New York: Anchor Books.

O'Connor, L., & Slater, S. (2006, October 11). Priest told cops of schemes, rationale. *Palm Beach Post*, p. 1B.

Pennsylvania Securities Commission. (1999). Securities Commission warns about religious "affinity fraud." Division of Enforcement and Litigation. Retrieved January 22, 2007, from http://www.psc.state.pa.us/newsroom/nr/nr9199.html

Pfeiffer, S. (2002, December 14). Despite departure, archdiocese faces "a real mess" in court. *Boston Globe*. Retrieved April 4, 2007, from http://www.boston.com/globe/spotlight/abuse/print3/121402_legal.htm

Ponton, L., & Goldstein, D. (2004). Sexual abuse of boys by clergy. In L.T. Flaherty (Ed.), *Adolescent psychiatry: Developmental and clinical studies*, Vol. 28 (pp. 209–229). Mahwah, NJ: Analytic.

Robinson, W.V., & Farragher, T. (2002, April 9). Files show law, others backed priest. *Boston Globe*, p. A1.

Rosoff, S.M., Pontell, H.N., & Tillman, R.H. (2002). *Profit without honor: White-collar crime and the looting of America*. Upper Saddle River, NJ: Prentice-Hall.

Seattle Post-Intelligencer. (2006, November 3). Pastor who fled U.S. is back for sentencing, p. B2.

Shupe, A. (1998). *Wolves within the fold: Religious leadership and abuses of power*. New Brunswick, NJ: Rutgers University Press.

Shupe, A., & Iadicola, P. (2000). Issues in conceptualizing clergy malfeasance. In A. Shupe, W.A. Stacey, & S.E. Darnell (Eds.), *Bad pastors: Clergy misconduct in modern America* (pp. 13–38). New York: New York University Press.

Slater, S. (2006, October 21). Records document priest's high-rolling lifestyle. *Palm Beach Post*, p. 1A.

Smith, S. (2007, July 23). Though an S.J. woman's murderer has pleaded guilty to the crime, the fight over Mary Marino-Starkey's remains is just beginning. *Recordnet.com*. Retrieved August 18, 2007, from http://www.recordnet.com/apps/pbcs.dll/article?AID=/20070723/A_NEWS/707230323/-1/A_COMM06

Southern Poverty Law Center (SPLC). (2001). Church vs. State: The seizure of Indianapolis Baptist Temple ends a standoff, but the "unregistered churches" movement is still in business. *Intelligence Report*. Retrieved March 22, 2007, from http://splcenter.org/intel/intelreport/article.jsp?aid=199&printable=1

Stewart, M. (2007, January 9). 10 years for "Dr. Dino." *Pensacola News Journal*. Retrieved March 22, 2007, from http://pensacolanewsjournal.com/aaps/pbcs.dll/article?AID=20070119/NEWS01/70

Terry, K., & Leland Smith, M. (2006). The nature and scope of the problem of sexual abuse of minors by Catholic priests and deacons in the United States: Supplementary data analysis for the U.S. Conference of Catholic Bishops. Washington, DC: U.S. Conference of Bishops. Retrieved June 4, 2007, from http://www.usccb.org/ocyp/johnjayreport.pdf

Thompson, P. (2006). Priest who stole millions to be arrested last but he won't be wearing handcuffs. *Daily Mail*. Ed Ire, p. 30.

U.S. Citizenship and Immigration Services (USCIS). (2006). Religious worker benefit fraud assessment summary. Office of Fraud Detection and National Security. Retrieved February 6, 2007, from http://www.ilw.com/articles/2006,0731-uscis.pdf

U.S. Conference of Catholic Bishops (USCCB). (2004). The nature and scope of the problem of sexual abuse of minors by Catholic priests and deacons in the United States: A research study conducted by the John Jay College of Criminal Justice. Retrieved June 4, 2007, from http://www.usccb.org/nrb/johnjaystudy

U.S. Conference of Catholic Bishops (USCCB). (2005). Charter for the protection of children and young people. Retrieved June 4, 2007, from http://www.usccb.org/ocyp/charter.shtml

U.S. Conference of Catholic Bishops (USCCB). (2006). Essential norms for diocesan/eparchial policies dealing with allegations of sexual abuse of minors by priests or deacons. Office of the Protection of Children and Young People. Retrieved June 5, 2007, from http://www.usccb.org/ocyp

U.S. Conference of Catholic Bishops (USCCB). (2007a). Office of Children and Youth Protection. What is the office and what is its function? Retrieved June 5, 2007, from http://www.usccb.org/ocyp/whoweare.shtml

U.S. Conference of Catholic Bishops (USCCB). (2007b). Report on the implementation of the Charter for the Protection of Children and Young People. Office of Child and Youth Protection, National Review Board. Retrieved June 5, 2007, from http://www.usccb.org/ocyp/whoweare.shtml

U.S. Department of Justice (USDOJ). (2007). Pastor sentenced to one year in prison for role in scheme to poach and smuggle leopard sharks. Retrieved February 8, 2007, from http://www.usdoj.gov/usao/can/press/2007/2007_01_23_Thompson.sentencing.press.html

Wells, K. (2003). A needs assessment regarding the nature and impact of clergy sexual abuse conducted by the Interfaith Sexual Trauma Institute. *Sexual Addiction and Compulsivity, 10,* 201–217.

Wides-Munoz, L. (2006, September 29). Police: 2 priests stole millions from their Palm Beach parish; 1 arrested, other sought. Associated Press.

Index